D1129181

A SEARCH FOR GOD
IN TIME AND MEMORY

➤➤ ◀◀

A Search for God
in Time and Memory

➤➤ ◀◀

JOHN S . DUNNE, c. s. c.

UNIVERSITY OF NOTRE DAME PRESS
Notre Dame, Indiana 46556

ACKNOWLEDGMENTS

Acknowledgment is made for permission to reprint extracts from "A
Dialogue of Self and Soul" from *The Collected Poems of W. B. Yeats,*
Copyright 1933 by The Macmillan Company, renewed 1961 by Bertha
Georgie Yeats, to The Macmillan Company, Mr. M. B. Yeats and Mac-
millan & Co., Ltd., London; and from "Finnegan's Wake" from *Irish
Street Ballads,* Colm O'Lochlainn, Copyright © 1960 Corinth Books, to
Corinth Books Inc., New York and The Sign of the Three Candles,
Dublin.

Library of Congress Cataloging in Publication Data

Dunne, John S   1929–
  A search for God in time and memory.

  Reprint of the ed. published by Macmillan, New York.
  Includes bibliographies.
  1. God—Knowableness. I. Title.
[BT102.D8 1977]   231'.042   76-20165
ISBN 0-268-01689-5
ISBN 0-268-01673-9 pbk.

Contents

PREFACE   vii

1. TIME OUT OF MIND   I

   Bringing Lifetime to Mind   2
   The Quest of the Earthly Jesus   8
   Bringing Deathtime to Mind   14
   The Quest of the Risen Jesus   19

2. THE LIFE STORY   33

   Paul and the Story of Deeds   34
   Augustine and the Story of Experience   45
   Kierkegaard and the Story of Appropriation   57

3. THE ALIENATED MAN   75

   The Loss of Spiritual Mediation   76
   The New Hell: Despair   83
   The New Purgatory: Uncertainty   93
   The New Heaven: Assurance   103

4. THE AUTONOMOUS MAN   119

     The Loss of Temporal Mediation   120
     The New Childhood: the Father of the Man   126
     The New Youth: the Unfinished Man and His Pain   135
     The New Manhood: the Finished Man among
          His Enemies   144
     The New Age: the Child of the Man   154

5. THE SEARCH THROUGH TIME AND MEMORY   169

     Life Stories and Stories of God   170
     Stories of the Past: Once There Was a God   179
     Stories of the Present: Now There Is No God   187
     Stories of the Future: Someday God Will Be   195

6. TIME WITHIN MIND   211

     INDEX   227

Preface

I WOULD LIKE TO PURSUE in this book a search for God in time and memory. It is a search that will carry us on quests and journeys through life stories, through hells, purgatories, and heavens, through ages of life, through stories of God. It is the sort of thing you might undertake if you were writing an autobiography or composing a personal creed.

Writing an autobiography would involve you in a process of bringing time to mind. You would start by trying to recall in as much detail as possible your past. As you began to put your past life into words, though, you would probably find that the story could be told in many different ways, depending on the kind of future you thought it was leading to. This would start you thinking about the possible relationships between your past and future. You would not be able to foresee the actual events of the future nor even, for that matter, to recall the entirety of the past, but you would have begun to think about your life as a whole, about all the elements of drama in it: the plot, the characters, the thought content, the modes of expression, the setting. Thinking this way would carry you to the edges of your life, backward to birth and forward to death; it would give you a sense of your lifetime being part of a larger time. It would make you wonder how your life fits into your times, whether it is a reenactment of

some typical modern life story. You might compare your life with
other lives that seem somewhat parallel; you might even compare
it with lives out of epochs long past. You might wonder how far
your story is simply the perennial human story, the everlasting
cycle of childhood, youth, manhood, and age, how far it is the
modern story and how far it is strictly your own story.

Composing a personal creed, besides engaging you in bringing
time to mind in this manner, would set you searching for something in memory. The object of the search would be your God.
The common creeds and declarations and manifestos describe the
shared faith of multitudes, but if you wished to know what you
personally believe in and act upon, to know what God really is to
you, your own memory and your own anticipations would have to
be consulted rather than public documents. To be sure, you
would be asking yourself how you stood personally on matters
that figure in the common creeds, especially, it might be, on
Christ and Christianity, but once you began consulting personal
instead of public sources, you might start to wonder how you
could be personally a disciple of Jesus without being contemporary with him or without his being somehow contemporary with
you. You would wonder about your basic state of mind and soul,
how certain or uncertain you are, how happy or unhappy,
whether you live in a state of inner assurance, a state of doubt, a
state of quiet desperation. You would ask yourself ultimately
about your mental image of God, what God once was to you,
what he is to you now, what you expect of him.

All these questions are quite personal and become very absorbing when you ask them. It is not easy, once you have become
concerned about them, to stand back and reflect upon all this
from a distance, to compare your questions and findings with
those of others. The awareness that comes, nevertheless, with
pursuing these very personal issues in your own life enhances
greatly your ability to understand lives other than your own. You
find yourself able to pass over from the standpoint of your life to
those of others, entering into a sympathetic understanding of
them, finding resonances between their lives and your own, and

coming back once again, enriched, to your own standpoint. Many things in your life become known to you only when resonances of this kind are generated. This process of "passing over," as I shall call it, is a method by which personal questions can be broadened and pursued in a much wider context than they would ordinarily be in an autobiography or a personal creed. It tends to bridge the gap between personal knowledge and public knowledge and to give the seeking and finding that occurs on the strictly personal level something of the communicability of public knowledge.

The method of "passing over" is the one I will be using in this book. In preparing for this book, I carried out the kind of self-examination that would go into an autobiography or a personal creed. I have not included that here but only the passing over to other lives. The reader who joins me in examining these lives, though, will find it very helpful to carry out a preliminary self-examination and perhaps to outline his autobiography and sketch out his personal creed. This will give him a starting point like mine and will enable us to go over together to one life after another.

We will begin by considering what is involved in bringing the lifetime to mind, how this is done from a biographical standpoint, and how it is done from an autobiographical standpoint. With this preparation we will pass over to the life of Jesus, endeavoring to go from the finished life described by Matthew, Mark, Luke, and John to the unfinished life as it might have appeared to Jesus himself and his disciples, before his death. Then we will consider the process of bringing what I shall call "deathtime" to mind, the time encompassing the lifetime. This will lead us back from the unfinished life of Jesus to a reconsideration of the finished life. After this we will consider various historic forms, which the life story has taken in the Christian era: first the story of deeds that appears in the New Testament itself, particularly in the writings of Paul; then the story of experience that appears in the *Confessions* of Augustine, the prototype of autobiography and, in its latter parts, the classical model of the search for God in time and memory; and then the modern story of appropriation that appears

in the writings of Kierkegaard, especially in his use of pseudonyms to represent partial and subordinate aspects of his personality.

From this point on we will be concerned only with the life
story in the modern era, beginning in the sixteenth century. We
will examine first the varieties of religious experience in this era,
from Luther to Kierkegaard, then the varieties of secular experience, from Rousseau to Sartre. We will relate the two kinds of
experience to the disappearance of human mediators between
man and God, the medieval "lords spiritual" and "lords temporal." Taking a cue from Luther, who compares hell, purgatory,
and heaven to despair, uncertainty, and assurance, we will treat
the modern cycle of religious experience as a kind of divine comedy, in which the modern man seeks to find his way from the hell
of despair and the purgatory of doubt to the heaven of assurance.
We will deal with the cycle of secular experience by examining
each of the ages of life as they appear in modern autobiography,
a childhood that is much more than the traditional prelude to the
"years of discretion," a youth that is prolonged far beyond that in
previous epochs, a manhood that comes relatively late in life, and
an old age that was a rare attainment in past history.

After examining the life stories, we will consider the stories of
God told in the modern era, tales of how "once there was a God,"
"now there is no God," "someday God will be." We will be seeking to discover what it is about the modern life story that makes
the human lifetime seem a pause in God's time. The dark God
that figures in the modern tales of God, the God hidden in the
darkness of the past and the future, we will compare and contrast
with the God of Jesus, the God whom Jesus called "Abba." This
will bring us full circle: We will end by considering what it
would be for a contemporary man to relate to the dark God as
Jesus related to Abba.

The method we will have used in doing all this, the process of
passing over by sympathetic understanding to others and coming
back to a new understanding of ourselves, may itself be the hint
of an answer to the questions we raise. It is by passing over that a

man makes contact with Jesus, becomes contemporary with Jesus, and it is by coming back to himself from this that Jesus in turn becomes contemporary with him. Passing over is the way a man discovers the shape of the life story in other ages, the story of deeds, and the story of experience, and coming back from this to his own time is how he discovers by contrast its current shape, the story of appropriation. This is how he makes up for the loss of spiritual and temporal mediation in the modern epoch, for passing over to others makes them mediators between himself and God, and yet coming back to himself from them places him once again in the modern situation of unmediated existence. This is ultimately how he brings time to mind, how he searches through time and memory, for passing over avails him of the time and memory of others, and coming back leaves his own time and memory enriched. In this process he goes from man's time, the time of life stories, to God's time, the greater and encompassing time which is that of the stories of God, and he experiences companionship with God in time. He discovers in this the greater dimensions of man, those which reach beyond the self and the individual life story. And he discovers the face underlying all, that of the compassionate God and the compassionate Savior.

The influences I have felt most strongly in writing this book are Lonergan's study of personal knowledge, *Insight*, Kierkegaard's works on the personal appropriation of Christianity, *Philosophical Fragments* and *Concluding Unscientific Postscript*, and Jung's autobiography, *Memories, Dreams, Reflections*. Then there is my own study of myth and mortality, *The City of the Gods*, where I compared societies in terms of their answers to death. What I did with societies there, I try in effect to do with individuals here.

A SEARCH FOR GOD
IN TIME AND MEMORY

$$\text{>>> } 1 \text{ <<<}$$

Time Out of Mind

It is easier to say "All the world's a stage and all the men and women merely players" than it is to say what parts are played on this stage and how they are allotted to the men and women who play them. Shakespeare has it that "one man in his time plays many parts, his acts being seven ages": infancy, childhood, youth, manhood, middle age, old age, and second childhood.[1] This may make it appear that life is only a process of aging, that "men must endure their going hence, even as their coming hither: Ripeness is all."[2] It could be, on the contrary, that something comes into being in the fullness of time in human life and human history. *Does becoming end in being or does it end in nothingness?* That is the question. If becoming ends in nothingness, then ripeness is indeed all. Life then is nothing but life; history is nothing but history. One who dies young, for example, is nothing but what he has accomplished up to that moment. If becoming ends in being, on the other hand, then life is not simply a matter of growing older. It is a matter of becoming someone. And it ends, whether one dies young or old, in being that someone, in being the one whom one is becoming.

Yet how can we ever hope, while we are still in the process of becoming, to determine whether becoming ends in being or whether it ends in nothingness? We are dealing here with time that is truly "out of mind," much more truly than the time that is counted so according to law. What we need is a method of bringing to mind the time that is out of mind. This would be a method first of bringing one's own lifetime to mind, of passing from the "immediate moment" in which one's concerns are confined to the present situation to the "existential moment" in which one's concerns are extended to one's future and one's past. Second, it would be a method of bringing what we might call one's "death-time" to mind, of passing from the existential moment in which one's concerns are confined to one's own lifetime to the "historic moment" in which one's concerns are extended to all time, both the future and the past. Bringing time to mind, thus understood, means dilating the present. When it leads toward nothingness, the moments of which we have spoken, immediate, existential, and historic, are like the "dialectical moments" on the way that Hegel followed in his *Phenomenology of Mind*, the way that he called the "path of doubt" and the "highway of despair."[3] When it leads toward being, they are dialectical moments in what we might borrow New Testament language to call the "quest of the way, the truth, and the life."

Bringing Lifetime to Mind

"To have been young, and then to grow older, and finally to die," Kierkegaard has said, "is a very mediocre form of human existence; this merit belongs to every animal. But the unification of the different stages of life in simultaneity is the task set for human beings."[4] The ages of man, it is true, could be compared with the metamorphoses that occur in the life history of any organism, whereas the task set for a man at any stage of his life is to unify the different stages of life in simultaneity, to live his whole life, the past through memory and the future through anticipation, at every present moment. The manner in which a man does this is different from one stage of his life to another. Each of his metamorphoses, suggesting as it does the task or role set for him at a particular stage of his life, is a mask of memory and of anticipation. What he has to remember when he is young is less than what he has to remember when he is old; what he has to anticipate when he is young is more than what he has to anticipate when he is old. The relationship between his past and his future defines his present, or better perhaps, is defined by his present.

The question about this relationship has been posed in two distinct ways by philosophers, "Will the future be like the past?" and "Is the past more necessary than the future?"[5] The first question was meant to be a question about nature, whether there are laws of nature that are uniformly valid for all times. The second question was meant to be a question about history, whether there is a cumulative past made up of events that have changed from being merely possible when they were future and merely contingent when they were present to being necessary now that they are past. Both questions, however, may be taken as questions about the lifetime of the individual man, as though an individual were to be asked, "Will your future be like your past?" and "Is your past more necessary than your future?" or more generally "What is your future to you?" and "What is your past to you?"

When the question is posed by the individual himself, it can become a question calling for a practical resolution. When it is posed by another, though, when it is biographical rather than autobiographical, this is not so. "Shall my future be like my past?" calls for a practical resolution on the future, either to model my future upon my past, to continue to act as before and to live according to the pattern by which I have lived, or else to free myself from the precedents of the past and to hold myself open toward all the possibilities of the future, to prevent what I have done from limiting what I can do. "Is my past to be more necessary than my future?" calls for a practical resolution on the past, either to treat the past as something about which I can do nothing, since it cannot now be otherwise, or else to treat it as something about which I can do something (e.g., repent or the like), since it could once have been otherwise. "Will his future be like his past?" and "Is his past more necessary than his future?" call for a different sort of answer, because none of these resolutions need be taken, and none of them, if taken, need be kept.

Perhaps this difference is the reason a man oftentimes encounters a considerable discrepancy between his image of himself and the image his friends and acquaintances have of him. To himself he may seem an undefined being, who is capable of any number of alternative courses of action. To his friends and acquaintances he may seem, on the contrary, a very well-defined being, who can be expected to act and react in a certain way and to say and think certain things in a given set of circumstances.[6] His image of himself arises from the fact that the answer to the question "Shall my future be like my past?" and "Is my past to be more necessary than my future?" has to be invented rather than discovered, while the image his friends and acquaintances have of him arises from the fact that the answer to the question "Will his future be like his past?" and "Is his past more necessary than his future?" has to be discovered rather than invented. Either image can become false if the mode of answering the question is confused with one of the answers, if he confuses the fact that he must invent the answer with the particular answer that is most indeterministic, namely *No*, or if his friends and acquaintances confuse the fact that they must discover the answer with the particular answer that is most deterministic, namely *Yes*.

Entire methods of arriving at self-knowlege have been based on the assumption that one or the other of these standpoints, of the man himself or of other men, is the true one. The method of existentialism is based on Kierkegaard's principle that "truth is subjectivity,"[7] according to which a man will arrive at the truth about himself only if he abandons the attempt to treat himself as though he were another person and takes instead the standpoint he alone can occupy with regard to himself. The method of psychoanalysis, by contrast, is based on Freud's ideal of freedom from illusion and delusion,[8] according to which a man will arrive at the truth about himself only if he abandons all purely subjective views of himself, whether these be "delusions" actually contrary to objective fact or simply "illusions" unsupported by any objective evidence.

If it were not possible to pass over from one standpoint to another, then the method of existentialism would be a valid method of arriving at knowledge of self but an invalid method of arriving at knowledge of others, a method Sartre, for instance, would be using validly in writing his autobiography but invalidly in writing biographies of Genet and Baudelaire, for a man could not occupy the standpoint of self in any person's life except his own. The method of psychoanalysis, on the other hand, would be a valid method of arriving at knowledge of other persons but an invalid method of arriving at knowledge of self or of assisting other persons to arrive at knowledge of themselves, a valid method of diagnosis but an invalid method of cure, for a man could not occupy the standpoint of an outsider with regard to his own life but only with regard to the lives of others.

If it is possible, however, to pass over from one standpoint to another, then another method is conceivable, a method based on the premises that (a) what is true or false is so from some standpoint or other, (b) no standpoint, whether it be the standpoint of the man himself or that of other men in regard to him, is true or false in itself, and (c) it is possible to pass over from one standpoint to another. This bears a certain resemblance to the dialectical method of Hegel, according to which a man will arrive at the truth about himself only if he abandons both his own purely subjective standpoint and also the purely objective standpoint of others and takes instead the absolute standpoint in which the subjective and the objective come into focus with one another. The difference would be that according to the method I am suggesting there would be no absolute standpoint, since no standpoint would be considered true in itself, though there would be the possibility of passing over from one relative standpoint to another. The personal discovery of the absolute standpoint, according to Hegel, would be the attainment of what Aristotle called the "knowledge of knowledge."[9] The personal realization that there is no absolute standpoint would be more like the attainment of what Socrates and Plato called the "knowledge of ignorance."[10]

The method of "passing over" would be a general method of arriving at self-knowledge of the Socratic type, the knowledge of one's own ignorance. It would also be a general method of arriving at a similar knowledge of others, the sort of knowledge Socrates himself used to produce through cross-examination. When I pass over from my standpoint to that of another, I go not only from my subjective view of myself to his objective view of me, but also from my objective view of him to his subjective view of himself. So when I come to realize that there is no absolute standpoint for me, I realize too that there is no absolute standpoint for him. I come to recognize his ignorance of himself and of me at the same moment that I come to recognize my ignorance of myself and of him. If I proceed in this manner to pass from my standpoint to that of one person after another, I will find myself cross-examining one person after another, as Socrates did, each time reexamining myself, as he also did, and each time coming to a fuller realization of my own ignorance and that of others.

Still, one might ask, is there such a difference between "passing over" and an "absolute standpoint"? Does not passing over itself serve as an absolute standpoint? A man who is sophisticated enough to be aware of the multiplicity of standpoints might pride himself on this and rely on this awareness and on his agility in passing over from one standpoint to another, just as he might have relied upon an absolute standpoint if he had thought that there was one. When Hegel describes what he means by "absolute knowledge" and the "absolute idea,"[11] it sounds as though he were describing the process of passing over. Absolute knowledge, according to him, is a knowledge of relative knowledge, a knowledge in which all the many relative forms of knowledge are preserved and surpassed. The absolute idea, and here he comes still closer to what we are saying, is not a particular idea with a particular content; it is simply the idea of the method itself. The absolute standpoint is thus a knowing or a method of knowing, or a knowing of this method of knowing that commands all other standpoints, from which all other standpoints can be derived, and in which all other standpoints can be united.

There is a radical difference between an "absolute standpoint" thus understood and what we have called "passing over" if and only if we hold fast to the principle that no standpoint is true in itself. The relativity of all standpoints can actually have a positive significance underlying its more obvious negative significance. It can point toward what we might call "mystery," meaning by that term not unintelligibility but inexhaustible intelligibility,[12] for the search from person to person involved in the process of passing over from standpoint to standpoint reveals each person as inexhaustible, incapable of being reduced to a single standpoint or to any sum of standpoints. If I keep in mind the relativity of standpoints as I pass over from one standpoint to another, therefore, I effectively hold myself open toward mystery. And my openness or orientation toward mystery becomes more and more explicit as the search goes on if I continue to hold fast to the relativity of all standpoints and do not allow passing over itself to become an absolute standpoint. The search thus becomes a positive quest of mystery, a quest, in New Testament terms, of "the way, the truth, and the life."

This description of a man searching from person to person for the way, the truth, and the life may sound rather odd, almost like a description of Diogenes with his lantern searching for an honest man. The difference between our searcher and Diogenes is that Diogenes goes from one person to another always failing to find what he is looking for, whereas our searcher, as he goes from one person to another, always finds what he is looking for, since each person is inexhaustible, each is a mystery, but he continues searching, nevertheless, because the further he goes, the more light is shed upon the mystery. It is not, therefore, a matter of looking for one person who will be the way, the truth, and the life, and rejecting all others, one by one. It is rather a matter of delving ever more deeply into the mystery of oneself and of others. And when it appears that Jesus is the way, the truth, and the life, as is said in the Gospel of John, "I am the way, the truth, and the life,"[13] this will be because in the person of Jesus one somehow finds a light on the mystery of oneself and others, which one can find in no other person.

The Quest of the Earthly Jesus

The quest of the way, the truth, and the life, based as it is on the principle that no standpoint is true in itself, is quite a different thing from the well-known "quest of the historical Jesus."[14] The quest of the historical Jesus, which was criticized by Schweitzer, was essentially a quest of the true standpoint on Jesus. The trouble was that there were many possible standpoints, that of Matthew, that of Mark, that of Luke, that of John. Which was the true one? On the whole it seemed that the true standpoint was that of Mark. In the last analysis, though, the quest of the true standpoint appeared to be hopeless, and the historical Jesus seemed to be forever hidden in the past. This was the conclusion on Jesus, but it could also be the conclusion on other personages, if the same zeal and rigor and exactitude were applied to finding the true standpoint on them. For instance, which was the true standpoint on Socrates? That of Plato, that of Xenophon, or that of Aristophanes? Or is Socrates, too, as has also been suggested, hidden forever in the past?

The real upshot, if our dialectic of standpoints is valid, is not that Jesus and Socrates and, for that matter, every other personage of the past and even of the present is simply hidden. It is rather that the kind of knowledge we can have of ourselves and others is a "knowledge of ignorance" instead of a "knowledge of knowledge." We can know what was true about Jesus from the standpoints of Matthew, Mark, Luke, and John, and we can know what was true about Socrates from the standpoints of Plato, Xenophon, and Aristophanes, even though we know that each of these standpoints is relative. We can pass over, furthermore, from these objective standpoints, relative as they are, to the subjective standpoints of Jesus and Socrates themselves, while realizing that these too are relative.

But can we say that the subjective standpoint of Jesus is relative? Is this not tantamount to denying his divinity? Actually to
say this neither affirms nor denies his divinity. It does affirm his
humanity. Let us consider, at any rate, what the life of Jesus
would look like if we should assume that his subjective standpoint
is relative, and if, going all the way, we should replace the "quest
of the historical Jesus" with the "quest of the way, the truth, and
the life." The relativity of the subjective standpoint is the fact
that there are as many subjective standpoints on a person's life as
there are different moments in his life. These standpoints always
differ quantitatively, the past and future being longer or shorter
according to the point where the person stands in his life, but
they differ qualitatively, the past and the future being taken
differently, before and after the turning points of the person's life.
The turning points in the life of Jesus, I would suggest, concern
his relations to John the Baptist.[15] At any rate, here again let us
consider what the life of Jesus would look like if we should assume that this is so.

The first great turning point in the life of Jesus would have
been his meeting with John the Baptist.[16] What this meeting did,
it appears, was raise in his life the issue of being God's son, God's
beloved. He came to John, apparently, in a considerably less
exalted state of mind, ready to undergo John's baptism of repentance and to be one among many sinners. When he was baptized,
however, he had a vision of the Spirit descending upon him, and
a voice was heard declaring him God's beloved son in whom God
was well pleased. Then he went into the desert and was tempted,
some of the temptations taking the form "if you are God's son.
. . ." The meaning of "God's son" here is probably the one suggested by the words "beloved" and "in whom I am well pleased,"
namely one who is God's beloved and in whom God is well
pleased. What happens here, this would imply, is that Jesus, who
is ready at this point to take his place among sinners, receives and
experiences unconditional acceptance from God. Now from the
standpoints of Matthew, Mark, Luke, and John, there can be no
question of Jesus taking his place among sinners, and then, too, he

is God's son in a somewhat different sense for each of them, but always in a stronger sense than this. It is possible, nevertheless, to pass over from their respective standpoints to that of Jesus at this point in his life by attending closely to the fact that he does, however paradoxical it seems, present himself to John for a baptism of repentance, and that the words declaring him God's son can be understood, however weak this seems in the light of later events, simply as God's favor.

Jesus evidently did not presume to be his own judge, either to condemn himself or to approve of himself. He came ready to accept condemnation of his past and received instead unconditional acceptance. Acceptance, however, was not without its problems, as the temptations immediately following demonstrated. The story of these temptations, as it was told from the standpoints of Matthew and Luke, was probably meant to show how Jesus overcame the temptations to which Israel had succumbed in the desert. This does not prevent them from having been very real and personal from the standpoint of Jesus himself.[17] Ready to undergo the baptism of repentance, he had been ready to accept condemnation of the past and to set the future against the past. Unconditionally accepted and looking toward the future anew, he was tempted to take advantage of his acceptance, but he refused to do so. Although he had been declared God's beloved like King David, he renounced the thought of an earthly kingdom, he resolved to live by God's word rather than by bread alone, and he determined not to presume upon God's acceptance or to put it to the test.

The second great turning point in the life of Jesus would have been the imprisonment of John the Baptist.[18] When John was imprisoned, as Mark tells us, or when Jesus heard that John was imprisoned, as Matthew tells us, Jesus went into Galilee and began to preach. The imprisonment of John, the stopping of John's preaching, was the signal for the beginning of Jesus's preaching. Significantly, too, as Matthew reports it, the message with which Jesus began was the same as the message of John, "Repent, for the kingdom of heaven is at hand." It is as though

Jesus felt called upon to take John's place, to proclaim the message that John was now prevented from proclaiming. The purport of John's message, however, would have been quite transformed when it came from the mouth of Jesus, transformed by the familiar relationship with God that grew out of unconditional acceptance. Jesus called God, not merely "Father" in formal terms as we translate it, but "Abba," the familiar form in Aramaic, an unprecedented usage.[19] What is more, he taught other men to speak of God and to God in this way, as though they too were unconditionally acceptable to God.

What Jesus saw himself as doing at this period of his life comes out, it seems, in his reply to the disciples of John the Baptist, who were sent by John from prison to ask Jesus "Are you the one coming or are we waiting for another?" Jesus replied "Go and tell John what you hear and see: the blind see, the lame walk, the lepers are cleansed, and the deaf hear, and the dead are raised and the poor receive the good news, and happy is he who is not scandalized at me."[20] This suggests a passage from the prophecy of Isaiah, the same passage with which Luke has Jesus begin his preaching.[21] It probably describes what Jesus at this time conceived to be the coming of the kingdom of God. From the standpoint of the evangelists the coming of the kingdom was probably much more than the coming of Jesus in his public life, it was his coming in glory, risen from the dead. From the standpoint of Jesus himself at this period, though, the coming of God's kingdom would be the new situation that comes about as he communicates to other men what he himself received at his baptism, God's unconditional acceptance.

The third great turning point in the life of Jesus would have been the death of John the Baptist. "When Jesus heard of it," Matthew tells us, "he withdrew from there in a boat to desert country by himself."[22] In John's death Jesus probably saw his own impending death. As John the Baptist was put to death by Herod, so also, Jesus and his contemporaries could see, was Jesus himself likely to be put to death. To begin his ministry, after the imprisonment of John, was to risk imprisonment; to continue it now, after the execution of John, was to risk death. As a matter of fact, Herod, thinking that Jesus was John the Baptist risen from the dead, wished to kill him. When Jesus was told of this, he said "Go and tell that fox, Behold, I cast out devils and do works of healing today and tomorrow, and on the third day I am finished. Yet today and tomorrow and the day after I must go on because it is not appropriate for a prophet to die outside of Jerusalem."[23] Perhaps he meant by this that he would presently finish his work in Galilee, Herod's jurisdiction, but that he was going on to Jerusalem, where he expected to die as had most of the prophets who were put to death. He dreaded the prospect. "Abba," he prayed in the garden of Gethsemani, "all things are possible to you, take away this cup from me, but not what I will but what you will."[24]

This prayer reveals the genuine attitude of Jesus towards his own death during this last period of his life. The death of Jesus probably made a great deal more sense from the standpoint of the evangelists than it did from his own standpoint at this time. It was not without meaning, however, from his own point of view, with his attitude toward God's will and his filial confidence in God. From the standpoint of the evangelists Jesus had to die so that by raising him from the dead God could reveal that Jesus was the Lord. From his own standpoint Jesus could probably have said something like what John the evangelist said: "Beloved, we are now children of God and it has not yet been manifested what we shall be."[25] Jesus had already received and experienced unconditional acceptance from God and lived on familiar terms with God, calling him "Abba," but from his present standpoint it had not yet been manifested what he was ultimately to be. He was led into temptation and his relationship with God was put to the test upon the cross, where he cried out "Eli, Eli, lamma sabachthani?" "My God, my God, why have you forsaken me?"[26] Still he did not despair, but was praying at the end, "Abba, into your hands I commend my spirit."[27]

Thus if we assume that the subjective standpoint of Jesus was relative, manifold, changing from period to period in his life, he appears to be fully and unequivocally human. His divinity, nevertheless, is not denied. Actually the full impact of the statement "Jesus is the Lord," the fundamental statement of Christian faith, cannot be felt without first grasping the reality of his humanity. It is only when one sees Jesus as fully and unequivocally human that his lordship and divinity appears for the staggering mystery that it is. This is the way it will have appeared to his original disciples, who will have known him first as a man, obviously a man, and only afterward, when he rose from the dead, will have perceived his lordship and divinity. In our culture, by contrast, where Jesus is the archetypal man, the culture hero,[28] it is necessary to move to a position where he can be seen as truly human. To feel the overwhelming mystery of the incarnation in our time, it is necessary to pass from the initial stage in which we find ourselves, where Jesus is the culture hero, through an intermediate stage, in which he becomes fully and unequivocally human for us, to a final stage, in which we can appreciate the unending wonder of the statement "Jesus is the Lord."

To reach this intermediate stage, where Jesus is fully and unequivocally human for us, we must pass over from the standpoint in which we are subjective and Jesus is objective (as culture hero) to the standpoint in which he is subjective. Luther, for example, attempted to enter into sympathy with Jesus by conceiving the abandonment experienced by Jesus on the cross to have been actual despair.[29] I believe that Luther was wrong on this, that Jesus did not despair, though he said, "My God, my God, why have you forsaken me?" but that he continued to the last to hope in spite of his experience of Godforsakenness, "Abba, into your hands I commend my spirit." Still Luther was able, notwithstanding this seeming error in the process, to pass over to the subjective standpoint of Jesus, to grasp the reality of Jesus' humanity and thus to feel the full impact of the Gospel that "Jesus is the Lord." Although we cannot be sure of our grounds, therefore, in passing over to the standpoint of Jesus, it is still supremely worthwhile to make the attempt and to accept the risks involved. For it is only in passing over in this manner, I believe, that the humanity of Jesus becomes real to us and we enter into a position where we can perceive the overpowering significance of the tidings that "God exalted him and gave him the name that is above every name."

Bringing Deathtime to Mind

The past consists largely of the lives of men and women whose very names have been forgotten. Almost nothing is known of individuals who lived in the long ages before writing was invented, and very little is known of those who lived in the first millennia of the recorded past. It would be something of a feat to give names to these nameless individuals; it would be like raising them from the dead. There is something that we can do, nevertheless, toward establishing their identities even without knowing their names or having their biographies at our disposal. We can at least determine how they went about identifying themselves, how they understood their identity, how they understood their individuality. We can describe the many parts a man would play in his time, even when we cannot name the actor who played them. Among the most primitive peoples, for example, the human life cycle is usually conceived to run through the following phases: from birth to naming; from naming to initiation; from initiation to death; from death to funeral; from funeral to the end of mourning, when all personal relations with the dead are severed; and from this severance to rebirth.[30] To become an individual, according to this notion of the life cycle, is to become a new instance of an original which has existed many times before and will exist many times again.

When a people make a practice of severing relations with their dead, as do most of the peoples who still live by hunting and food-gathering, their past does not accumulate, and the only passage of time they find significant is the passage that occurs in the ordinary human lifetime. Almost from the beginning of man's existence on earth, though, there have been peoples who have allowed the past to accumulate, who have maintained relations with their dead, who have buried their dead in caves, or who have set up megaliths or built pyramids, or who have made and recorded history. If history is the cumulative past, then these peoples have been creating history in the shape of a community of the dead outnumbering the community of the living and always growing in number through fresh additions from among the living. To become an individual among these peoples has meant more than becoming one of the living; it has meant becoming one of the dead. Life for them has not been a process of being born, named, and initiated into the community of the living, nor has death been an opposite process of relapsing into the state of the uninitiated, the anonymous, and the unborn. Instead, life has been a process of becoming a human being, and death has been considered its point of completion. The fully individuated man has not been the initiate but the dead man, and the mask a man has been called upon to wear ultimately has not been the animal face of his totem but his own death mask.

There have been thinkers in these historically minded civilizations, nevertheless, who have maintained that the lifetime is the only time that should have significance for man, that centuries and millennia can have significance only for a god or for a man who is attempting to be a god, and that each generation of men has the same task to accomplish in life as every previous generation.[31] All generations, according to this, are contemporary, in that the lapse of time between one and another is not significant. The millennia separating me from Abraham, to use one of Kierkegaard's examples, are insignificant beside the three days it took Abraham to reach the top of the mountain where he was to sacrifice Isaac, for the millennia are not a time in someone's lifetime whereas the three days are such a time and a crucial time at that. As a result Abraham and I are contemporaries in that no significant lapse of time separates us from one another.

The contemporaneity of generations is in effect a negative answer to the question "Is the past more necessary than the future?" where the cumulative past is an affirmative answer. A man who maintains the contemporaneity of generations differs, to be sure, from the primitive hunter and food-gatherer who has no conception of a cumulative past, because it is one thing never to have thought of the cumulative past and quite another thing to have thought of it and to have consciously and deliberately rejected the idea. This conscious and deliberate rejection, though it is a rejection of the heritage of the time in which he lives, does not place a man in a position of revolt against his time. Rather it places him in a position of withdrawal. To revolt against his time, a man must accept the idea of a cumulative past but reject the idea of a conformable future. He must, in effect, say *Yes* to the question "Is the past more necessary than the future?" but *No* to the question "Will the future be like the past?" When a modern revolutionary, for example, expresses the hope that he will be vindicated by history, he is assuming that the future will eventually become part of the cumulative past which he calls "history," and he is guessing that when it does, it will prove to have been different from what was already past.

A further possibility would be to combine the idea of novelty in time with the idea that man's time is strictly the human lifetime. This is the view that pervades process thinking like that of Bergson and Whitehead. The future is not like the past, according to this, and the past accumulates, but the time encompassing the lifetime is God's time rather than man's time. The greater time, as Whitehead envisions it,[32] instead of being merely the time of mankind or of society, is that of God's adventure, and the individual man is God's companion for a short time along the way. A man's own adventure in time is only lifelong, and yet as God's companion he incorporates the greater past into his life and his own adventure gets incorporated into the greater future. The past accumulates, so to speak, in the divine memory. It enters into the individual life insofar as the living person relates himself to the dead. In turn his life itself enters in the same manner into the future, having attained immortality in the memory of God.

When it comes to judging among these various views and deciding whether the encompassing time is man's time or God's time, whether the past is cumulative, whether the future is novel, perhaps we should have recourse once again to the relativity of standpoints. The individual man can pose these problems about the greater past and future with as much practical significance for his own life as he can the parallel problems about his own past and future. He can make them biographical questions, situating his life in time, or he can make them autobiographical questions, construing time in terms of his life. There may be, in fact, a close link between his attitudes concerning time and those concerning his lifetime. And it will probably consist in his way of taking the relationship between the dead and the living. For the basic issue in questions about his past and his future is that of becoming one of the living, while in those about *the* past and *the* future it is that of becoming one of the dead. Questions concerning the lifetime are summed up in this, "Who am I becoming among the living?" those concerning the greater time in this, "Who am I becoming among the dead?"

These two issues, that of becoming one of the living and that of becoming one of the dead, have been variously conceived and dealt with in existentialism and psychoanalysis. Kierkegaard handled them by distinguishing two standpoints, the standpoint of life and the standpoint of death, the one being the standpoint from which a man is in the process of becoming and the other the standpoint from which the process of becoming is finished, and he concluded that the standpoint of death is illusory, since it involves the assumption that life is over for the man who occupies the standpoint.[33] Freud, on the other hand, postulated two kinds of instincts, the life instincts and the death instincts, the one kind governing the process of becoming one of the living and the other governing the process of becoming one of the dead, and his conclusion was that the life instincts are subordinate to the death instincts since the final outcome of life is always death.[34]

Actually Kierkegaard's notion of "standpoint" involves fewer dubious assumptions than Freud's notion of "instinct," and for that reason seems more appropriate. Instead of being a struggle between life instincts and death instincts, with the death instincts ultimately victorious, life would be more plausibly a process that can be regarded from two standpoints, that of life itself and that of death. There seems to be this much truth in Freud's method, though, that becoming one of the dead should be considered as much a process as becoming one of the living. The standpoint of life and the standpoint of death, instead of differing as the standpoint of becoming and the standpoint of being finished, as they did for Kierkegaard, would differ as the standpoint of becoming one of the living and the standpoint of becoming one of the dead. Thus it would be possible for a man to pass over from the standpoint of life to the standpoint of death without treating himself as though he were already dead. It would be possible, that is, provided he does not conceive the process of becoming one of the dead as it is conceived among the primitive hunting and food-gathering peoples to begin with the moment of death rather than to run through life.

The question that would arise for a man when he passes over from the standpoint of life to the standpoint of death would be something on this order: "If I must someday die, what can I do to satisfy my desire to live?"[35] The problem is, if I must become one of the dead, how I am to become one of the living, or reversing it, if I am to become one of the living, how I can become one of the dead. When a man passes over from an objective standpoint on his life to an objective standpoint on his death, his death will appear to him as an objective fact, an occurrence that will someday be historically verifiable but that is not verifiable as yet. When he passes over from a subjective standpoint on his life to a subjective standpoint on his death, however, his death will appear to him as a subjective certainty, the certainty that "I will die" comparable with the very certainty that "I am." Thus passing over from the standpoint of life to the standpoint of death means coming to the objective probability or to the subjective certainty of one's death and is analogous to the act of dying.

And if passing over from the standpoint of life to that of death is like dying, passing over from the standpoint of death to that of life is like rising from the dead. When a man passes over from an objective standpoint on his death to an objective standpoint on his life, he sees life as a fact in spite of the fact of death. Likewise when a man passes over from a subjective standpoint on his death to a subjective standpoint on his life, he sees that the certainty that "I am" stands in spite of the certainty that "I will die." The problem of death becomes a problem for the individual when he passes over from the standpoint of life to that of death; the solution becomes a solution for him when he passes back from the standpoint of death to that of life. To understand another man, therefore, I must die with him and rise with him again; I must pass over with him from the standpoint of life to that of death, and then I must pass back with him from the standpoint of death to that of life. I must do in his regard something analogous to what Paul would have the Christian do in regard to Christ: be buried with him in death in order to be raised with him unto life.[36]

What I will discover when I do this is ignorance, the sort of ignorance Socrates used to bring to light in himself and in others. If indeed the principles underlying our dialectic of standpoints are valid, then neither the standpoint of life nor the standpoint of death is true in itself. So to pass over from the standpoint of life to that of death and back again will be to discover my ignorance of the meaning of my life. When I do this with another, I will come across a different version of the problem of death and a different solution of the problem, but what I will ultimately discover is another man's ignorance and a new dimension of my own ignorance. "If Christ be not risen from the dead,"[37] ignorance and more ignorance is all that I could ever hope to discover, and the knowledge of ignorance will ultimately have been vain. But if Christ be risen from the dead, then the knowledge of ignorance will not have been vain. If Christ be risen from the dead, it will be possible to "pass over from death to life,"[38] and in passing over to discover an inexhaustible meaning in life and in death.

The Quest of the Risen Jesus

"Christ!" exclaims Vladimir, "What has Christ got to do with it? You're not going to compare yourself to Christ!" "All my life

I've compared myself to him," answers Estragon in Samuel Beckett's tragicomedy, *Waiting for Godot*.[39] Time in this play is "out of mind," immemorial like time before the arbitrary boundary fixed by law as 1189. "Have you not done tormenting me with your accursed time!" Pozzo cries, "It's abominable! When! When! One day, is that not enough for you, one day he went dumb, one day I went blind, one day we'll go deaf, one day we were born, one day we shall die, the same day, the same second, is that not enough for you?"[40] But the boundary that separates time out of mind from time within mind is not quite so arbitrary as 1189; it is the very boundary that separates B.C. from A.D. The characters in the play are lost, as it were, in B.C., waiting for A.D. to come. They are contemporary with us, and yet they are living before Christ. It is as though we ourselves were living before Christ instead of after him.

Maybe living in "our era," as the A.D. period is called, does not come naturally to us. Maybe it is something we have to attain to. And maybe we are lost, lost in time out of mind, until we attain to it. Christ is the hero of our era, the archetypal man.[41] But there is a seemingly insoluble problem involved in living according to this archetype. "The passion of man," Sartre has said, "is the reverse of that of Christ, for man loses himself as man in order that God may be born."[42] What Sartre apparently means is that man attempts to do away with the concerns and anxieties that make him human, either by fulfilling his desires or else by hardening himself to pain and deprivation or else by renouncing his hopes and fears, in order that the fulfilled or hardened or detached being that he conceives to be divine may be born. This is what seems to prevent us from entering the A.D. period and finding our way to the present. We lose ourselves as human beings in order that God may be born. We are like the two bums, Vladimir and Estragon, who are waiting for Godot. We are oriented toward the future, waiting for the future to dawn. We live in B.C., waiting for A.D. to come, waiting for God to be born. Vladimir and Estragon wait and wait again, but Godot never comes. The future is always ahead, always still to come. Complete fulfillment, complete hardening, complete detachment, are always out of reach. "We lose ourselves in vain," Sartre concluded, "man is a useless passion."[43]

What is missing here, I believe, is the humanity of Christ, the fact that the passion of God, the reverse of what Sartre called the "passion of man," God losing himself as God in order that man may be born, is also a human passion. The passion of God, in fact, is the passion to be human, just as the passion of man is the passion to be divine. Although man is not God and therefore in a sense cannot lose himself as God, he can very well have the desire to be God, to be God through fulfillment or through hardening or through renunciation, and so he can lose himself as God by aiming at being man rather than at being God. The lost pathway into the present, if this is correct, is the path of the "kenosis," the "emptying" of self described in the first half of the great hymn about Christ:

> *Being in the form of God*
> *He counted not as plunder*
> *Equality with God,*
>
> *But emptied himself,*
> *Taking the form of a servant,*
> *Coming to be like men;*
>
> *And found in shape as a man,*
> *He humbled himself*
> *Becoming obedient unto death,*
> *even the death of the cross.*[44]

Every man can participate in this, passing over from the standpoint of life to the standpoint of death, because he can aim at being a man, even a mortal man, instead of aiming at being God. And if he does this, he empties himself, and, passing back again from the standpoint of death to the standpoint of life, he finds his way into the present, which is defined by the "exaltation" described in the second half of the hymn:

Therefore God also exalted him
And gave him the name
That is above every name,

That in the name of Jesus
Every knee should bend
In heaven, on earth,
     and below the earth,

And every tongue should confess
That Jesus Christ is Lord
To the glory of God the Father.

The logic of the exaltation is this, that the man who loses himself as God in order that man may be born is undergoing the passion of God, for it is the passion of God to lose oneself as God in order that man may be born. So the "name that is above every name" belongs to such a one, that is, the name of the Lord.

This implies that there is a unity between the passion of God and the passion of man. What man attempts to accomplish, losing himself as man in order that God may be born, is actually accomplished when he loses himself as God in order that man may be born. Hegel took this unity to be that of a single standpoint, the absolute standpoint, the standpoint of what he called "absolute knowledge" and "absolute idea." The double process of man losing himself as man in order that God may be born and God losing himself as God in order that man may be born, the "Golgotha of absolute spirit,"[45] as Hegel called it, is the ultimate theme of Hegel's *Phenomenology of Mind,* and the knowledge of this process is what he there called "absolute knowledge." It is also the ultimate theme of his *Science of Logic,* and the idea of this process is what he there called "absolute idea."

The trouble with Hegel's conception of the "Golgotha of absolute spirit" is that it involves what seems to be an illusion about the extent to which we can understand the passion of God and the passion of man. The illusion is that grasping the unity of the divine and the human passion amounts to comprehending them fully. In reality man, although he can grasp this unity, does not fully understand what he is doing when he loses himself as man in order that God may be born. Nor does he fully understand what he is doing when he loses himself as God in order that man may be born. The "Golgotha of absolute spirit," once one realizes this, is replaced by the Golgotha of a spirit which is not possessed of any absolute knowledge or absolute idea but only of a knowledge of its own ignorance. The knowledge a man has when he realizes that he does not know what he is doing in losing himself as man in order that God may be born is like the knowledge of ignorance professed by Socrates. The corresponding knowledge a man has when he realizes that he does not know what he is doing in losing himself as God in order that man may be born is like the consciousness of mystery shown by Jesus when he cried out, "My God, my God, why have you forsaken me?"

It is the acknowledgment of ignorance, the openness toward mystery, that authenticates both the passion of man and the passion of God. We can understand what it is to desire to be God through fulfillment of desire or through hardening against pain and deprivation or through renunciation of hope and fear, and so we can understand conversely what it is to aim at being man rather than God. When we make humanity our aim, however, and enter thereby into a sympathetic understanding of the passion of Christ, we discover that the fulfilled or hardened or detached being that we had imagined to be divine on the basis of our own desire to be God is not the genuine God, but the genuine God is the one who loses himself as God in order that man may be born. It appears to us then that if Socrates, for example, had merely engaged in what he (or Plato) called the "practice of dying,"[46] the practice of detaching himself from the objects of hope and fear, he would have been on the wrong track. He would have been losing himself as man in order that a false god might be born. What put Socrates on the right track, it appears, then, is that he engaged in this practice acknowledging his own ignorance, opening his mind and heart toward mystery, and thus in effect seeking the way, the truth, and the life.

That Jesus, on the other hand, truly undergo the passion of

God, losing himself as God in order that man might be born, it was necessary not only that his subjective standpoint be relative, as we have seen, changing from one turning point to another in his life, and thus that he be genuinely human, but also that he be conscious of this relativity, and thus that he be consciously and deliberately human. Otherwise he will have become man, but becoming man will not have been his aim. The conscious relativity of his standpoint appears in the consciousness of mystery that he showed on the cross, asking God why he had forsaken him, or beforehand in the garden, asking God if it were possible that the cup of his suffering might pass from him, or earlier, refusing to presume upon God's acceptance or to make of it a claim to earthly authority, or still earlier, refusing to be his own judge, either to condemn or to approve of himself, and being ready to take his place among sinners by undergoing the baptism of repentance.

All during the life of Jesus the kenosis was taking place, the process of consciously living a human life and ultimately dying a human death. At the same time, however, the exaltation was going on in the shape of the acceptance he was receiving and experiencing from God. This acceptance was conscious too, as appears in the fact that Jesus lived on familiar terms with God, calling him "Abba." The process of becoming as kenosis ends in being human, in being Jesus; as exaltation it ends in fellowship with God, in being the Lord. Looked at the one way, the life of Jesus is the process of the Lord becoming Jesus; the other way it is the process of Jesus becoming the Lord. It is from various standpoints on the completed life that the evangelists, Matthew, Mark, Luke, and John, speak of Jesus, standpoints from which it is true purely and simply that "Jesus is the Lord." If we pass over from their standpoints to the subjective standpoint of Jesus himself during his life, though, we pass over to a standpoint in which Jesus is in the process of becoming who he is, a standpoint in which Jesus himself has not yet experienced or fully understood what it is to be the one whom he is becoming.[47]

Saying this, however, does not amount to saying what the

Arians said in the classical controversies on Christ, which took place in the fourth century, namely that "there was a time when he was not."[48] The Lord as understood here is the Lord of the Old Testament, the figure whom the Israelites called "Yahweh." This name, the name Yahweh, is "the name that is above every name," the name God gave Jesus in exalting him.[49] The statement "Jesus is the Lord" means "Jesus is Yahweh," and the life of Jesus was thus a process of Jesus becoming Yahweh and Yahweh becoming Jesus. The life of Jesus, nevertheless, is comparable with the life of any other man in that the final statement, "Jesus is Yahweh," is true as a result of Jesus's life and would not be true, in spite of the preexistence of Yahweh, if Jesus had never lived. The divinity of Jesus lies where the uniqueness of any man lies. Socrates and I are fellow men, and yet I cannot become Socrates. Likewise Jesus and I are fellow men, and yet I cannot become Jesus, nor can I become the Lord.

The passion of Christ, accordingly, cannot be legitimately generalized and the individual Jesus left out of it, as though we fully comprehended it and could repeat it at will. Instead we have first to pass over from our standpoint to his, and only then will we be able, passing back to our own standpoint, to participate in his kenosis and his exaltation. When we pass back from the standpoint of Jesus to our own standpoint, when we come to ourselves and to our lives, seen in the light of a sympathetic understanding of his life, we find the "power to become sons of God,"[50] spoken of in the Gospel of John, but we find simultaneously that this power to become sons of God is exercised by becoming flesh as "the Word became flesh."[51] The power to become a son of God for Simon is the power to become Peter; for Saul it is the power to become Paul. It is after he recognized that Jesus is the Christ, "You are the Christ, the Son of the living God," that Simon learns that he himself is Peter, "You are Peter."[52] The exaltation for Simon is to become Peter, but the kenosis is to become Simon. The exaltation for Saul is to become Paul, but the kenosis is to become Saul. The outcome of life for Jesus is that Jesus is the

Lord, Yahweh; the outcome for Simon is that Simon is Peter; the outcome for Saul is that Saul is Paul.

There are the beginnings in all this of an answer to our original question "Does becoming end in being or does it end in nothingness?" The term *becoming* has changed meaning twice in the course of our inquiry. Our starting point was the ordinary meaning of becoming as the relationship between one immediate moment and another, between one point in life and another. On this level life looked like a simple process of going from infancy to childhood to youth to manhood to middle age to old age to second childhood. Our first move, then, was to dilate the present, passing from the immediate moment where concern is confined to the present situation to the existential moment where concern is extended to one's past and future. On this new level, the level of lifetime, becoming appeared to be the relationship between one existential moment and another, between one's whole life taken one way at one point and one's whole life taken another way at another point. Here it seemed that no one way of taking one's life was exhaustive, that life could not be exhausted from any standpoint, subjective or objective, or from any sum of standpoints. This seemed already to belie the notion that becoming ends in nothingness, that life is nothing but life. It also seemed to belie any quest of the true standpoint on a person such as the quest of the historical Jesus or the quest of the historical Socrates and seemed to call rather for what we have termed a "quest of the way, the truth, and the life."

Our second move was to dilate the present once again, passing from the existential moment, where concern is confined to one's lifetime, to the historic moment, where concern is extended to all time, both the past and the future. On this level, the level of what we have termed "deathtime," becoming appeared to be the relationship between one historic moment and another, between one's lifetime as it appears in the context of all time from one point in one's life, and one's lifetime as it appears in that context from another point in one's life. On the level of lifetime becoming appeared as the process of becoming one of the living; on the level of deathtime it appeared as the process of becoming one of the dead. As what Sartre called the "passion of man," losing oneself as man in order that God may be born, becoming one of the dead appeared to be aimed at nothingness, the nothingness at least of man. As a passion like that of Christ, on the other hand, which Sartre called the "reverse" of the passion of man, losing oneself as God in order that man may be born, becoming one of the dead appeared to be aimed at being, the being at least of man. Now it appears that this last way of becoming is the way into the fully dilated present, the A.D. period, the time created by the kenosis and exaltation of Christ. This is the road that should lead from time out of mind to time within mind.

NOTES

CHAPTER I. TIME OUT OF MIND

1. *As You Like It,* Act II, scene 7, lines 139 ff.
2. *King Lear,* Act V, scene 2, line 11.
3. Hegel, *The Phenomenology of Mind,* tr. by J. B. Baillie (New York, Macmillan, 1961), p. 135.
4. Sören Kierkegaard, *Concluding Unscientific Postscript,* tr. by David Swenson and Walter Lowrie (Princeton, N.J., Princeton University Press, 1941), p. 311.
5. The question "Will the future be like the past?" is posed by Hume in his *Treatise on Human Nature,* Book 1, part 3, chapter 12. The question "Is the past more necessary than the future?" is posed by Kierkegaard in his *Philosophical Fragments,* 2nd ed. by Niels Thulstrup, tr. by David Swenson, rev. tr. by H. V. Hong (Princeton, N.J., Princeton University Press, 1962), pp. 89 ff. (the Interlude).
6. Cf. Roy Pascal, *Design and Truth in Autobiography* (Cambridge, Mass., Harvard University Press, 1960), p. *vii.*
7. Set forth by Kierkegaard in the *Concluding Unscientific Post-script,* pp. 169 ff.
8. Set forth by Freud in *The Future of an Illusion,* tr. by W. D. Robson-Scott (New York, Doubleday, 1964).
9. Aristotle, *Metaphysics,* Λ, 1074b35. Cf. also *ibid.,* 1072b18-31 which Hegel quotes to conclude his own *Encyclopedia* (second edition).
10. Plato, *Apology,* 21 ff.
11. Hegel discusses "absolute knowledge" in the last chapter of the *Phenomenology of Mind* and the "absolute idea" in the last chapter of the *Science of Logic.*
12. Cf. my definition of "mystery" in *The City of the Gods* (New York, Macmillan 1965) as an "inexhaustible source of soluble problems," p. 4.
13. John 14:6.
14. Albert Schweitzer, *The Quest of the Historical Jesus* (London, Macmillan, 1911). For the present state of the question cf. James M. Robinson, *A New Quest of the Historical Jesus* (London, Allenson 1959).

15. For the positions that have recently been taken on the role of John the Baptist in the life of Jesus cf. Robinson, *op. cit.*, p. 114, note 1 and pp. 116 ff.
16. Matthew 3:13 ff.; Mark 1:9 ff.; Luke 3:21 ff.
17. Bultmann, after recognizing the possible connection between the temptations ascribed to Jesus and the temptations of Israel in the desert, goes on to argue as follows: "But there is no clue why these three events were told as three temptations of the Son of God, i.e., the people of God, and that this was the basis for them being ascribed to Jesus; for the Jewish tradition, though it certainly knew stories of temptation by Satan, knew none about the temptation of the Messiah, nor could it have ever recounted anything of the kind," *History of the Synoptic Tradition*, tr. by John Marsh (New York, Harper 1963), pp. 256 f. Bultmann's conclusion is that the temptation story shows Hellenistic influence. But one might use these same considerations to argue that the story, in spite of Old Testament echoes, reflects an actual event in the life of Jesus or perhaps reflects the types of temptation that ran through his whole life.
18. Matthew 4:12; Mark 1:14.
19. On the significance of this term and its use by Jesus cf. Joachim Jeremias as quoted in Robinson, *A New Quest*, p. 24, note 1.
20. Matthew 11:1 ff.; Luke 7:18 ff.
21. Isaiah 61:1 ff. in Luke 4:18 f.
22. Matthew 14:13. For recent discussion of the significance of John's death in the life of Jesus cf. Robinson, *A New Quest*, p. 114, note 1.
23. Luke 13:31 ff.
24. Mark 14:36.
25. I John 3:2.
26. Matthew 27:46; Mark 15:34.
27. Luke 23:46.
28. Cf. *infra*, note 41.
29. Cf. Luther's commentary on Psalm 22:1 in *Opera* (Jena, Germany, Richtzenhainus and Rebartus 1566), II, 227 ff. Cf. my discussion of this in *The City of the Gods*, p. 186.
30. Cf. G. Rachel Levy, *The Gate of Horn* (London, Faber and Faber, 1948), pp. 65 ff. on the contrast between the cave-dwelling peoples of paleolithic times, who maintained relations with their dead and the surviving hunting, and food-gathering peoples, who make a practice of severing relations with the dead. She sees the practice of maintaining relations with the dead as part of the culture that carried through from the paleolithic cave-dwellers to the neolithic village-dwellers and the early historical city-dwellers.
31. Cf. especially Kierkegaard, *Fear and Trembling*, tr. by Walter

Lowrie (New York, Doubleday, 1954), pp. 129 ff. (the Epilogue), and *Philosophical Fragments,* pp. 111 ff. Cf. also Martin Heidegger, *Being and Time,* tr. by John Macquarrie and Edward Robinson (New York, Harper, 1962), pp. 424 ff.

32. Cf. Whitehead, *Process and Reality* (New York, Harper, 1960), especially the conclusion pp. 531 ff.

33. Cf. Kierkegaard, *Concluding Unscientific Postscript,* pp. 74 ff. (the true standpoint as the standpoint of becoming); pp. 131 and 141 (as the standpoint of life rather than death); pp. 267 ff. (as the standpoint of existence); and p. 273 (the alternative standpoint calls logically for suicide).

34. Freud set forth his view on life and death instincts first in *Beyond the Pleasure Principle* (1920), tr. by James Strachey (New York, Bantam, 1959).

35. I have attempted to trace the solutions given to this problem by different societies in *The City of the Gods.* This formulation of the problem occurs there in the preface (p. *v*) and in the conclusion (pp. 217 ff.).

36. Romans 6:3 ff.

37. I Corinthians 15:17.

38. John 5:24; I John 3:14.

39. Samuel Beckett, *Waiting for Godot* (New York, Grove, 1954), p. 34.

40. *Ibid.,* p. 57.

41. "Our discourse necessarily brings us to Christ, because he is the still living myth of our culture. He is our culture hero, who, regardless of his historical existence, embodies the myth of the divine Primordial Man, the mystic Adam." C. G. Jung, *Aion (The Collected Works of C. G. Jung,* IX, 2) tr. by R. F. C. Hull (New York, Princeton University Press, 1959), p. 36.

42. Jean Paul Sartre, *Being and Nothingness,* tr. by Hazel Barnes (New York, Philosophical Library 1956), p. 615.

43. *Loc. cit.*

44. Philippians 2:6 ff. On the division into two strophes and into stanzas of three lines cf. F. W. Beare, *A Commentary on the Epistle to the Philippians* (New York, Harper, 1959), pp. 73 ff.

45. This phrase occurs on the last page of *The Phenomenology of Mind.*

46. *Phaedo,* 61 ff.

47. On the difficulty of dealing with an issue such as this in terms of traditional scholastic categories cf. Karl Rahner, *Theological Investigations,* tr. by Cornelius Ernst (Baltimore, Taplinger, 1961), I, 149 ff.

48. Some codices add a condemnation of this sentence to the Nicene

creed in the acts of the Council of Nicea. Cf. Denzinger-Umberg, *Enchiridion Symbolorum* (Barcelona, Herder, 1948), p. 30.

49. The Greek word *Kyrios,* "Lord," the title given to Jesus in the hymn of Philippians 2:6 ff. and generally in the New Testament, is the word for Yahweh in the Greek version of the Old Testament, the Septuagint.

50. John 1:2.

51. John 1:14.

52. Matthew 16:16 ff.

2

The Life Story

"IN EACH PERIOD," Whitehead has said, "there is a general form of the forms of thought; and, like the air we breathe, such a form is so translucent, and so pervading, and so seemingly necessary, that only by extreme effort can we become aware of it."[1] There is, I would suggest, not only what Whitehead called a "form of the forms of thought," but there is also what might be called a "form of forms of life," equally translucent, equally pervading, equally necessary to all appearances, and equally difficult to become aware of in each of the great period of history. When Yeats, for example, speaks of "our culture with its doctrine of sincerity and self-realization,"[2] he is articulating to some extent, it seems, both the modern form of the forms of thought and the modern form of the forms of life. The modern form of the forms of life, as we shall see, appears to be the form of self-appropriation, the form of a transition from a state of alienation to a state of autonomy, which the life story characteristically exhibits in modern times. The modern form of the forms of thought, accordingly, as can be seen in idealism, Marxism, existentialism, psychoanalysis, and many other modern ideologies, is characterized by the problems of alienation, autonomy, and appropriation.

Now the "quest of the way, the truth, and the life" of which we have spoken seems to have taken different forms in different periods of history according to the different prevailing forms of thought and life. In the New Testament period, when life, at least in some milieus, was still conceived as a story of deeds, the quest, for instance the quest that carried Paul from Pharisaism to Christianity, tended to involve a man in the problem of faith and works. In a later period, when life was conceived as a story of experience, the quest, for instance the quest that carried Augustine from Manichaeism to Christianity, tended to involve a man in the problem of the gamut of experience. In the modern period when life is conceived as a story of appropriation, the quest, for instance the quest that carried Kierkegaard from Hegelianism to Christianity, tends to involve a man in the problem of alienation and autonomy. If it is only by extreme effort, as Whitehead said, that we can become aware of the form of the forms that prevails, especially in our own time, it will be worthwhile for us to trace the quest through these different forms, hoping to come thereby to a genuine awareness of the modern form and of its historical relativity.

Paul and the Story of Deeds

Paul, both Paul the Pharisee and Paul the Christian, appears to have conceived the problem of death to be a problem of unrighteousness. "The sting of death is sin,"[3] he said to the Corinthians. Thus the solution of the problem for Paul was righteousness, at first the righteousness that comes through fulfillment of the law, the righteousness of the Pharisee, afterward that which comes through reliance upon Christ, the righteousness of the Christian. For if unrighteousness gives death its sting, then righteousness and righteousness alone can take the sting out of death. What Paul meant by unrighteousness he described in detail in the famous passage on the wrath of God in his epistle to the Romans, where he listed the unrighteous deeds of the pagans. How unrighteousness gives death its sting he says in the last line of that passage: "Knowing the ordinance of God, that those who do these things are worthy of death, they not only do these things but they even countenance those who do them."[4] Evidently unrighteousness gives death its sting by making a man worthy of death and making him know that he is worthy of death. The sting is the consciousness that one is worthy of death. What righteousness does, consequently, is not to eliminate death itself but to eliminate this worthiness of death.

Righteousness thus understood was not a problem in the eastern religions, Buddhism and Hinduism, because it is the question of man's standing before God, and without a God like that of the Bible, this kind of question never arises. It is a recurrent problem, though, where the Biblical tradition has prevailed. Witness, for instance, the centrality of the problem in the Protestant Reformation. And it remains a problem even after the existence of the Biblical God has been called into doubt. For instance, Kant, who lived at a time when the existence of God had already been very seriously questioned, and who took this doubt into his own reckoning, had an idea about being worthy of happiness that is quite parallel to the idea of being worthy of life or not being worthy of death. When he posed what he considered the primary question of conscience and posed it in its simplest form, in terms of deeds, "What should I do?" his answer, which he tried to put in equally simple terms, was "Do what will make you worthy of happiness."[5] His meaning was that one should not strive for happiness itself, whether because this motive was too selfish to be ethical, or because it was impossible to make oneself happy by one's own deeds, or because the existence of the God who would confer happiness was in doubt; but that one should strive only to make oneself worthy of happiness.

The existence of God was not in doubt at the time of Paul but the existence of the afterlife in the shape of resurrection was very much in doubt. Among the Jews of his time the Sadducees denied the resurrection, while the Pharisees affirmed it. Paul himself, being at first a Pharisee and then afterward a Christian, maintained the doctrine of resurrection throughout his life. He was aware, though, of those who denied it and plunged himself into arguments with them: on one occasion setting Pharisees against

Sadducees on the question of the resurrection, on another provoking the scorn of pagans by maintaining the resurrection, and on
others arguing with Christians who thought to deny the resurrection.[6] To deny the resurrection was in Paul's eyes to stultify
righteousness. In the eyes of Paul the Pharisee it was to stultify
fulfillment of the law; in the eyes of Paul the Christian it was to
stultify reliance upon the risen Christ. "If the dead do not rise,"
Paul argued as a Christian to Christians, "then Christ has not
risen either; and if Christ has not risen, your faith is madness, you
are still in your sins."[7]

When not only the resurrection of the dead but the very existence of God has come into doubt as it has in modern times, this,
one might think, would no longer be pertinent. Yet Kant, reflecting on the modern doubt about God's existence, was able to come
forward with an argument very similar to that of Paul. To the
question "What should I do?" he had answered "Do what will
make you worthy of happiness." To what he considered the other
principal question concerning the realm of action, "What may I
hope?" he answered "To be happy," in fact "To be everlastingly
happy." The modern doubt about the existence of God has its
roots, Kant believed, in the rather sober answer that must be
given to the question about the realm of thought that goes before
these questions about the realm of action, the question "What can
I know?" The two practical issues, though, "What should I do?"
and "What may I hope?" are connected for Kant much as righteousness and resurrection are connected for Paul. If the endeavor
to make oneself worthy of happiness makes sense, he reasoned,
then the hope for happiness must also make sense.[8]

The ultimate question, therefore, is whether or not the quest of
this worthiness, worthiness of life or worthiness of happiness, is
inherently futile. The quest of righteousness is the thing that
carries through from Paul's days as a Pharisee to his days as a
Christian. The conviction that the quest of righteousness cannot
be futile is the conviction that remains constant in his life both
before and after his conversion to Christianity. It is very likely the
thing in him that laid him open to the illumination and inspira-

tion that brought about his conversion. It is almost as if there were a kind of general principle for him like the beatitude pronounced by Jesus, "Blessed are those who hunger and thirst for righteousness, for they shall be satisfied."[9] Paul hungered and thirsted for righteousness all his life, both when he was a Pharisee and after he became a Christian. When he was converted to Christianity, he came to believe that this hunger and thirst of his would never be satisfied through the kind of efforts he had made as a Pharisee to fulfill the law. But this did not mean to him that his hunger and thirst had been vain. Rather it was to be satisfied by reliance upon the risen Jesus.

The quest of righteousness is by its inner logic a quest of divine acceptance. The fully meaningful life is the unconditionally acceptable life, so that when a man goes in quest of a fully meaningful life he is in quest of unconditional acceptance. Unconditional acceptance, though, is something that one cannot give to oneself. Nietzsche saw very rightly that to accept one's own life unconditionally is superhuman, that only a superman can accept his own life so fully as to be willing to live it over and over again in eternal recurrence. Paul, for his part, never, even as a Pharisee, thought that he could confer unconditional acceptance upon himself. He always sought it from God and from God alone. What he thought as a Pharisee was that full acceptance was given only to the man who fulfilled the law of God. The only life that could be accepted without reservation, he believed then, was the life that was lived in perfect conformity with the law. The man who lived such a life was the righteous man. This was the man who deserved to live, the man who did not deserve to die.

The enigma for the Pharisee was that many live who deserve death and some die who deserve life. The enigma was carried to the last extreme in the riddle of Jesus, who was put to death as a criminal and whose disciples claimed nevertheless that he was unconditionally acceptable to God, that he was the chosen one of God. It appears, for instance, in the words of the two thieves hanging on crosses beside Jesus: One said to Jesus "If you are the Christ, save yourself and us"; the other replied "Do you not fear

God, that you are in the same judgment? And we indeed justly, for we receive what our deeds have deserved, but this man has done nothing amiss."[10] To Paul the Pharisee either Jesus could not be the chosen one of God or else the whole basis of life as he had known it hitherto was undermined. It was enough of a problem that many live who deserve death and some die who deserve life, but to think that the chosen one of God could be executed as a criminal, this was the end of the world of Pharisaism. "Cursed is the man that hangs on a gibbet," Paul later quoted from the book of Deuteronomy in setting out the enigma of Jesus to the Galatians.[11] The complete reversal of Pharisaism was that the cursed man could be the man unconditionally accepted by God.

A modern man with a Pharisaical mentality would at this point question the existence of God. If many live who deserve death and some die who deserve life, how can there be a God? The question implies a demand for what has come to be called "poetic justice." If there were a God, the reasoning goes, then there would be poetic justice in the world; God would see to it that righteousness is rewarded and unrighteousness punished in the drama of life, just as the poet might see to it the drama of the stage. The evident lack of poetic justice in the drama of life, therefore, proves that there is no God, or it proves perhaps that if there is a God he is not a just God, justice being defined as poetic justice, or perhaps it proves that if there is a God he is not related to life as a dramatist is related to a drama he composes. At any rate, "There is no God," when it is asserted on these grounds, means "There is no poetic justice in the world."

Paul, instead of questioning the existence of God on these grounds that many live who deserve death and some die who deserve life, reversed the reasoning. If all men must someday die, he concluded, then all men must deserve to die. Unrighteousness must be universal. The role of the law in actual fact, he concluded further, is not to make men righteous through their fulfillment of it, but to make them aware of their unrighteousness through their failure to fulfill it. "Through the law," he told the Romans, "there comes the knowledge of sin."[12] Paul could con-

clude to all this so readily because he was dealing with righteousness as a positive thing, the fulfillment of the law, and unrighteousness as a negative thing, the failure to fulfill the law. If he
had been dealing with innocence and guilt, it would have been
a different matter, for then innocence would have been the negative thing, the lack of responsibility, and guilt would have been
the positive thing, the positive responsibility for evil deeds. It
would have been rather difficult to infer that all men are guilty
simply from the fact that all must die, even on his principle "the
wages of sin is death,"[13] and it would have been equally difficult
to infer that the role of the law was to make men aware of their
guilt.

It is not impossible, though, thinking in this modern fashion in
terms of personal responsibility, to arrive at conclusions about
innocence and guilt that parallel in some degree, though only in
some degree, Paul's conclusions about righteousness and unrighteousness. At first, to be sure, this seems impossible since the problem of death in "our culture with its doctrine of sincerity and
self-realization," when it is conceived as a problem of unrighteousness, is conceived as a problem of God's unrighteousness
rather than man's. For the doctrine of sincerity and self-realization, with its demand that every man be true to himself, seems to
presuppose the innocence of man. The self to whom a man is
called upon to be true appears to be a self who deserves to be
realized, not a self who deserves to die. If man must die, on this
presupposition, in spite of the fact that he is not deserving of
death, then, as Camus argued in *The Rebel*, there must be a fundamental lack of justice in the scheme of things. Still it is not
impossible to come to something corresponding to the unrighteousness of man within the perspectives of sincerity and self-
realization. Camus himself, in his later works, especially *The Fall*,
abandoned his position on the innocence of man and put forward
the contrary thesis that "no man is innocent." Sincerity on this
thesis consists in admitting one's guilt, and self-realization consists
in shouldering the burden of one's guilt.

Paul came up against the problem of God's seeming unrighteousness in the enigma of Jesus's death on the cross. Although Paul did not proceed to question the existence of God, he did what amounted to the same thing, he questioned a concept of God. It amounts to the same thing, for to question the existence of God is to question the existence of a certain God conceived a certain way, for instance a God who is conceived to be just according to the standards of poetic justice. What Paul questioned was the Pharisaical concept of the righteous God. The news about Jesus, he believed, was the revelation of a God who was righteous in a way quite different from that which would have been expected by a Pharisee. "I am not ashamed of the gospel," he said, announcing the theme of his epistle to the Romans, "for it is the power of God unto salvation to every one who believes, to the Jew first and to the Hellene. For the righteousness of God is revealed in it from faith to faith, as it is written, 'The righteous man lives by faith.' "[14]

The gospel of the death of Jesus strikes the modern man too, who is thinking in terms of guilt and innocence as a challenge to his ideas about the kind of justice that ought to prevail in the world. "Christianity's bitter intuition and legitimate pessimism concerning human behavior," Camus said in *The Rebel*, "is based on the assumption that over-all injustice is as satisfying to man as total justice. Only the sacrifice of an innocent god could justify the endless and universal torture of innocence. Only the most abject suffering by God could assuage man's agony. If everything, without exception, in heaven and earth is doomed to pain and suffering, then a strange form of happiness is possible."[15] If everything, without exception, in heaven and earth is doomed to death, including God himself, we could paraphrase, then a strange form of happiness is possible. The strangeness of it could give one pause, enough to reject the gospel or to be ashamed of it were one to accept it.

Camus said all this, however, when speaking for a multitude of modern thinkers, he still maintained the "innocence of man." The death of Jesus would look somewhat different in the light of his later thesis that "no man is innocent." Paul saw the death of Jesus

in the light of the parallel thesis that no man is righteous before
God. Thus Paul has it that Jesus not only shared in man's fate, his
doom to pain and suffering and death, but also that he shared
somehow in man's sinfulness. "Christ delivered us from the curse
of law," he told the Galatians, "by becoming a curse for us, as it is
written, 'Cursed is the man that hangs on a gibbet.' " God "made
him sin for us, him who knew not sin," he told the Corinthians,
"that we might become God's righteousness in him." And "God
by sending his son in the likeness of the flesh of sin and on
account of sin," he told the Romans, "condemned the sin in the
flesh that the decree of the law might be fulfilled in us."[16]

When the death of Jesus is seen by a modern man in the light
of the thesis that "no man is innocent," a somewhat analogous
conclusion tends to be drawn. "Say, do you know why he was
crucified—the one you are perhaps thinking of at this moment?"
the narrator asks in Camus' novel, *The Fall*.

> Well, there were heaps of reasons for that. There are always reasons
> for murdering a man. On the contrary, it is impossible to justify
> his living. That's why crime always finds lawyers, and innocence
> only rarely. But, beside the reasons that have been very well ex-
> plained to us for the past two thousand years, there was a major one
> for that terrible agony, and I don't know why it has been so care-
> fully hidden. The real reason is that he knew he was not altogether
> innocent.[17]

The participation of Jesus in man's sinfulness is perhaps more
startling when it is put this way in modern terms of positive
responsibility than when it is put in terms of the failure of works
to justify man before God. The basic idea, though, in either terminology is the same. It is that becoming man meant for Jesus not
merely becoming a participant in abstract human nature but becoming a participant in the concrete human situation, sharing in
our inability to justify ourselves or in our responsibility and guilt.

Jesus's own way of envisioning his participation in the human
situation was probably much nearer to Paul's than to a modern
man's, though Jesus did not share in Paul's Pharisaic background,
for it seems to have been common among men of that time to

think of life as a story of deeds or of "works" (*erga*), as they are called in the New Testament. John, for example, the other main creator of theology besides Paul in the New Testament, seems to have agreed with Paul in thinking of life as a story of works, though in his Jewish background he was probably more closely connected with the Essenes than with the Pharisees or Sadducees.[18] Both John and Paul use the term *works* occasionally to describe evil deeds. Paul's special usage of the term, however, is to describe deeds done in fulfillment of the law of Moses, and in this sense he sets works against faith in Jesus as alternative ways to righteousness. John's special usage of the term is to describe the deeds of Jesus, and in this sense he makes works the basis of faith in Jesus, the works of Jesus being the reason for believing him.[19] John's way of saying that Jesus participated in the human situation with its sinfulness was to say that "the Word became flesh" or that "Christ came in the flesh"—this appears if we set these beside such other statements of his about what he calls "flesh" as this one, "the Spirit is what gives life; the flesh profits nothing."[20]

Passing over from a modern standpoint to a New Testament standpoint amounts, it seems, to passing over from a standpoint where we appear to be responsible for making our lives unacceptable or only conditionally acceptable to a standpoint where we appear to be unable to make our lives unconditionally acceptable. The unconditional acceptance, which is called *Agape*, "love," in the New Testament, and which, according to the New Testament, comes to us through Christ, means in the New Testament itself unconditional acceptance of us in our inability to make ourselves acceptable, but when we pass back to a modern standpoint it means unconditional acceptance of us in our responsibility for making ourselves unacceptable. Christ in the one standpoint appears to have willingly shared in our inability to make ourselves acceptable and in the other appears to have willingly shared in our responsibility for making ourselves unacceptable and in both, by his willingness to be our fellow, appears to have brought unconditional acceptance to us. The condition elim-

inated in the one standpoint is that we make ourselves acceptable; the condition eliminated in the other is that we not be
responsible for our unacceptability. The one is the condition that
appears when life is envisioned as a story of deeds, for it consists
of the deeds required to make a life fully acceptable; the other is
the condition that appears when life is conceived as a story of
appropriation, for it consists of the responsibility from which a
life must be free to be fully accepted.

The standpoint of the New Testament is the standpoint of men
who stand before God. There are such standpoints of that time,
though, as that of Plutarch's *Lives*, where life is envisioned as a
story of deeds, but men stand before other men rather than before God. The standpoint of man before God as it figures in the
New Testament is also a standpoint of man before men, because
the unconditional love that is described in the New Testament
comes to a man through other men. It is before God and not
merely before men in that the love is unconditional. The standpoint of man before men, on the other hand, as it figures in the
lives of the illustrious Greeks and Romans of whom Plutarch
wrote, is not also a standpoint of man before God, for the acceptance the illustrious men enjoy is a conditional one, dependent
upon their illustrious deeds.

The standpoint of man before men figures also in the modern
problem of appropriation in that a modern man faces the possibility of identifying himself with what he is to other men, the
possibility of identifying himself with what he is to himself, and
the possibility of trying to become to himself what he is to others
and trying to become to others what he is to himself. The modern
man who stands before men, however, is judged by his sincerity
and self-realization, by whether he really is what he is to others or
really is what he is to himself or is to others what he is to himself
or is to himself what he is to others. The ancient man, on the
contrary, is judged by the rightness of his deeds, by whether he
has done anything worth remembering or whether he has not
done anything better forgotten. But then the ancient judgment
and the modern judgment are both overturned by the principle

"Judge not that you be not judged,"[21] which comes with unconditional acceptance.

The standpoint of man before God and that of man before
men do not differ simply as one standpoint and another, each
possessing its relative truth. They differ rather as a relativized and
an absolutized standpoint, and so there is something to choose between them. A sure sign of an absolutized standpoint, whether it
be ancient or modern, is the possibility of passing judgment upon
a man from that standpoint, and a sure sign of a relativized standpoint is the impossibility of doing so. The fulfillment or nonfulfill-
ment of the conditions in conditional acceptance is the basis of
judgment. Unconditional acceptance overturns all such judgment
and for that reason can itself be called "judgment" as it often is in
the New Testament, but it is not what would ordinarily be called
judgment. It is more a judgment of judgment.

There is a passage in the Gospel of John which seems to sum-
marize the viewpoint of the New Testament, not only the viewpoint of John himself but that of Paul too, in terms of the three
concepts "sin," "righteousness," and "judgment": "If I do not
leave," Jesus tells his disciples, "the Paraclete will not come to
you, but if I go I will send him to you. And when he comes he
will refute the world on sin, on righteousness, and on judgment:
on sin because they do not believe in me, on righteousness because I go to the Father and you will see me no longer, and on
judgment because the ruler of this world is judged."[22] The problem of death in Paul, as we have seen, is a problem of sinfulness,
the problem of being worthy of death. Paul uses the term *sin* as
the Pharisees used it to mean failure to fulfill the law of Moses,
but he rejects the view of the Pharisees that man can be without
sin. John redefines the term accordingly to mean the rejection of
Jesus—this is the real and avoidable sin for him, refusing to accept
Jesus and what comes to man through Jesus. Paul also uses the
term *righteousness* as the Pharisees used it to mean worthiness of
life before God, but he rejects the view of the Pharisees that it
can be attained by fulfilling the law. John redefines the term
accordingly to mean, instead of being worthy to live, laying down

life—what Jesus did. Finally Paul uses the term *judgment* as the Pharisees used it to mean the acceptance or condemnation of man by God, but he rejects the view of the Pharisees that man's deeds are its basis. John redefines the term accordingly to mean the act of God that overturns all human judgments and their basis—the judge of this world is judged. Thus the effect of Jesus upon the world, what Paul calls the "Spirit" and John also calls the "Paraclete," is not simply to solve the world's problem but to overturn the problem and the solution.

As long as life was conceived and lived according to the form it takes in the memory of men (or in the memory of gods or of God), namely as a story of memorable deeds,[23] these and similar conceptions of sin, righteousness, and judgment were at work in the world. Another way of conceiving and living life, however, had been developing for some time, and was to prevail soon after New Testament times. According to this new way of conceiving it and living it, life took essentially the shape it takes in personal memory, that of a story of experience.[24] Sin and righteousness thus came to be conceived more in terms of experiences than in terms of deeds. Man's lower and more bodily experiences came to constitute his sinfulness as in Manichaeism or at least his imperfection as in Neoplatonism, while his higher and more spiritual experiences came to constitute his righteousness or his perfection. The judgment of judgment, consequently, had to take a new form in this new age. Judgment had to take the form of an experience of experience, a recollection of experience. The judgment of judgment had to take the form of an experience of nonexperience, a recollection of nothingness and of creation from nothingness.

Augustine and the Story of Experience

There is a kind of pattern, a path of personal quest, a journey of the soul, which can be traced through the first great autobiography, the *Confessions* of Augustine, and through one subsequent autobiography after another down the ages. The pattern may simply be due to the fact that Augustine's autobiography stands at the head of the literary tradition of autobiography in Western civilization.[25] But more likely it is due, at least in part, to the genuinely archetypal character of the events Augustine narrates, the actual recurrence of such events in human lives. The story of his life has an archetypal quality about it because it is told as a story of experience, of the running of a gamut of experience, rather than as a tale of unique deeds and achievements. When life is conceived to be a story of deeds as it was in the time of Paul and earlier, its generalization tends to take the form of law, a list of deeds to be done and not to be done. But when it is conceived to be a story of experience, its generalization tends to take the form of a gamut of experience to be run.

The gamut that appears in the *Confessions* might well be described in terms of the experience of time, especially since Augustine carries out an elaborate search through memory in Book Ten and a search through time in Book Eleven, which takes him all the way back to the beginning of time in Books Twelve and Thirteen. The autobiography proper, which occupies the first nine books, covers only the first thirty-three years of Augustine's life. He wrote it, however, when he was in his forties. The last four books appear to reflect the expansion of his concerns over time, the expansion which led in his later years to the thoughts and feelings expressed in *The City of God*, where his interests and concerns have the past and future of mankind as their object. In the light of this later development, his early development, with its problem of rising above what he called the "bodily" level in thinking and living, appears to be a movement from what we would call the "immediate" to the "existential" level of experience. Running the gamut of experience involved first rising from the level where his concerns were confined to the immediate present to the level where they were extended to his past and future, and then rising from there to the level where they were extended beyond the confines of his own lifetime to the past and future of man. The first phase was that of the first generation, the first thirty-three years, of Augustine's life, the second was that of the second generation, or really the remaining forty-three years of his life.

The division of a life according to the length of a generation, the time it ordinarily takes for father to be succeeded by child, is a very obvious one. The problem of the first generation in a man's life is the problem of what Yeats called "the unfinished man and his pain," while the problem of the second half of life is that of what he called "the finished man among his enemies."[26] The division can be seen in the great classics of autobiography written in modern times, Rousseau's *Confessions*, Wordsworth's *Prelude*, and Goethe's *Poetry and Truth*. Rousseau divides his autobiography into two parts, the first dealing with the first thirty years of his life and the second dealing with the following twenty-three years. Wordsworth and Goethe give unity to their autobiographies by dealing only with the first generation: Wordsworth deals only with the first twenty-eight years of his life, and Goethe deals only with the first twenty-six years of his. In each case the story of "the unfinished man and his pain" is felt to be quite a different story from that of the "finished man among his enemies."

Where the *Confessions* of Augustine differ from these modern autobiographies, and not only from these but also from ancient counterparts like the *Meditations* of Marcus Aurelius, is in the standpoint which Augustine occupies, the standpoint of man before God. Augustine had not always been able to occupy such a standpoint when speaking of himself and his own life. In his *Soliloquies*, written during the two years after his conversion to Christianity, during his thirty-third and thirty-fourth years, he was unable, it seems, to stand before God in this manner. The *Soliloquies* begin with a prayer, it is true, and also include two brief prayers the language of which foreshadows the language of the *Confessions*,[27] but they consist mainly of dialogue between Augustine and his own reason. He stands before himself like Marcus Aurelius in his *Meditations*, the original title of which was *To Himself*. Passing over from the standpoint of man before himself to the standpoint of man before God was no easy matter, demanding as it did the transformation of his inner conversation with himself into a conversation with God. The process seems to have required the whole decade that elapsed between his finishing the *Soliloquies* and his beginning the *Confessions*.

The standing before God was connected in Augustine's mind with the bringing of time to mind, the process that created the autobiography and structured the life itself. He expected, according to what he said in Book Ten of the *Confessions*,[28] to find God in his memory, as though the fully recollected man and the man standing before God were one and the same. Perhaps what he meant was something like this: The difficulty of standing before God is the difficulty of communicating with God. It is easy enough to address to God the questions one would ordinarily address to other men or to oneself. It is easy enough to do this for a moment or for an experiment, that is. But it is difficult to keep it up when no answer seems forthcoming from God. Augustine apparently believed that an answer is to be found in the events of one's life, that these events are a revelation of God's will or purpose in one's regard. Thus the man who is recollected, who has his life before him, or has the time of his life in mind, is in a position to discern a response to his prayer. He can question God and be questioned by God; he can answer God and be answered by God.

A clue to Augustine's thinking on this would be Plato's view that time is the "changing image of eternity."[29] Augustine, as far as I know, never quotes Plato to this effect, but the view itself is pervasive in Augustine's writings. On the simplest level the view means that the eternal truths are exemplified in every particular here and now. Turned around, this statement means that if one endeavors to find meaning on the immediate level of experience, what one finds is timeless truths. On a second level the view means that one's eternal vocation is revealed in the events of one's life. Turned around, this statement means that if one endeavors to find meaning on the existential level of experience, the level where one's lifetime is brought to mind, what one finds is no longer timeless truths but an eternal call addressed to oneself. In the *Soliloquies* Augustine was still largely occupied with his immediate situation and with the discovery of timeless truths and the general discovery of the timelessness of truth, and so he was unable to sustain communication with God but had to communicate rather with his own reason. In the *Confessions*, however, where he was systematically engaged in bringing his lifetime to mind, he was occupied with the discovery of God's call addressed to himself, and so he was drawn into communication with God.

On a third level the view means that the eternal logos is revealed in the events of history. Turned around, this statement means that if one endeavors to find meaning on the historic level of experience, the level where all time is brought to mind, what one finds is the rational principle in history or the Word of God, which, according to the Christian gospel, is incarnate in Jesus Christ. In the last books of the *Confessions* Augustine did become engaged in bringing all time to mind, in searching through time back to the very beginning of time, and he was drawn further into communication with God, to the point where he took the eternal Word as addressed to himself and to each man personally and was responding in prayer to it or to the God who spoke it, especially to the Word conceived as that "in which all things were made and without which nothing was made that has been made."[30] He stood perhaps even more firmly on this level in writing *The City of God* in his later years, from the age of fifty-nine to that of seventy-two, but he was not drawn into communication with God in the same manner, or if he was, he did not set it out in writing as he did in his autobiography.

A gamut of experience like this cannot be comprehended from a single fixed standpoint but requires for its understanding a continually shifting standpoint, a dialectic, to follow along with the shifting standpoints of the life itself. Augustine had at his disposal the most developed form of dialectical thinking in ancient times, the Platonic type of dialectic, which was designed to follow man's ascent from passion for the individual to ecstasy in contemplation of the universal and ideal. We have at our disposal the kind of dialectic that has developed in modern times, the Hegelian type of dialectic, which is designed to follow man's

ascent from the immediate to the existential and from the existential to the historic level of experience. The ancient and the modern dialectic can be brought into cooperation with one another,
and their cooperation can enable us to pass over from our own
standpoints to those of antiquity and back again, if we take advantage of the notions that are common to both of them, particularly the notion of "recollection."

Recollection is the shape that thinking and living appear to
take from a shifting standpoint, i.e., in a dialectic. In a Platonic
dialectic, although there is an awareness of the recollection of the
past, interest is focused on the recollection of the eternal, since
this is the kind of thinking and living involved in ascending from
passion for the individual to ecstasy in contemplation of the universal and ideal. In a Hegelian dialectic, contrariwise, while there
is an awareness of time as the changing image of eternity and
thereby of the recollection of eternity in time, interest is focused
on the recollection of time itself, since this is the kind of thinking
and living involved in ascending from the immediate to the existential and from the existential to the historic level of experience.
The difference in interest is ultimately the difference between
concern about running the gamut of experience and concern
about appropriating one's life, the difference between the ancient
story of experience and the modern story of appropriation.

On the primary level, the recollection of immediate states, the
problem of recollection is the problem of character and its discovery. One can trace the history of the problem all the way from
Socrates, saying that he did not yet know himself and wondering
whether he was "a monster more complicated and more furious
than Typhon or a gentler and simpler creature to whom a divine
and quiet lot is given by nature,"[31] to Nietzsche, wondering
whether he was or should become the Dionysian type, creative
and passionate and unrestrained, or the Apollonian type, critical
and rational and self-controlled.[32] In fact, the two characters
envisioned by Socrates seem quite similar to the two envisioned
by Nietzsche, the monster swollen with passion to the Dionysian
type and the gentler and diviner creature to the Apollonian type.

However characters have been divided and classified, though, they have usually been conceived to be formed or at least manifested in the repetition of immediate states, in recurrent patterns of reaction to immediate situations. To discover his character, a man has had to recollect his past behavior in immediate situations, particularly, as Aristotle would have it, the balance of passion and caution his behavior has exhibited.

When Augustine set about in the first half of his *Soliloquies* to discover the state of his soul, this is what he did. His goal, as he stated it in the beginning, was "to know God and the soul." So he could not stop at the mere recollection of his immediate states, but neither could he reach his goal without first carrying this through. Part of it was the need to understand the state of the soul in order to understand the soul itself; part of it was the need of the soul to be in an appropriate state before it could understand God. His inquiry and dialogue with himself on this question was continued, according to the literary form of his meditations, over two days. On the first day he was quite optimistic about the state of his soul: ever since he had originally been inspired by reading Cicero at the age of nineteen to pursue wisdom, he had abandoned all passion for wealth, and more recently he had managed to give up his passion for woman while his passion for company and friendship had changed into the simple desire to help others and be helped by them in the pursuit of wisdom. On the second day, however, after feeling again during the night the intensity of his passion for woman, he was considerably more pessimistic about the pursuit of wisdom prevailing over passion.[33]

Whatever be the result of the endeavor to discover one's character or state of soul, whether it be encouraging or discouraging, it tends to be unsatisfactory as self-knowledge. At best one has discovered what type of man one is. One has yet to discover who one is. Socrates discovered more about himself in discovering his ignorance of himself than he would have if he had succeeded in determining whether he was Dionysian or Apollonian. For in discovering his ignorance of himself in the attempt to classify himself, he was able to do better than classify himself; he was able to relate himself to himself, to others, and to the unknown beyond himself. His ignorance of himself meant that he was fundamentally a mystery to himself, that this was his real and ultimate relationship to himself. It meant secondly that his relationship to others had to be fundamentally ironic, that what has become known as "Socratic irony" was the appropriate attitude for him in communication, a willingness to learn from others arising from his awareness of his own ignorance and leading to a manifestation of the ignorance of others. It meant finally that the eternity of his unknown self, which reappeared in every immediate situation and was called to mind in the discovery of his ignorance, was a question.

This was the question to which Augustine devoted the second half of his *Soliloquies*. Recollection became for him here the Platonic recollection of timeless truth. Later on, to be sure, when he wrote his *Retractations,* he took back what he said about recollecting timeless truths insofar as it involved the implication that the soul has become acquainted with the timeless truths in a previous existence.[34] At this point, however, he was ready to take recollection in the literal sense of recall. His argument for the immortality of the soul was the timelessness of truth together with the fact that the soul was the abode of truth. He seems to have been dissatisfied with his own reasoning, and he left the *Soliloquies* unfinished. He had succeeded in the course of them, nevertheless, in discovering something about himself. He had related himself to others in his effort to discover the state of his soul, how he stood with regard to woman and with regard to his friends. He had related himself to himself throughout in the very form of his dialogue with his own reason. And he had related himself to God in his quest throughout to know God and the soul, "that I may know myself, that I may know Thee," "that I may return into myself and into Thee."[35]

There are many ways, however, of relating self to self, to others, and to God. This is what comes to light when it is existential states rather than merely immediate states that are repeated in living and recollected in thinking. The problem in a Platonic dialectic is that of "conversion";[36] in an Hegelian dialectic it is that of "mediation."[37] Ascending from passion for the individual to ecstasy in contemplation of the universal and ideal is a matter of "conversion" or "turning" from the individual to the universal and ideal. Ascending from the immediate to the existential and from the existential to the historic is a matter of "mediation" or the abolition of immediacy. Actually a series of conversions are required for the Platonic ascent, and a series of mediations for the Hegelian ascent, a series of transitions from one existential state to another. Repetition here is the fact that one's whole lifetime, past and future, is present in each successive existential moment through all the changes in orientation of self to self, to others, and to God. Recollection, accordingly, means bringing not simply one's lifetime to mind but bringing to mind the successive changes the orientation of one's life has undergone.

The kind of recollection in which Augustine engages in the *Confessions* is this sort. In the first two books, it is true, he speaks of his infancy and childhood and youth, and perhaps leads the reader to expect that the whole account will be a recollection of immediate states, infancy, childhood, youth, manhood, and age. This impression begins to prove false by Book Three, where he speaks of his becoming a Manichee. The actual subject of his recollection then turns out to be his existential states, childhood Christianity, Manichaeism, Skepticism, and Neoplatonism, philosophical and ecclesiastical Christianity. Each of these was a complete orientation of his whole life and the transition from one to another was in each instance a "conversion." The great conversion in Augustine's eyes was the one to Christianity, but he was also interested in his turning from childhood Christianity to Manichaeism and in his turning away from Manichaeism. In spite of his conversion from childhood Christianity to Manichaeism, he was able to see in his life a kind of general movement of conversion toward the God of Christianity because of the pursuit of wisdom that began just before his conversion to Manichaeism when he was nineteen years of age. Indeed his ultimate conversion to Christianity at the age of thirty-two was seen and described by him at the time as a conversion to philosophy.[38] Only later, when he wrote the *Confessions* in his forties, from the standpoint of a more ecclesiastical Christianity, did he see it as a conversion to something transcending philosophy.

That an eternal call is manifested in such a succession of existential moments or situations, as Augustine thought, seems to be a specifically Biblical idea. Socrates spoke of the *daimonion*,[39] the divine or supernatural something, which made itself felt at various junctures in his life, commanding him, according to Xenophon's report, or merely forbidding him, according to Plato's, to do certain things in certain situations. Similar claims were made as late as the Renaissance, for example, by Cardano in his autobiography, *The Book of My Life*.[40] Later still, Goethe in his autobiography spoke of the "demonic" that reveals itself in nature and in the lives of great men, and which revealed itself also, he believed, in his own life.[41] What Hegel said of the *daimonion* of Socrates, however, seems to have been true in each of these instances, namely that Socrates searched in his own thought for what was worthy and good, and looked to his *daimonion* merely to determine how he should act in various contingencies.[42] The "demonic" of which Goethe spoke was actually contrary, according to Goethe, to the moral order of the world. Maybe to see the concrete situations of one's life as the revelation of something like the will of God requires that one stand already on the historic level of experience and see the existential situations in terms of the historic revelation of God described in the Bible.

It was probably because he did stand to some extent on the historic level of experience that Augustine, when he wrote the *Confessions*, was able to see his call as emanating from the God of Christianity and the Bible, rather than from some unknown or obscure source conceived after the fashion of the *daimonion* of Socrates. He did not elaborate his theory of the call until later in his controversies with the Pelagians on predestination, but he so perceived at this time the pattern of vocation in his life that he was drawn into communication with the God who was acting and permitting things to happen in his life, who was ever commanding, forbidding, and inviting him. To see one's life as a succession of immediate states, as he did when he wrote the *Soliloquies,* is to stand not on the immediate but on the existential level of experience. It is to be concerned not merely about the immediate present in which one finds oneself but about one's past and one's future. Likewise, to see one's life as a succession of existential states, childhood Christianity, Manichaeism, Skepticism and Neoplatonism, philosophic and ecclesiastical Christianity, as he did when he wrote the *Confessions,* is to stand not on the existential level but on the historic level of experience. It is to be concerned not merely about one's own past and future but about one's involvement in the diverse currents of thought and life flowing out of the past and into the future of mankind.

There is a problem, however, about assuming that the fully recollected man and the man standing before God are one and the same. They are one and the same in Augustine's theory and practice in the *Confessions.* Yet what are we to say about Rousseau's *Confessions* or Wordsworth's *Prelude* or Goethe's *Poetry and Truth* or most other autobiographies? In all of these we seem to have the fully recollected man, but in almost none of them do we seem to have man standing before God. There are some works, to be sure, like Pascal's *Thoughts,* where the fully recollected man does stand before God. Yet what about most products of the fully recollected man? What about ancient expressions of the fully recollected man like the *Enneads* of Plotinus or the *Meditations* of Marcus Aurelius?

Recollection in none of these works, we could say in reply, is carried to such lengths as it is carried in Augustine's *Confessions.* Augustine's search through memory and time takes him all the way back to the beginning of time. The idea of creation from nothingness, moreover, pervades the recollection of his own life from the time when he was a Manichee to the time when he became a Christian, from the time when he repudiated the idea of creation to the time when he accepted it. Maybe there is some kind of oblivion of createdness, some kind of forgetfulness of the contingency of human existence, like the "oblivion of being" of which Heidegger speaks,[43] which Augustine overcame, and which is not ordinarily overcome. Maybe it is only the man who overcomes this oblivion, this forgetfulness, who is fully recollected.

If Augustine had remained a Manichee, he would have been trying to recollect his former existence in the world of light prior to his fall into the world of darkness. If he had remained a Neoplatonist, he would have been trying to recollect his former existence in the world of ideas. As a matter of fact, it took him some time after his conversion to Christianity to get rid of the Manichaean notion that the soul is passed on from generation to generation through the act of procreation, and to get rid of the Neoplatonic notion that learning is remembering truths learned in a former existence.[44] When he had finally thought his way through all of this, however, and become convinced that there was no preexistence of souls, he set out to recollect the nothingness from which he came.

The recollection of nothingness, the full realization of the contingency of his own existence, was apparently the thing that brought Augustine into the presence of God as creative power. The standing before God in the *Confessions* was genuine, was more than the mere rhetorical device of putting the discourse into the form of second person address to God, because it occurred in the light of such recollection. It was not yet possible for him to do this when he wrote the *Soliloquies*, because at that time he still had a strong sense or illusion of preexistence. Only when this sense or illusion was overcome through the confrontation with nothingness could his interior conversation with himself become a conversation with God. A man could be free of any illusion of preexistence and yet not have an explicit sense of the contingency of his existence, but a man like Augustine, who did have some kind of sense of preexistence and convinced himself that it was an illusion, could not do so without becoming fully aware of his contingency and the nothingness that lay at his origin. Thus Augustine was led to carry recollection to lengths far beyond what

previous or subsequent autobiographers attempted. The nothingness out of which he came was the same nothingness out of
which his world came, and in recollecting it, he found himself in
some real sense contemporaneous with the beginning of time.

Kierkegaard and the Story of Appropriation

Repetition, Kierkegaard believed, is the modern counterpart of
the ancient ideal of recollection. "Say what one will, it is sure to
play a very important role in modern philosophy; for *repetition* is
a decisive expression for what 'recollection' was for the Greeks.
Just as they taught that all knowledge is a recollection, so will
modern philosophy teach that the whole of life is a repetition."[45]
This he said in a book called *Repetition*, with the subtitle "An
Essay in Experimental Psychology." The concept of repetition
was to become important later on in the actual development of
psychology in the twentieth century, when Freud came to the
conclusion that the principle of repetition was more fundamental
in human behavior than even the pleasure principle, the principle
that the aim of psychological processes is pleasure. "Enough is
left unexplained," he said in a late work called *Beyond the Pleasure Principle*, "to justify the hypothesis of a compulsion to repeat
—something that seems more primitive, more elementary, more
instinctual than the pleasure principle which it overrides."[46]

Freud and Kierkegaard, to be sure, meant different things
when they used the term *repetition*. Freud had in mind such
occurrences as the repetition of unpleasant experiences in traumatic neurosis and in child's play, repetition, we might say, on
the level of immediate experience. Kierkegaard, on the contrary,
had in mind repetition on the level of existential experience. The
feelings on the immediate level would be, for instance, fear or
courage in the face of immediate danger, hope or despair in the
face of immediate difficulty, pleasure or pain at immediate good
or evil, and the like. The corresponding feelings on the existential
level would be the dread of nothingness and the courage to be,
hope or despair in the face of one's mortality, joy or suffering

arising from the meaning or meaninglessness of one's life, and the like, all of which have for their object the whole of a man's life, past, present, and future, rather than the immediate present. Repetition of immediate experiences, therefore, would be quite a different thing from repetition of existential experiences. There is, nevertheless, as much relationship between the two as there is between the corresponding feelings, so much that the corresponding feelings have been given the same names.

Freud's examples are all instances of what he called "the compulsion to repeat."[47] Children tend to repeat both their pleasant and their unpleasant experiences in the form of games they invent. Adults who suffer from traumatic neuroses, neuroses caused by injuries and fright, tend to relive the traumatic experience in their dreams. Adults, moreover, who are not neurotic but "normal" find repetitive patterns in their lives such that all of their human relationships have the same outcome. There is the benefactor who seems doomed to suffer ingratitude, each of his protégés abandoning him after a time in anger or disgust. There is the man whose friendships always end in his being betrayed by his friend. There is the man who again and again raises someone else to a position of great responsibility and then, after a time, himself undermines the person's position and replaces him with another. And there is the lover each of whose love affairs follows the same pattern of stages and ends always in the same conclusion. There are also more spectacular instances, reminiscent of folklore, for example, a woman who married three successive husbands, each of whom became ill soon afterward and died.

Kierkegaard's examples are all of voluntary rather than compulsive repetition and are all, in spite of pseudonyms and fictional alterations, taken from his own life.[48] The voluntary character of the repetition is underlined by the fact that in each instance he failed to achieve the repetition. There was, first of all, his attempt to repeat a pleasant experience on the immediate level, to make a trip to Berlin and to relive the experience he had once had there with the place itself, his lodgings, and the theater. The attempt was a failure, nothing was the same, and his final attempt to experience a repetition at least by returning to a pleasant experience of home in Denmark was upset by his servant, who was in the process of cleaning house in his absence. All this he describes in a light vein, but then he describes in a serious vein his attempt to repeat an experience on the existential level. This was his endeavor to end his love affair with Regina Olsen and to begin it again in a new form. He wished to end it in its original form, because he believed that he was making her dependent upon himself. He wished to begin it anew as love of two free and independent persons. The breakup of the original affair led instead to Regina's engagement to another man. This was clearly not the outcome Kierkegaard was anticipating when he began writing his book on repetition. When it did happen, he altered the ending of the book so that the only repetition he experienced was that after the love affair was over, he was himself again.

The purpose of repetition, according to Freud, is apparently the assimilation of one's experience.[49] The child repeats his pleasurable experiences in the form of games, one might think, in order to taste the pleasure again and again. But why does he do the same with his unpleasurable experiences? The same question could be asked about the neurotic who relives his traumatic experiences in his dreams. The purpose of dreams, Freud believed, is ordinarily wish-fulfillment. The reliving of an unpleasant experience in a dream, on this view, could only mean that some deeper purpose than pleasure and wish-fulfillment is at work. The assimilation of an unassimilated experience is the most likely possibility. When it comes to the repetition that occurs in the lives of normal adults, where human relationships tend to follow the same course and have the same outcome, the explanation tends to become a general explanation of the structure of a human life. One age in life is the repetition of another: Age is a repetition of manhood, manhood is a repetition of youth, youth is a repetition of childhood, and childhood is a repetition of infancy. Thus infancy and the events that occur in infancy, one's relationships with father and mother, brother and sister, are repeated, according to Freud's way of thinking, throughout the subsequent course of one's life. The goal of the repetition would be the full and complete assimilation of those primordial experiences that were so mysterious to the human being when he first underwent them.

According to Kierkegaard the purpose of repetition is quite similar. His term for assimilation is *appropriation*. That repetition has this purpose in his thinking appears not so much in his book on repetition as in the whole structure of his authorship. Many of his works are deliberate repetitions of others: *Stages on Life's Way* is intended to be a repetition of *Either/Or; Concluding Unscientific Postscript* is intended to be a repetition of *Philosophical Fragments*, and so forth.[50] The purpose of such repetition, as he conceived it, was the further assimilation of the matter in question. The purpose of his whole authorship, as he described it in *The Point of View of My Work as an Author*, was the personal appropriation of Christianity.[51] Each of his works was a fresh effort at this appropriation, and so it was natural that one should be written as a repetition of another. Probably he conceived the purpose of repetition in a similar manner when it came to his love affair with Regina. The new love affair was to be related to the old, as one of his "religious" works, as he called them, was related to the corresponding one of his "aesthetic" works. It was to be an assimilation of the original relationship on a higher level. What had been merely an aesthetic experience was to become a religious experience.

Thus repetition, whether as Freud or as Kierkegaard conceived it, would be more than a mere matter of the wheel turning. It would be a matter of the vehicle moving forward because the wheel is turning.[52] The repetition itself would be the turning of the wheel; the forward movement of the vehicle would be the assimilation or appropriation that is taking place. Perhaps it is characteristically modern to conceive movement on every level, the immediate, the existential, and the historic, in this manner. The distinction between the levels, too, and the movement from one level to another exhibit this same conception. To move from the immediate level, where one's concerns are confined to the immediate situation, to the existential level, where they are extended to one's past and future, is to appropriate one's own life or lifetime. To move from the existential level to the historic level, where one's concerns are extended to the past and future of mankind, is to appropriate one's times and all history. The whole process of "bringing time to mind" with which I am concerned in this book, in other words, has this structure of repetition and appropriation.

If it is characteristically modern to think of life and to live it in this manner, then the modern man would not have phases in his existence in the same way as an ancient man who was trying to run a gamut of experience or a medieval man who was trying to climb a ladder of experience. "Become what you are" would be the modern man's maxim. There would be becoming in his life in that he would be in a process of assimilating or appropriating his life, but the becoming would be a repetition, a becoming of what he already is. The phases of his life, consequently, would all have the same ultimate content instead of having different contents like the phases in the life of a man running a gamut of experience or climbing a ladder of experience. This may be the reason a modern man cannot take a division of life into five ages (as in Roman law), or seven ages (as in Shakespeare), or the like, as seriously as could a medieval man or an ancient man. The difference between one phase of life and another, for a modern man, would be a difference in modality, a difference in the degree or manner in which the content is appropriated.

Kierkegaard with his many pseudonyms is perhaps an embodiment of the modern man's difference from men of former times. The modern man, like Kierkegaard, knows all about stages in life, has many theories about them, but does not have stages in his own life. Instead of stages like those of the ancient man running a gamut of experience or those of the medieval man climbing a ladder of experience, the modern man has subordinate personalities or identities or points of view. Kierkegaard's pseudonyms, Victor Eremita, Johannes the Seducer, Frater Taciturnus, the Judge, Quidam, Johannes de Silentio, Constantin Constantius, Johannes Climacus, Virgilius Haufniensis, Nicolaus Notabene,

Hilarius Bookbinder, William Afham, Anti-Climacus, all possess distinctive points of view, distinctive identities, distinctive personalities, and distinctive styles of thinking and writing. Kierkegaard himself, however, according to what he said in his *Point of View of My Work as an Author*, had only one ultimate point of view throughout his whole authorship, namely the point of view that appears in the works he signed with his own name rather than a pseudonym, the point of view of a religious author.

All of this, the lack of stages with distinct contents, the subordinate identities and the overriding identity, arises most probably from an ideal of life, the ideal of being true to oneself. Yeats has it that the modern man looks to the mirror rather than to the mask to discover what he should do and who he should try to become.[53] The man of the Renaissance and the Middle Ages, Yeats thought, looked to a mask, endeavoring to imitate Christ or some classical hero. The man who lives in the modern epoch "with its doctrine of sincerity and self-realization" looks instead to the mirror and strives to become himself rather than to imitate another. The older ideal was also an ideal of appropriation or assimilation. It was the appropriation or assimilation of the identity of Christ or of the classical hero. The newer ideal is different in that it is the self that is to be appropriated or assimilated. This self is the content that is common to all the phases in the modern man's life. The different ways in which he can take himself or relate to himself are the different identities or points of view that figure in his life. The relation to himself in which he is true to himself, or else the self to which he feels called upon to be true, is the overriding identity.

The ideal of being true to oneself figures in the life and teaching of Kierkegaard as the ideal of "willing one thing." *Purity of Heart Is to Will One Thing* is the title of one of his works. One can read through this work, where he shows how one attitude after another is not willing one thing, and still wonder what it is to will one thing. The one thing, it seems, is one's true self, and willing one thing means willing to be oneself or being true to oneself. The relation of this to Kierkegaard's religious point of view appears in his definition of faith in *Sickness unto Death:* "By relating itself to its own self, and by willing to be itself, the self is grounded transparently in the Power which constituted it."[54] What he seems to mean by this is that unconditional acceptance of self places a man before God. As long as self-acceptance is only conditional, a man does not yet will one thing but wills the many things implied by the condition: "If things go this way, then I will accept my life, but if things go that way, then I will not accept it." When he accepts himself or accepts his life without qualification or condition, though, then he wills one thing. If his willing is unconditional in the further sense that it is not crippled by a despair of being himself, then it involves a positive reliance on the Power that constitutes the self.

The possibility of willing to be oneself even though one despairs of being oneself, however, shows how the modern ideal can exist also in a nonreligious form. The nonreligious form with which Kierkegaard was familiar was the Hegelian form, in which the self is found at the end of what Hegel called "the path of doubt" and "the highway of despair."[55] But there was a much earlier version of the path of doubt in Descartes. The skepticism arising from the decay of medieval institutions, such as one finds in Montaigne, became the way in Descartes to the modern self. By subjecting the existence of everything, God, world, and self, to a process of "methodic doubt," Descartes was able to find a certainty about the self that could subsist in doubt itself.[56] Doubting the existence of the world or of God is possible without affirming their existence, but doubting the existence of the self is not. For if I doubt, I am. In an atmosphere of doubt and skepticism, therefore, the atmosphere accompanying the decline and fall of medieval institutions and the rise of modern scientific inquiry, it is possible to be sure of oneself. What is more, it is possible to be sure of oneself at the very moment when one is doubting oneself.

Kierkegaard's relation to Hegel is much like Pascal's relation to Descartes. For Descartes, running the gamut of skepticism ends in self-certainty. For Pascal, on the contrary, it ends in a faith in God, a reliance upon God rather than self. "It is necessary to have these three qualities," Pascal said, "Pyrrhonian, geometer, submissive Christian."[57] At least this was the combination that occurred in Pascal himself. Faith in God, to be sure, does not arise for Pascal out of the doubt of God's existence, as though to doubt God's existence were not possible without affirming it. Rather it arises in the face of skepticism about God, in the face of universal skepticism. Faith of the stark kind that Pascal had could not emerge, in fact, until a man's skepticism was universal. He did not reject the more ordinary kind of faith, which is based, as he thought, on unexamined and unquestioned custom and tradition. His own faith, nevertheless, had universal skepticism for its background and could appear for what it was only against that background. Skepticism was its foil, and it could not be felt as faith unless skepticism too was felt.

The kind of faith Kierkegaard spoke of had despair as its foil and could not be felt as faith except in the face of despair. The gamut of despair as Hegel described it was quite parallel to the gamut of skepticism in Descartes. Where Descartes would have a man methodically doubt the existence of the world, the existence of God, and the existence of self, Hegel would have him despair of each in turn. The despair was ultimately a despair in view of death, "the sovereign master" of the world as Hegel called it.[58] As long as man hopes to escape death, he is enslaved by his fear of it. When he gives up hope, on the other hand, he frees himself from its sovereignty. First he despairs of any deliverance from death that might come to him from the world. Then he despairs of God, the last hope outside of himself. Finally he despairs of himself, but when this occurs, something occurs which is similar to what occurs when a man doubts his own existence. The despair turns back upon itself as doubt turns back upon itself. Despair and doubt, in fact, are the same for Hegel. His way is a "path of doubt" as much as it is a "highway of despair." When doubt is doubted, a man finds himself in a state of "absolute knowledge." When despair is despaired of, he is "absolute spirit."

If we define them this way, Descartes' self-certainty and Hegel's self-certainty could be taken as forms of faith, and Descartes and Hegel could call themselves men of faith and Christians. If faith is the opposite of doubt, then the doubt of doubt looks like it might be faith, and if faith is the opposite of despair, then the despair of despair looks like it too might be faith. Pascal's faith, however, was a faith in the face of all doubt, including the doubt of doubt. Kierkegaard's faith, likewise, was a faith in the face of all despair, including the despair of despair. Thus Kierkegaard, thinking like Hegel of despair at one's mortality, thought that all forms of despair were forms of "sickness unto death," modes of life in which death is the sovereign master. Hegel, as Kierkegaard saw, thought that despair was the cure,[59] at least when despair ran its course and became the despair of despair, which occurs at the end of the highway of despair. Luther, and the Lutheran tradition in which both Hegel and Kierkegaard stood, was perhaps ambiguous, coupling faith in God with despair of self.[60] Hegel took this one way, making the final moment a despair of despair. Kierkegaard took it the other way, making the final moment, after the gamut of despair has been run, a faith in the face of all despair.

It was not that the gamut of despair or gamut of skepticism was a gamut of experience that it would take a life to run. The spirit of universal doubt or universal skepticism or universal despair pervaded the world in which Descartes and Pascal, Hegel and Kierkegaard lived and thought. This spirit has become in the twentieth century a sense of cultural relativity and a sense of the relativity of all standpoints. In and before the time of Descartes and Pascal there had been developing a sense of the rigorous and exact natural science which could be gained by fixing and holding a standpoint. This was related perhaps to the development of perspective in art and point of view in literature. The consciousness with which the standpoint or perspective or point of view was chosen may have accompanied the spirit of skepticism that was growing at the same time. In the time of Hegel and Kierkegaard there was developing a sense of the dialectical comprehension of human affairs which was possible from a shifting standpoint. This was related to revolutionary movements in society, and the consciousness with which the shifting of standpoints was carried out probably went with the spirit of despair that was emerging at that time. The sense of a complete relativity of standpoints, however, a relativity such that no standpoint, fixed or shifting, is the true standpoint, seems characteristic of the twentieth century.

This was the kind of relativity with which we were dealing in Chapter 1 of this book. The kind of faith that seemed appropriate there should perhaps be described now as a faith in the face of relativism. To take what was there called the "knowledge of ignorance," the realization of the relativity of all standpoints, for faith would be like taking the self-certainty of Descartes or Hegel for faith. Considering Pascal and Kierkegaard, one would be led to identify faith rather with the acceptance of oneself and one's life, which is possible in an awareness of the relativity of all standpoints to oneself and one's life, and ultimately with the commitment to Christ that is possible in an awareness of the relativity of all standpoints on Christ. Faith like this would parallel the faith of Pascal and Kierkegaard. It would differ from theirs in that the relativism that is its background and foil would go further than skepticism or despair. The despair with which Hegel and Kierkegaard dealt seems to have reached deeper into human living than the skepticism with which Descartes and Pascal dealt. The relativism of the twentieth century in turn seems to reach deeper into human thinking than the despair of the nineteenth.

The self that comes to light at the end of the gamut of skepticism, despair, and relativity—the self of which Descartes was certain, the self in which Hegel was confident, the self we ourselves knew to be ignorant—is the same as the self of faith, and yet it is different. Consider once more Kierkegaard's description of the self of faith: "By relating itself to itself and by willing to be itself, the self is grounded transparently in the Power which constituted it."[61] The self of skepticism, despair, and relativity relates itself to itself and wills to be itself, and yet it is not grounded transparently in the Power that constituted it. The self of which Descartes spoke, "I think, therefore I am," related itself to itself in that it doubted its own existence and found evidence of its own existence in the very doubting of it, the "I think"; it willed, furthermore, to be itself in that it consciously and deliberately asserted its own existence, the "I am." The self of which Hegel spoke related itself to itself in that it despaired of itself and found its despair to be despair of despair; it willed to be itself in that the despair of despair is a confidence, a self-confidence, unshakeable by despair in any form. The self with which we were dealing in Chapter 1 of this book related itself to itself in that it became conscious of the relativity of all standpoints on itself and its life and found in that relativity its own irreducibility; it willed to be itself in that it refused to reduce itself to what it was from any one standpoint or sum of standpoints. Neither the self of skepticism nor that of despair nor that of relativity, nevertheless, is grounded transparently in a Power constituting it.

The self of faith, on the other hand, is grounded transparently in the Power that constituted it. Pascal and Kierkegaard seem to stand not merely before themselves like Augustine in the *Soliloquies,* but before God like Augustine in the *Confessions.* Perhaps the self of faith stands before God in this manner because it wills to be itself in a much more radical way than the self of skepticism or despair or relativity. The Cartesian self-affirmation grounded in doubt, the Hegelian self-confidence grounded in despair, and the contemporary refusal of self-reduction grounded in the consciousness of relativity seem pale up against the willing to be oneself which is grounded in reliance upon a creative Power. What such reliance seems to involve, if we put everything together, is understanding life as a becoming which goes from nothingness to being, as a process of creation. Willing to be oneself would mean willing to become oneself now and to be oneself in the end. It would mean appropriating the creative power that could draw being out of nothingness. It is not that such power is supposed to be given as an element in human experience. The experience would be of becoming and of the orientation that becoming has from nothingness toward being. The experience of reliance upon creative power would be an experience of willingly becoming, of willingly moving away from nothingness toward being, of willingly being created.

There is a suspension of judgment that occurs in running the gamut of skepticism, the gamut of despair (insofar as the "high-way of despair" can also be called a "path of doubt"), and the gamut of relativity. The suspension is itself suspended, however, in the end, and judgment does occur, judgment of the most far-reaching sort wherein a man evaluates his own life and the lives of others. It is at this point that a modern man is in a position to receive a judgment upon judgment, if the Spirit that came to "refute the world on sin, on righteousness, and on judgement"[62] is at work in the modern world. It is only after a Cartesian judgment upon life has been passed that a Pascalian faith in a judgment overturning such judgment becomes significant; it is only after a Hegelian judgment upon life has been passed ("world history is the world's court of justice"[63]) that a Kierkegaardian faith in a judgment overturning such judgment becomes significant; and it is only after a relativistic judgment upon life has been passed that a faith of the contemporary kind in a judgment also overturning this judgment becomes significant.

When the existence of God is doubted in the gamut of skepticism, when God is despaired of in the gamut of despair, when God is relativized in the gamut of relativity, then, as Hegel said in his *Phenomenology of Mind*, "God is dead" for the modern man.[64] But when a modern man believes in the face of doubt, as did Pascal, or in the face of despair, as did Kierkegaard, or in the face of relativity, as does the contemporary man of faith, then he experiences a victory over death, even over the death of God. This is an experience comparable perhaps to the Easter faith of the original disciples of Jesus, a faith in the face of the death of Jesus and the apparent failure of his life and his lifework. What this faith would be for the modern man is an acceptance of the judgment upon all human judgment, the judgment upon doubt and despair and relativity, the judgment that is the unconditional acceptance of man. Such faith can arise consciously and explicitly only when doubt is universal, as it was for Pascal, or when despair is universal, as it was for Kierkegaard, or when relativity is universal, as it may be for a contemporary man. "This is the victory which overcomes the world," John said, "our faith."[65] A faith like that of Pascal or Kierkegaard is a victory which overcomes the modern world. Yet only the man who stands on the leading edge of modern experience, as did Pascal or Kierkegaard, can taste that victory.

NOTES

1. A. N. Whitehead, *Adventures of Ideas* (New York, Macmillan, 1937), p. 14.
2. W. B. Yeats, *Per Amica Silentia Lunae* (London, Macmillan, 1918), p. 26.
3. I Corinthians 15:56. I will use as sources here only the letters of Paul that are undoubtedly genuine: Romans, I and II Corinthians, Galatians, Philippians, I Thessalonians, Philemon. Cf. Bultmann, *Theology of the New Testament*, tr. by Kendrick Grobel (London, SMC Press, 1952), I, 190.
4. Romans 1:32.
5. Kant, *Critique of Pure Reason*, tr. by Max Muller. (New York, Doubleday, 1961), p. 473.
6. Acts. 17: 18 and 32 (provoking scorn of pagans by maintaining resurrection); 23:6 ff. (setting Pharisees against Sadducees on the question); I Corinthians 15:12 ff. (against Christians who would deny the resurrection).
7. I Corinthians 15:16.
8. Cf. Kant, *op. cit.*, pp. 473 ff.
9. Matthew 5:6.
10. Luke 23:39 ff.
11. Deuteronomy 21:23 in Galatians 3:13.
12. Romans 3:20.
13. Romans 6:23.
14. Romans 1:16 f.
15. Albert Camus, *The Rebel*, tr. by Anthony Bower (New York, Vintage, 1956), p. 34.
16. Galatians 3:13; II Corinthians 5:21; Romans 8:3.
17. Camus, *The Fall*, tr. by Justin O'Brien (New York, Vintage, 1956), pp. 111 f. Cf. also his *Exile and Kingdom*, tr. by Justin O'Brien (New York, Knopf, 1958), p. 55.
18. On the relation of John to the Essenes cf. Raymond E. Brown, *The Gospel according to John I–XII* (*The Anchor Bible*) (New York, Doubleday, 1966), LXII ff.
19. The term *works* is used to describe evil deeds in John 7:7 (the works of the world); I John 3:8 (the works of the devil); Gala-

tians 5:19 (works of the flesh); Romans 13:12 (the works of darkness). Paul's special usage of the term to describe deeds done in fulfillment of the law occurs in Romans 3:27, 4:2 and 6, 9:11 and 32, 11:6; Galatians 2:16, 3:2 and 5 and 10. John's special usage of the term to describe the deeds of Jesus occurs in John 5:20 and 36, 7:3, 9:4, 10:25 and 32 and 37 f., 14:10 ff., 15:24.

20. John 1:14 ("the Word became flesh"); I John 4:2 f. and II John 7 ("Christ came in the flesh"); John 6:63 ("the flesh profits nothing"). Cf. also John 8:15 ("you judge according to the flesh").

21. Matthew 7:1.

22. John 16:7 ff.

23. On memorable deeds and the immortal past as a solution to the problem of death in the classical world cf. my book, *The City of the Gods*, 81 ff.

24. On the transition from memorable deeds and the immortality of the past to the uniformity of life and running the gamut of experience as a solution to the problem of death in the Roman empire cf. *ibid.*, 141 ff.

25. On the place of Augustine's autobiography in the history of autobiography cf. Georg Misch, *A History of Autobiography in Antiquity*, tr. by E. W. Dickes (London, Routledge and Paul, 1950), I, 17 and II, 625 ff. and 681 ff. Cf. also Roy Pascal, *Design and Truth in Autobiography*, pp. 21 ff.

26. "A Dialogue of Self and Soul" in *The Collected Poems of W. B. Yeats* (New York, Macmillan, 1951), pp. 231 f.

27. *Soliloquies*, I, 1 (opening prayer); II, 1 and 6 (brief prayers).

28. *Confessions*, X, 24 ff. Cf. *ibid.*, 5 ff.

29. *Timaeus*, 37 D ff.

30. *Confessions*, XI, 6 ff. Cf. John 1:3.

31. *Phaedrus*, 230 A, tr. by H. N. Fowler in the *Loeb Classical Library*, no. 36 (London, Heinemann, 1960), p. 423.

32. Nietzsche makes this distinction in *The Birth of Tragedy*. Cf. *The Complete Works of Friedrich Nietzsche*, ed. by Oscar Levy (New York, Russell, 1964), I, 22 ff.

33. *Soliloquies*, I, 14.

34. *Retractations*, I, 4 referring to *Soliloquies* II, 20.

35. *Soliloquies*, II, 1 and 6.

36. The idea of conversion figures prominently in the parable of the cave in *Republic*, VII, 514 ff. The terms for it are especially *periagoge* (518) and *metastrophe* (532B). The imagery of the cave is suggested in Augustine's *Soliloquies*, I, 14. Augustine would have encountered the Platonic idea of conversion in the Neoplatonists if not in the Academics and Cicero.

37. Hegel sets forth the idea of mediation in the preface to his *Phenomenology of Mind*, 82 f.

38. *Against the Academics*, II, 5 and 6. There are five early descriptions of his conversion: *ibid.*, II, 2, 3, 9; III, 14; *On the Happy Life*, Dedication; *On Order*, I, 3, 5; *On the Ways (Morals) of the Church*, II, 19, 20; *On the Use of Believing*, I, 2; VIII, 20. On this particular one cf. Misch, *op. cit.*, II, 633, note.
39. Plato, *Apology*, 31D; Xenophon, *Memorabilia*, I, 1, 4 and IV, 8, 1.
40. Cardano, *The Book of My Life*, tr. by Jean Stoner (New York, Dutton, 1930), pp. 240 ff.
41. *Goethe's Autobiography, Poetry and Truth from My Own Life*, tr. by R. O. Moon (Washington, Public Affairs Press, 1949), pp. 682 ff.
42. Hegel, *Phenomenology of Mind*, p. 719.
43. Cf. Heidegger's essay "The Way back to the Ground of Metaphysics," tr. by Walter Kaufmann in *Existentialism from Dostoevsky to Sartre* (New York, Meridian, 1956), pp. 207 ff.
44. Cf. what he says in *Retractations*, I, 4 where he takes back what he had said in the direction of preexistence in the *Soliloquies* and refers to his refutation of the idea in his work *On the Trinity*, XII, 15, 24.
45. Kierkegaard, *Repetition* (published in 1843 under the pseudonym Constantine Constantius), tr. by Walter Lowrie (New York, Harper, 1964), p. 33.
46. Freud, *Beyond the Pleasure Principle* (originally published in 1920), tr. by James Strachey (New York, Bantam, 1959), p. 47.
47. *Ibid.*, pp. 28 ff. (traumatic neuroses); pp. 32 ff. (child's play); pp. 44 f. (normal adults).
48. Kierkegaard, *Repetition*, pp. 54 ff. (his trip to Berlin); pp. 82 ff. (the attempt to repeat the love affair); pp. 125 ff. (the repetition as being oneself again). For the corresponding events in Kierkegaard's life cf. *The Journals of Kierkegaard*, tr. by Alexander Dru (New York, Harper, 1959), pp. 86 (May 10, 1843—the repetition experience or attempt at Berlin) and pp. 86 f. (May 17, 1843—the failure of the affair with Regina).
49. Cf. Freud, *Beyond the Pleasure*, pp. 39 f. on the relationship between repetition and recollection—how the physician wants the patient to remember events so that the patient will not have to repeat them. Conscious assimilation, according to Freud, is preferable to unconscious assimilation and can take its place. Cf. *ibid.*, pp. 41 ff. on repetition of unpleasurable experience as proof that the purpose of repetition is not pleasure.
50. Cf. the use of the concept of repetition in the *Concluding Unscientific Postscript* (published in 1846 under the pseudonym Johannes Climacus), tr. by David F. Swenson and Walter Lowrie (Princeton, N.J., Princeton University Press, 1941), pp. 253 ff. (how one work of his is a repetition of another and how this

relates to his basic thesis that truth is inwardness and is attained through a process of appropriation).

51. *The Point of View of My Work as an Author* (written in 1848 under his own name), tr. by Walter Lowrie (London, Oxford University Press, 1939), pp. 41 ff. and 53 ff. on how the problem of the *Concluding Unscientific Postscript* is *the* problem for Kierkegaard. Cf. *The Concluding Unscientific Postscript*, pp. 23 f., for a definition of the problem as a problem of appropriation, the personal appropriation of Christianity.

52. Cf. Toynbee's use of this as an image of history in *Civilization on Trial* (New York, Meridian, 1958), p. 25.

53. Yeats, *Per Amica*, p. 26.

54. This definition occurs in the opening and concluding words of *The Sickness unto Death*. See *Fear and Trembling* and *The Sickness unto Death*, tr. by Walter Lowrie (New York, Doubleday, 1954), pp. 147 and 262.

55. Hegel, *Phenomenology of Mind*, p. 135.

56. Descartes sets forth his method of universal doubt in his *Discourse on Method*, IV, and his *Meditations on First Philosophy*, I and II.

57. Pascal, *Pensées*, p. 461 in Pleiade edition of Pascal, *Oeuvres Completes* (Paris, Editions de Pleiade, 1957), 1218, footnote.

58. Hegel, *Phenomenology*, p. 237. Cf. my discussion of this in *The City of the Gods*, pp. 188 ff. and 191 ff.

59. "Despair is conceived as the sickness not as the cure," Kierkegaard said in the preface to the *Sickness unto Death*, p. 143.

60. Luther speaks of the necessity of despairing of oneself to have faith in God in the *Heidelberg Disputation*, thesis 18, tr. in Jaroslav Pelikan and Helmut T. Lehman, *Luther's Works* (Philadelphia, Fortress, 1957), XXXI, 51 f.

61. Cf. *supra*, note 54.

62. John 16:8.

63. Cf. Hegel, *The Philosophy of Right*, tr. by T. M. Knox (Oxford, Clarendon Press, 1965), p. 216.

64. Hegel, *Phenomenology of Mind*, pp. 753 and 782. Cf. my discussion of this in *The City of the Gods*, pp. 185 ff.

65. I John 5:4.

3

The Alienated Man

I$_T$ IS A REMARKABLE FACT that Christ has been able to remain the archetypal man of Western civilization in its transition from medieval to modern form. The fact itself can be ascertained from the lives of outstanding men and women of modern times. Its explanation is perhaps that Christ, the mediator between God and man, could be the prototype not only of medieval mediators, the medieval "lords spiritual" and "lords temporal," but also of modern men who have no mediators. For the mediator himself has no mediator—Christ's own relationship to God was an unmediated one. Christ, especially in his passion, can readily be taken as the prototype both of the man who for lack of mediation feels too close to God, who feels that he has "fallen into the hands of the living God," and of the man who for lack of mediation feels out of touch with God, who feels that God is silent or absent or dead. The words "My God, my God, why have you forsaken me?" which Christ uttered upon the cross, have become meaningful to the modern man in his unmediated existence in a way that they could not be to the medieval man living in the hierarchical world of mediation.

The mediation, whether spiritual or temporal, was mediation between man and God and thus between man and all reality, and all men in the Middle Ages could experience it, including the mediators themselves. Its breakdown, the breakdown of spiritual mediation in the Reformation and the breakdown of temporal mediation in the Revolution, meant a fundamental change in the structure of human life. The tremendous impact of the change is revealed in the fact that each stage in the breakdown of the medieval form issued into a period of unlimited warfare, the religious wars of the sixteenth and seventeenth centuries and the revolutionary wars of the eighteenth, nineteenth, and twentieth centuries.[1] The nature of the change, however, is most clearly revealed in the changing quality of the individual life story. This is what I would now like to study, tracing in this part the effects of the loss of spiritual mediation on individual lives from Luther to Kierkegaard and tracing in the next part the effects of the loss of temporal mediation on individual lives from Rousseau to Sartre.

The Loss of Spiritual Mediation

The Black Death, the virulent form of plague that ravaged Europe in the fourteenth century, was the beginning of the end of the medieval system of spiritual mediation. The meaning of the medieval categories "spiritual" and "temporal" related to the idea of God as God of the living and of the dead. The temporal mediators, the "lords temporal," were mediators between men and God as God of the living; the spiritual mediators, the "lords spiritual," were mediators between men and God as God of the dead, or rather between men and God as a God of the living to whom the very dead were alive. When the Black Death swept Europe, there came into being a new sense of death disrupting the order of the world. The system of spiritual mediation embodied in the church had made death a part of life. With the disruption caused by the Black Death and also the inner decline of the system of spiritual mediation, death became a problem in a new fashion. The new feeling for death found expression in the Dance of Death depicted by painters or described by poets or actually performed by actors in which men danced with their skeletons or, later, in which Death, as a skeleton, led skeletons to the grave.

The problem of death which was dramatized in the Dance of Death was the problem of common mortality, the problem of all distinctions vanishing in the face of death.[2] Each of the ranks in the hierarchical society used to be represented in the dance, clergy, nobility, and commons, and all danced with their own skeletons or were led by the skeleton of death to their graves. It was the same idea that appeared in the monuments of the period, the double tombs in which a nobleman or clergyman would be represented by two effigies, one an effigy of himself in the costume of his rank, the other an effigy of his skeleton or his half-decayed cadaver. Significantly, the Dance of Death and the double tombs were current during the fourteenth, fifteenth, and sixteenth centuries, from the time of the Black Death to the time of the Reformation, from the time when the problem became explicit to the time when the new solutions emerged. In the interim the old solution, the system of spiritual mediation, became increasingly unsatisfactory, and already in the fourteenth and early fifteenth centuries there were the beginnings in the teachings of Wycliffe and Hus of the new solutions which were to be formulated in the sixteenth century by Luther and Calvin.

The effect the medieval system of spiritual mediation had once been able to have upon individual lives appears most strikingly in the life of Dante, especially when his autobiography, *The New Life*, is compared with the account of his imaginary journey through the world to come, *The Divine Comedy*, written almost on the eve of the Black Death. In his autobiography Dante divides his life into two great phases, his "old life" and his "new life." What separates the old life from the new life is an experience of love, his love for Beatrice. What then divides the new life itself is an experience of death, the death of Beatrice. In the last and longest part of his life, the one that begins with her death, Dante seems to live in touch with the world of the afterlife and with Beatrice in that world, so much so that he could imagine making a journey through the different regions of the land of the dead, hell, purga-

tory, and heaven, with Vergil as his guide through hell and purgatory and Beatrice as his guide through heaven. Although Dante
places many of the lords spiritual in hell, he does not question the
system of spiritual mediation. It is taken for granted throughout
and it makes itself felt throughout in the relationship that holds
between the living and the dead, in the fact that Dante could live
in touch with Beatrice, the object of his admiration, even after
her death and transfiguration.

It was only when it began to fail, when it began to seem
ineffectual before the all-conquering power of death, that the
system of spiritual mediation was at last examined, attacked, and
defended. The particular points at issue in the Reformation can
be grouped together in different ways according to the different
viewpoints of the various contending theologies of the time, but
the viewpoints themselves, as well as the various issues common
to them, can all be related to one another in terms of the problem
of death and the failure of spiritual mediation.[3] In these terms
there were five major points at issue: first, the relationship between the present life and the afterlife, the issue underlying the
debates about predestination, faith, grace, and good works; second, the authority of the spiritual mediators, the issue underlying
the debates about submission to the hierarchical church, confession made to priests, obedience to the precepts of the church,
criticism of the words and lives of the lords spiritual, and continuing divine guidance of the teachings of the hierarchical church;
third, the life of those "dead to the world" (monks and nuns,
counted as already dead in medieval law), the issue underlying
the debates about monasticism, "evangelical counsels," and vows
of poverty, celibacy, and obedience; fourth, the attitude toward
the dead themselves in purgatory and heaven, the issue underlying the debates about purgatory, indulgences, and veneration of
saints; and fifth, the presence of the dead and risen Christ, the
issue underlying the debates about the Mass.

How Luther experienced the loss of spiritual mediation shows
up in the *Ninety-five Theses*, which he nailed to the door of the
church at Wittenberg in 1517, particularly in Theses 13 to 16. "By

death," he said in Thesis 13, "the dying pay all, and they are already dead to the laws of the canons, having as they do a right to release from them."[4] This assertion, limiting the authority of the church to this side of death, is most significant if it is set alongside the fact that the church as an institution in the Middle Ages was supposed to mediate between man and God as God of the dead or better, as we have said, between man and God as a God of the living to whom the very dead are alive. "The imperfect health of soul or the imperfect love of a dying person," he went on to say in Thesis 14, "brings with it great fear, all the greater the more imperfect it is," and "This fear and horror," he added in Thesis 15, "is sufficient by itself (not to mention other things) to constitute the pain of purgatory, since it verges on the horror of despair." Here he is describing the feeling of a man for whom the prospect of death is no longer mitigated by any sense of spiritual mediation—his own feeling during his temptation, his *Anfechtung*. "Hell, purgatory and heaven," he concluded in Thesis 16, "appear to differ as despair, near-despair and security." Dante's journey through hell, purgatory, and heaven was no longer possible in Luther's time, but neither was it any longer necessary, for hell, purgatory, and heaven now existed in the despair, the uncertainty, and the assurance of this life.

Distrust of God, lack of the confidence in God that he termed *fiducia*, Luther believed, was the motive behind the system of spiritual mediation, the motive behind the desire to have something human interposed between man and God. Perhaps we could turn this around and say that the breakdown of spiritual mediation that Luther experienced in his time was the source of his own feelings of distrust and lack of confidence in God before he found his solution to the problem that the breakdown posed. These early feelings of his distrust and lack of confidence he considered an experience of the "wrath" of God. His later feelings of trust and confidence in God when he had found his solution, the way of *fiducia*, he considered an experience of the "grace" or graciousness of God. The experience of God's wrath in his early life and its recurrence in his later life he considered an experience of hell. The experience of God's grace which he first tasted when he entered upon the way of trust and confidence he considered an experience of heaven. The transition from the one to the other, especially the painful road he had to travel to first discover the way of trust and confidence, he considered an experience of purgatory.

The life of Luther is a kind of paradigm of the course history has taken in modern times, the breakdown of spiritual mediation followed by a falling back upon temporal mediation followed finally by a breakdown of temporal mediation. In the first half of his life, when he was "the unfinished man with his pain," Luther experienced the loss of spiritual mediation in the fullest measure. In his temptation, his *Anfechtung*, he learned what it was to be abandoned by God and also what it was to fall into the hands of God. In the second half of his life, when he was "the finished man among his enemies," he had to fall back upon the temporal authority of the German princes for his own protection and he had to appeal to the ruling class to bring about the reformation to which the spiritual authority of the church was opposed. Also he saw the specter of a loss of temporal mediation in the revolt of the peasants in Germany, the foreshadowing of the breakdown that was to occur in later revolutions, and he gave his full support to the repression of this revolt by the temporal authority. Yet he had a taste in this, a foretaste, of what it would be to stand before God as the contemporary man does without any mediation whatsoever, spiritual or temporal.

The loss of mediation, at least the loss of spiritual mediation, did not mean for Luther a decline in the significance of Christ as mediator between God and man. On the contrary, it meant a rediscovery of Christ, a new image of Christ, and this too was paradigmatic for the subsequent course of history. "Christians must be exhorted," he said in the ninety-fourth of his ninety-five theses, "to seek to follow Christ their head through pains, deaths and hells." The new image of Christ was that of the man who experiences unmediated existence, who undergoes the hell of despair, the purgatory of uncertainty, and the heaven of assurance.

Commenting on the words Christ uttered on the cross, "My God, my God, why have you forsaken me?" Luther maintained that Christ experienced the wrath of God on the cross and underwent the pains of the damned in hell.[5] Christ, the mediator between God and man, had no further mediator to stand between himself and God, and so was exposed to the naked wrath of God as well as to the boundless graciousness of God. Ironically, therefore, as Luther saw, it could be that it is not by having a spiritual mediator, a lord spiritual, standing between himself and God that a man comes into relation with Christ but rather by not having a mediator and by being exposed to the hell, the purgatory, and the heaven that Christ experienced.

The falling back upon temporal mediation, however, and the recoil at the prospect of a loss of temporal mediation that we find in the life of Luther suggest that his life has its limitations as a paradigm of the course of history. His life indicates the course taken by the decline and fall of the medieval system of spiritual mediation, but perhaps there is more to the modern history of mediation than this, perhaps there is a *ricorso* corresponding to the *corso* like a reverse cycle in Vico's philosophy of history, perhaps the decline of mediation in its old form is accompanied or followed by the rise of mediation in a new form. There are lives like that of Newman that point toward a movement of this sort. The fundamental experience in these lives too is unmediated existence, but the response to it is a search for mediation. In the first half of his life Newman experienced the inadequacy of the reliance upon temporal mediation that he encountered in the Church of England and the need for a restoration of spiritual mediation such as was envisioned in the Tractarian movement. In the second half of his life he found it necessary to have recourse to Roman Catholicism for the recovery of spiritual mediation, since the authorities of the Church of England appeared to him to have repudiated it. The restoration he envisioned, though, was so far from being medieval that he was afterward claimed as the father of what came to be known as Modernism.

The search for mediation, understood as something other than

an endeavor to restore the medieval lords spiritual, may lead to
the solution of an unsolved problem about the new image of
Christ as the man who experiences unmediated existence. The
problem is that if a man is exposed to God's wrath and to God's
graciousness without the mediation of any human being, then he
seems to be the Christ himself and seems to have no need of
Jesus. It can be argued, of course, that this experience of his puts
him into relation with Jesus, but it could be argued equally well
that it also puts him into relation with every other man who has
experienced unmediated existence. Maybe in reality the modern
man is confronted with a choice of undergoing the hell, the purgatory, and the heaven of unmediated existence by himself and
thus in effect trying to be the Christ himself or else of undergoing
it all in sympathetic association with Jesus and in this way experiencing mediation and letting Jesus be the Christ. Whether or not
he experiences mediation in this sense, though, he will experience
unmediated existence.

There may be in this a fundamental clue to the nature of
religious experience in the modern period. William James, to be
sure, called his classic study of religious experience, based mostly
on personal documents from the modern period, *The Varieties of
Religious Experience*, and, with his feelings on pluralism, he
wished to lay emphasis on the word *varieties*. Yet if the lives of
the religious personages he examined are reconsidered in the light
of our clue it may seem more appropriate to speak of a "unity of
religious experience." The modern categories of the "religious"
and the "secular" appear to be the reciprocals of the medieval
categories of the "spiritual" and the "temporal." The modern
man's religious experience entails a sense of loss of the spiritual
mediation involved in the medieval man's spiritual experience.
The modern man's secular experience entails a parallel sense of
loss of the temporal mediation involved in the medieval man's
temporal experience. Spiritual mediation as it was experienced by
the medieval man meant that there was always something human
between man and God, something that at once united man to
God and separated him from God. In the higher reaches of me-

dieval mysticism this human something could be reduced to a "cloud of unknowing" ("in which cloud a soul is united to God"[6]), consisting of human ignorance at once separating man from God and uniting him to God, but it was still there. To understand the religious experience of the modern man, we must consider what it would be to negate this human something and leave nothing either to unite man to God or to separate him from God.

The New Hell: Despair

The first phase of religious experience, according to Luther's formula relating hell, purgatory, and heaven to despair, near-despair, and security, would be the phase of despair, the modern man's descent into hell. The inscription over the gates of Dante's hell was "abandon all hope you who enter."[7] The same inscription stands over Luther's hell. What is more, the road to heaven passes through hell for Luther as truly as it did for Dante. "It is certain," he said in Thesis 18 of the *Heidelberg Disputation*, "that to obtain the grace of Christ, a man must utterly despair of himself."[8] Explaining the thesis, he went on to say "This is what the Law wants, that a man despair of himself, as it leads him down to hell and makes a pauper of him and shows him to be a sinner in everything he does." Without this descent into hell, he believed, there could be no ascent into heaven. "The man who does what he can and thinks that he does something good," he argued "does not appear to himself to be altogether nothing, nor does he despair of his own powers, but rather is presumptuous enough to rely upon his own powers for grace."

This doctrine of despair was contested by Luther's contemporary, Erasmus, especially in the work he wrote against Luther, *On Free Will*. "To avoid the Scylla of arrogance," Erasmus said, "one should not fall into the Charybdis of despair."[9] Erasmus proposed instead what he called a "middle solution," midway between "despair" and "presumption." Luther, as far as Erasmus could see, was speaking in "hyperboles" and "paradoxes." On the one hand Luther called for a distrust of self, which he exaggerated to the point of despair. On the other hand he called for a trust in God, which he exaggerated to the point of presumption. Taken separately each of these two exhortations was a hyperbole. Taken together they were a paradox. Indeed if we compare the thesis of Luther, which we quoted, "It is certain that to obtain the grace of Christ a man must utterly despair of himself," with the thesis that immediately precedes it on Luther's list, "Saying this does not amount to giving cause for despair but rather for humility and to arousing eagerness to seek the grace of Christ," we get the impression that Luther was merely speaking in hyperboles and that the conjunction of opposing hyperboles formed a paradox.

This was not Luther's own feeling on the matter, however, for he not only answered Erasmus with a large work entitled *On Enslaved Will*, in which he reaffirmed his hyperboles and paradoxes with great vehemence, but he afterward developed his mature theology of Law and Gospel, in which the hyperboles became literalities and the paradoxes became ambivalences. The situation of the man in despair as Luther himself diagnosed it was due to the unconditional demand made upon man by the Law of God, the demand for a man's whole heart and whole mind and whole soul, when that demand was felt without feeling the unconditional acceptance offered to man by the Gospel, the good tidings of man's salvation. This is substantially the way he formulated it in his preface to Paul's epistle to the Romans, the preface that was still powerful enough two centuries later to be the occasion of John Wesley's conversion. The situation Luther described here and elsewhere was the one in which he found himself during his trial and temptation as a young man. It was the situation of unmediated existence. To experience unconditional demand upon oneself is truly to fall into the hands of the living God; and to fail to experience unconditional acceptance is truly to sense the loss of God, the hiddenness, the silence, the absence of God.

The situation Luther was describing was one in which there is nothing between man and God to cushion the impact of God's demand upon man. In this situation man experiences God's demand as a boundless demand, and this compels him to despair of his own ability to satisfy it. Erasmus, on the contrary, rejecting the hyperboles and paradoxes that describe the situation of unmediated existence, was speaking of a situation in which God's demand is humanized and limited, i.e., in which it is mediated. In effect what Erasmus stood for, the humanistic reformation of Christianity, was a movement toward mediation rather than away from it. Luther was in no position to sympathize with such a movement. In Luther's eyes the basic flaw in the old system of spiritual mediation, the "theology of glory" as he called it,[10] was that it was a system of limiting and humanizing both God's demand and God's acceptance. The alternative, his "theology of the cross," amounted in his eyes to recognizing and feeling the full demand of the Law and the full power of the Gospel.

Such later figures of the Protestant tradition as John Bunyan in the seventeenth century and John Wesley in the eighteenth century felt a resonance between their experience and that of Luther without finding themselves in complete agreement with his theology. Bunyan's trial and temptation as he describes it in his autobiography, *Grace Abounding,* was not so much the Lutheran experience of the Law and the Gospel as the Calvinist experience of the absolute sovereignty of God, the sense of an uncontrollable power, which may have set a man aside for eternal perdition as easily as it may have set him apart for eternal life. Bunyan thought, nevertheless, that there was a similarity between his own temptations and the ones Luther had described "shewing that the law of Moses, as well as the Devil, Death, and Hell, hath a very great hand therein; the which at first was very strange to me, but considering and watching, I found it so indeed."[11] Perhaps this is an indication that the Calvinist experience and the Lutheran experience are comparable, that Luther's theology of the Law and the Gospel and Calvin's theology of the sovereignty of God are different ways of construing a common experience.

Luther's descent into hell was an experience of despair over his ability to fulfill God's demand. Bunyan's descent into hell was an experience of despair at God's apparent rejection of him, and his autobiography was meant to describe, among other things, as he has it on the title page, "how he despaired of God's mercy."[12] The two forms of despair seem at first to be very different, as different as despair of self and despair of God, and the second, that of Bunyan, seems far more similar to the kind of despair that was traditionally ascribed to the damned in hell. Both Luther and Bunyan, however, were in despair at what they called the "wrath of God." For Luther the wrath of God was the wrath of a demanding God who could not be satisfied no matter what a man did, since everything a man did would inevitably lack the whole-heartedness, the whole-mindedness, and the whole-souledness that God demanded. For Bunyan the wrath of God was the wrath of a sovereign God who could with perfect justice reject a man and might well do so, since this man, like any other man, was unable to meet his demands.

The wrath of God and the two forms of despair were a problem, as a matter of fact, not only in Protestantism but also in seventeenth century Catholicism, especially in the controversies between the Jesuits and the Jansenists. Pascal in his *Provincial Letters* attacked the Jesuits both for trying to mitigate the sovereignty of God in the bestowal of grace and for trying to mitigate God's demand, and he defended the Jansenists against the charge of driving man to despair either by making God's commandments impossible to fulfill or by excluding some men from God's mercy. The Jesuits were apparently trying to mitigate the Protestant conceptions of the wrath of God, to mitigate the wrath as Law with their casuistry and to mitigate the wrath as sovereignty with their doctrine that all men receive sufficient grace to be saved. The Jansenists, on the other hand, were as emphatic as Lutherans about God's demand and so had to defend themselves against the charge of driving man to despair by making God's commandments impossible to fulfill. And they were as emphatic as Calvinists about God's sovereignty in the bestowal of grace and so had to defend themselves against the charge of excluding some men from God's mercy.

The Jesuits, it seems, with their casuistry and their doctrine of "sufficient grace," were holding in effect for mediation, a mediation that would render God's demand possible of fulfillment and would be universal enough to make salvation accessible to all men. The Jansenists, in defending themselves against the charge of driving man to despair, were perhaps doing no more than Luther was doing when he said "Saying this does not amount to giving cause for despair but rather for humility and to arousing eagerness to seek the grace of Christ." Pascal himself, though, as appears in his *Pensées*, wished to affirm simultaneously the "grandeur of man" and the "misery of man," to affirm the grandeur of man "without inflating" and to affirm the misery of man "without despair."[13] The double affirmation resembles Luther's double affirmation that man is at once a sinner standing under the unconditional demand of the Law and a saint standing under the unconditional acceptance of the Gospel, but the "without inflating" and "without despair" is reminiscent of Erasmus and his middle way between arrogance and despair.

To render God's demand possible of fulfillment and to render salvation accessible to all, the basic concerns of the Jesuits in the seventeenth century, became basic concerns in the Protestantism of the eighteenth century, particularly in the evangelical movements of Pietism and Methodism, but not along the lines of a middle way of mediation. John Wesley underwent his experience of conversion at Aldersgate on the occasion of hearing Luther's preface to Romans where Luther sets forth his doctrine of Law and Gospel.[14] Later on, to render God's demand possible of fulfillment, Wesley found it necessary to take issue with Luther. When he did take issue, though, it was not over the situation of unmediated existence but over the idea of faith as assent to the Law and the Gospel as doctrines. A man could assent to these doctrines and yet remain in despair, as the example of a man like John Bunyan abundantly proved. Bunyan had certainly believed in the sovereignty of God and also in the Law and the Gospel as doctrines when he despaired of God's mercy. In fact, it would be difficult to envision him despairing without believing in these doctrines, for they were the source of his despair as much as they were afterward the source of his assurance.

To overcome despair and attain holiness, Wesley maintained, it was not enough to assent to the Law and the Gospel as doctrines, but it was necessary to actually undergo an experience of the "assurance of faith." Before his conversion at Aldersgate, where he first began to experience that assurance himself, Wesley had seen it exemplified by the Moravian Pietists and he had felt it lacking in himself. This was his hell, to have only the kind of faith that is ascribed in Scripture to the devils ("the devils also believe and they tremble"), a faith that consisted merely of assent to the Law and to the Gospel as true doctrines. "If it be said that I have faith (for many such things have I heard from many miserable comforters)," Wesley wrote, before he had undergone the experience of his conversion, "I answer: 'So have the devils—a sort of faith—but still they are strangers to the covenant of promise.' "[15] As long as there was trembling, Wesley thought, his faith was still no better than the faith of the devils. "By the most infallible of proofs, inward feeling," he wrote at that time, "I am convinced of unbelief—having no such faith in Christ as will prevent my heart from being troubled, which it could not be if I believed in God and rightly believed also in Christ."[16]

Something like the hell Wesley experienced was known also in the contemporary Catholicism of the eighteenth century, but it was construed in somewhat different terms. It was taken to be a problem of conscience rather than one of faith. Saint Alfonso de Ligouri, the leading Catholic theologian of the period and the only one to be subsequently given the title Doctor of the Church, was a moral theologian and his *Moral Theology* had its beginning and foundation in his treatise on conscience. His life, too, was a drama of conscience, especially toward the end, when he experienced all kinds of scruples of conscience and temptations to despair. If it was also a drama of doctrine, it was a drama of doctrine on conscience. The most important change of opinion he underwent during the course of his life was his change from a rigorous view favoring "law" over "liberty" to a more moderate view balancing the two.[17] What he feared in rigorism, he said in his preface, was that it "urges souls unto ruin through erroneous conscience and despair."[18] This is apparently what almost happened to Ligouri himself during his last temptation.

The type of question with which Ligouri dealt, that of the boundary line between law and liberty, involved the assumption that both law and liberty were limited. Law was evidently not being conceived as unconditional demand, nor was liberty being conceived of as unconditional acceptance. Instead of balancing an unrestricted Law against an unrestricted Gospel, as Luther had done, Ligouri was attempting, with limited success, to balance a limited law against a limited liberty. Take away the limitation, and the problem of arriving at certainty of conscience between law and liberty becomes the problem of arriving at assurance of salvation between Law and Gospel. The latter was Wesley's concern. Ligouri was part of the continuing effort in Catholicism to render God's demand possible of fulfillment by limiting it and humanizing it. Wesley was attempting the much more ambitious task of rendering God's demand possible of fulfillment without placing any limit on the demand itself. This was an ambitious thing to attempt within Protestantism, because it required that he go beyond Luther and do more than simply balance the Law's demand with the Gospel's acceptance.

The difficulty Wesley had already sensed in Luther's balancing of Law and Gospel, that it was too much a matter of merely assenting to the Law and the Gospel as doctrines, was felt still more acutely in the next century by Sören Kierkegaard. With the breakdown of temporal mediation in the French Revolution and the removal of the mitigating influence that temporal mediation had evidently had upon the relations between man and God, the problem of despair entered a new phase, and assent to doctrine seemed still less adequate to solve it. Luther, who in the breakdown of spiritual mediation had fallen back upon temporal mediation, now received considerable criticism from within Lutheranism itself. Kierkegaard said of Luther, "he is an extremely important patient for Christianity, but he is not the doctor; he has the patient's passion for expressing and describing his suffering and what he feels the need of as an alleviation, but he has not got the doctor's breadth of view."[19] The sickness Kierkegaard had in mind when he spoke of "doctor" and "patient" was that which he treated in *The Sickness unto Death,* namely the experience of despair. He himself had been a patient, too, with this kind of sickness, and when he describes it, he shows that he, too, has the patient's passion for expressing and describing his suffering and what he feels the need of as an alleviation. The question is whether he also has the doctor's breadth of view.

Luther's diagnosis of despair was that it was due to the unconditional demand made upon man by the Law of God; his cure for it was the unconditional acceptance offered to man by the Gospel. Kierkegaard, however, has it that Christianity is not a doctrine, the double doctrine of Law and Gospel as Luther supposed, so much as a person, the person of Jesus Christ.[20] Although all that Luther says about despair is true as far as it goes, according to Kierkegaard, the ultimate cause of despair is the "offense" contained in the individuality of this person, in the fact that one finds a person where one would expect to find a doctrine, an individual where one would expect to find something communicable and universal. This has the effect of hurling one back upon oneself as an individual, somewhat as happens in everyday life when one comes up against the barrier of another person's privacy or another person's idiosyncrasy. Despair already exists prior to the experience of the offense, Kierkegaard thought, in one's unconsciousness of having a self or in one's unwillingness to be oneself. The Law is the demand that one be oneself, and when it is experienced without the acceptance that is offered to the self by the Gospel, then there is despair consisting of an unwillingness to be oneself. Despair becomes acute, though, when one encounters the Gospel and one is hurled back upon oneself as an individual by one's collision with the individuality of Jesus Christ.

Kierkegaard would have no mitigating of this experience through what Hegel called "mediation."[21] A synonym for "mediation" in Hegel's vocabulary was "reflection." By reflection, by rising in consciousness above the immediate here and now, one can dissolve the singularity that gives offense in the encounter with another person and transmute it into a universal and communicable idea. Since reflection puts one at a remove and at the same time puts one in touch, Hegel's "mediation" appears to have some affinity with "mediation," as we have been speaking of it here. This is borne out in the thought patterns of Newman, a contemporary of Kierkegaard's, who felt the loss of mediation in the sense in which we have been using the term, and who was in search of such mediation. Newman is enough like Hegel, perhaps indirectly influenced by him, to speak of Christianity as an "idea" and to speak of the "development" of that idea. What the idea turns out to be for Newman, as also for Hegel, is the idea of the Incarnation,[22] and thus something corresponding to a person rather than to a doctrine like that of the Law and the Gospel, only the person is reflected in an "idea" or even a "doctrine."

Thus the "offense" involved in Christianity, the individuality of Jesus Christ, is mitigated in Newman's thinking as it is in Hegel's by means of reflection, by taking Christianity as an idea capable of development. Newman, however, in contrast with Hegel, distinguishes between the "notional assent" one would give to a mere doctrine and the "real assent" one could give to a doctrine or an idea like that of Christianity, which is expressive of an individual reality.[23] Hegel's way of mediation was, as he himself termed it, a "highway of despair,"[24] for in advancing to greater reflection, one despairs, so to speak, of the stage of awareness one leaves behind. Such despair is a notional despair like that of a scientist or mathematician who leaves a more restricted theory behind him when he advances to a more comprehensive theory. Real despair, the kind of despair with which Kierkegaard was concerned, would be an alternative to real assent, and in its acute form would be caused by the offense involved in Christianity. Among its less acute forms real despair would include all the alternatives to real assent, not only notional despair but also a merely notional assent.

The history of despair in modern times, if Kierkegaard was not exaggerating, is a history of sickness, the "sickness unto death." In the present century it has become common to speak, as for instance William James did, of the "sick soul" and to construe the contemporary man's descent into hell as mental illness.[25] The experience of men like Luther, Bunyan, Wesley, and Kierkegaard, if this is valid, must be classified as pathological. A pragmatic approach like that of William James, however, which looks to the fruits rather than to the source of religious experience, allows one to say that much religious experience has a pathological origin and yet has a value, that it can arise from sickness of mind and yet be luminous, reasonable, and helpful. It allows one to maintain, for instance, that religious experience and mental disorder are parallel, that both can entail a great emotional crisis and both can mean an attempt of the mind to reorganize itself, and that the difference between them is in the outcome of the crisis, the success or failure of the attempted reorganization. Where the outcome is successful, the experience will ordinarily be called "religious." Where it is unsuccessful, it will ordinarily be called "pathological." This was the thesis of Anton Boisen, a man who was himself the victim of a severe mental crisis, who made a religious recovery, and who devoted himself afterward to the study of mental illness and religious experience.[26]

Where the pragmatic approach has been deficient, it seems, is in bringing to light the problem that the modern man's religious experience solves and that his mental illness fails to solve—the problem, I would say, of unmediated existence. Each of the figures we have just considered solved more or less successfully the problem of despair, some of them, Luther, Bunyan, Wesley, and Kierkegaard, within the situation of unmediated existence, and some of them, Erasmus, Pascal, Ligouri, and Newman, by recourse to mediation in some form. The cause of despair they have generally found in the exposure of man to the wrath of God, to the boundless demand of God's Law, to the absolute sovereignty of God in the bestowal of grace, to the offense involved in the individuality of Jesus Christ. We could generalize and say that the cause of despair is the situation of unmediated existence, but this would imply that only recourse to mediation in some form—balancing law and liberty, walking the middle path between despair and presumption, removing the offense by reflection—would be an adequate solution. It could still be, nevertheless, that it is necessary for the modern man to descend into hell before he can emerge from it in one of these ways.

The New Purgatory: Uncertainty

The second phase of religious experience, according to Luther's formula relating the cycle of religious experience to hell, purgatory, and heaven, is what he called *near-despair*, the experience corresponding to purgatory. The near-despair he himself experienced in his period of trial and temptation as a young man consisted of fear about his standing before God. Dante's purgatory had been a seven-story mountain, which the soul climbed after death while it was purified of the seven deadly sins, pride, envy, anger, sloth, avarice, gluttony, and carnality. Luther's purgatory was the uncertainty a man experiences during life as to whether his seeming good works are not in reality deadly sins. "The works of the righteous would be deadly," he said in the *Heidelberg Disputation*, "if they were not feared as deadly by the righteous themselves out of pious fear of God," and "the works of men are much more deadly when they are done without fear and with mere and evil self-assurance," and "presumption cannot be avoided nor can true hope be present unless the damning judgment is feared in every work."[27] Purgatory in medieval thinking had also been the place where "venial" as distinct from "mortal" or "deadly" sins were expiated. "Only then are sins truly venial before God," Luther contended, "when they are feared as mortal by men."[28]

This is the way, and these are the terms in which Luther experienced dread when he was a young man. In the light of his mature theology the reason for his uncertainty was the dualism of the Law and the Gospel. Standing under two principles, the principle of the Law and that of the Gospel, a man cannot be certain whether he is acting on the one or the other. If he is acting on the principle of the Gospel, this means that he finds strength in the Gospel to fulfill the Law, that he finds strength in the boundless acceptance God offers him to meet the boundless demand God makes upon him. If he is acting rather on the principle of the Law, this means that he is attempting to fulfill the Law by his own strength, that he is striving to meet the boundless demand God makes upon him in order to win for himself God's acceptance. If he is acting on the principle of the Gospel, his seeming good works are truly good. If he is acting on the principle of the Law, however, his seeming good works are actually no good, for the Law is a principle that condemns them, just as an unattainable ideal condemns by its own loftiness all attempts to reach it.

Erasmus tried to formulate the difference between Luther and himself on works in the following propositions: Luther was saying in effect, "man can do nothing without the grace of God, and so man's good works are null," while Erasmus was saying, "man can do everything with the aid of grace, and so all human works can be good."[29] Actually it seems that Luther could make both of these statements, and the real difference between him and Erasmus seems to have been in this, that Luther could make both, while Erasmus had to make one or the other. Luther, perhaps we could say, was describing the ambiguity of unmediated existence, while Erasmus was speaking for the resolution of ambiguity that comes about through mediation. When, as Luther assumed, man finds himself torn between God's demand and God's acceptance, torn between God's wrath and God's grace, he does not know how to evaluate his works. They may proceed from God's grace, and then again they may proceed from his own ability. If they proceed from God's grace, they are good and holy. If they proceed from his own ability, they are worthless and deadly.

When, as Erasmus would have it, man's ability is taken to be no more and no less than the ability he has by God's grace, this ambiguity is resolved. Then it no longer makes sense to ask whether his works proceed from his own ability or whether they proceed from God's grace. For to proceed from the one is to proceed also from the other. Luther thought this was a sophism. "If you add this unhappy qualification that apart from God's grace it [free will] is ineffective," he said to Erasmus, "you take away all its power."[30] As far as Erasmus could see, though, Luther was describing the situation of a man who is torn between despair and presumption, despair at God's demand and his own inability to fulfill it, and presumption upon God's acceptance. Despair and presumption thus understood are compatible with one another, and they go with an uncertainty about the value of one's works. Erasmus, trying to find a middle road between despair and presumption, came up against uncertainty too, but it was not the kind of uncertainty that arose like Luther's out of despair of man's ability. It was the kind that arose out of the endeavor to avoid presumption upon God's grace.

The ambiguous relationship with God implied in the dread and the uncertainty of which Luther spoke was a problem in Calvinism as well as Lutheranism. "The truth is," Max Weber has said, "that both Luther and Calvin believed fundamentally in a double God."[31] Both believed in a God who had two faces, a wrathful face and a gracious face. The wrathful countenance of God and the gracious countenance alternate throughout the Bible, especially in the Psalms, but one has the feeling that these are only different expressions, so to speak, which the same face can assume. With Luther and Calvin, however, the opposition of God's wrath and God's grace is carried so far that it is rather like two faces. The religious experience for which they speak, it seems, is characteristic of modern man and of his situation of unmediated existence. In that situation, where there is nothing and no one to stand between man and God, nothing and no one to unite man to God or to separate him from God, man is at once too close to God and too far from God. And the ambivalence of man's situation is an ambivalence of his God in this situation. The God who is too close and too far is a God with two faces, a face of grace and a face of wrath.

The double God in Lutheranism is that implied in the dualism of Law and Gospel, the God who makes unconditional demands of man and the God who offers man unconditional acceptance. The double God in Calvinism is that implied in the concept of the absolute sovereignty of God in the bestowal of grace, the God of gratuitous acceptance and the God of gratuitous rejection. The uncertainty of Luther was a doubt as to his seemingly good works, as to whether they proceeded from his own ability (or rather inability) under the Law or whether they proceeded from God's grace under the Gospel. The uncertainty of a Calvinist like John Bunyan was a doubt whether God had gratuitously accepted him or whether he had gratuitously rejected him. Bunyan went through several periods of temptation to despair, according to the account he gives in his autobiography, each time falling into despair from reading passages in the Bible that seemed to imply that he was rejected by God, and each time emerging once more after reading passages that seemed to imply that he was accepted.

In Catholicism, where one would expect to find simply the old system of spiritual mediation preserved into modern times—or at most, in the wake of the old system's breakdown, the new search for mediation—one finds a sense of uncertainty which was, at least in principle, still stronger than that in Lutheranism and Calvinism. Against Luther's doctrine of assurance of one's salvation through faith, the Council of Trent had maintained that a man could not be certain, even by faith, of being in God's favor or of persevering to the end of his life in God's favor.[32] This radical uncertainty had been a point of theology in the Middle Ages, but it became in modern times the characteristically Catholic way of experiencing and understanding the situation of unmediated existence. In terms of Luther's formula relating hell, purgatory, and heaven to despair, uncertainty, and assurance, this uncertainty in which the Catholic had to live amounted to living neither in heaven nor in hell, but in purgatory. "The greatest pain of purgatory," Pascal said too, "is the uncertainty of the judgement."[33]

The double God in Catholicism, therefore, insofar as there is one, would be the God implied in the doctrine of man's uncertainty as to whether he stands in God's grace and will persevere in God's grace. In all three of the classic modern religious traditions, Lutheranism, Calvinism, and Catholicism, the ultimate unity of God is affirmed and the doubleness comes down finally to an ambiguity in man's relationship to God. The foundation of the ambiguity in Lutheranism and Calvinism, however, is in God, in God's demand and acceptance or in his absolute sovereignty, while in Catholicism it is in man, in man's uncertainty about himself before God. The nature of the ambiguity is such that one alternative is compatible with the other in Lutheranism, man is at once just by the Gospel and a sinner by the Law, while one excludes the other in Calvinism and Catholicism, man is either in God's grace or out of it. The character of the ambiguity is such that man cannot resolve it in Catholicism and Lutheranism—he remains uncertain, or he remains both just and sinful—while he can resolve it in Calvinism—he can make certain of God's choice in his regard.

However it is understood, the ambiguity of man's relationship with God is likely to cause horror in the religious man, and the double God is likely to seem a hideous idol. All three versions of the double God, in fact, were rejected outright in the evangelical movements of the eighteenth century, Pietism and Methodism. Perhaps it is the essence of the evangelical movements to have been movements to abolish all ambiguity in religious experience. John Wesley, in setting forth his idea of an unambiguous religious experience, the experience of the "assurance of faith,"[34] found it necessary to criticize all three of the classic religious traditions.[35] His criticism of Catholicism was directed against the doctrine of uncertainty, because to experience the assurance of faith, a man had to be certain of being in God's favor and persevering in it. His criticism of Lutheranism was directed against the doctrine of being at once just and sinful, because to experience the assurance of faith, as he understood it, was not merely to assent to the doctrine of justification by faith but to attain a holiness that was incompatible with sin. And his criticism of Calvinism was directed against the doctrine of predestination, because it would be impossible to experience the assurance of faith, he believed, if God were thought to be a God who could as gratuitously reject a man as accept him.

In spite of all this emphasis on the assurance of faith, though, and in spite of his opposition to ambiguity in all its forms, Wesley found himself unable to go as far as the Moravian evangelicals of his time, who excluded all uncertainty from the experience of faith. The question that ultimately arose between Wesley and the Moravians, after lengthy association, was whether it was true as the Moravians asserted "that no doubting could consist with the least degree of true faith; that whoever at any time felt any doubt or fear was not weak in faith but had no faith at all."[36] Wesley, though he continually sought an assurance that would eliminate all doubt and all trouble of heart, came to believe after his experience of assurance at Aldersgate that there were "degrees of faith,"[37] because even after his experience of assurance he continued to be troubled. Once degrees of faith were admitted, there was something between the hell of no assurance and the heaven of absolute assurance, something very like a purgatory with degrees of purification, a seven-story mountain like Dante's, but one that was to be climbed in this life rather than the next, on the way to a heaven that could be experienced in this life.

The problems about the assurance of faith that arose in the evangelical movements of the eighteenth century paralleled the problems about certainty of conscience that had arisen in seventeenth- and eighteenth-century Catholicism. The assurance of faith had already been ruled out in Catholicism by the stand the Council of Trent had taken in the sixteenth century against the possibility of being certain by faith of being in God's grace and of persevering in grace until death. An assurance of conscience, however, was compatible with a lack of assurance about one's salvation, just as, vice versa, a lack of assurance of conscience, like Luther's dread and uncertainty about the value of his works, was compatible with an assurance of one's salvation, like Luther's reliance upon God's acceptance. As an experience, nevertheless, acting with a certain conscience was very much like acting with assurance of one's salvation, and acting with a doubtful conscience was very much like acting without such assurance. It is not surprising, therefore, that the assurance of faith as Wesley understood it included an assurance of conscience rather than a dread and uncertainty like Luther's about the value of his works.

The principle was maintained by the Catholic moralists of the seventeenth and eighteenth century that a man should always act with a certain conscience and never with a doubtful one. This was an apparently uncompromising principle, like the evangelical principle requiring certainty of salvation for genuine faith and allowing no room for doubt or trouble of heart. Something corresponding to the "degrees of faith" had to be admitted, though, in order to deal with actual experience. Ligouri was typical in this matter. He began with the principle about the need for certainty of conscience, arguing from Paul's assertion, "whatever is not from faith is sin." Then he went on to a lengthy discussion of the "scrupulous conscience," the "doubtful conscience," and the "probable conscience."[38] The result was a purgatory of conscience, a process of purification through which a man had to pass in dealing with his scruples and his doubts and his opinions in order to reach the heaven of a clear and certain conscience. The basic difference between the "moral systems" for arriving at certainty of conscience and the evangelical "methods" of arriving at the assurance of faith is perhaps that the moral systems were merely an attempt to resolve ambiguity in the mediated state of existence, leaving the ambiguity of the unmediated state, the uncertainty as to one's salvation, unresolved.

An uncertainty that affected not only the question of one's salvation, as did the Catholic uncertainty, not only the question of one's works, as did the Lutheran uncertainty, but both of them at once, would be an uncertainty indeed. This is the sort of uncertainty Kierkegaard describes in *The Concept of Dread*, the work of his that has had perhaps the greatest influence on twentieth-century existentialism. The background of this extreme uncertainty is the breakdown of the system of temporal mediation in the nineteenth and twentieth centuries, intensifying the ambiguity that had been created by the breakdown of the system of spiritual mediation in the sixteenth and seventeenth centuries. When he describes dread, Kierkegaard shows again, as he does when he describes despair, that he himself is a patient and has the patient's passion for expressing and describing his suffering and what he feels the need of as an alleviation. He describes himself as "a poor man who from childhood up has fallen into the most wretched melancholy, an object of dread to himself."[39] The question again is whether, besides being a patient, he is also a doctor and has the doctor's breadth of view.

His understanding of dread did show a breadth of view that went beyond the question of certainty about one's salvation and certainty about one's works to that of certainty about the truth of Christianity.[40] There was the dread that was the "original sin" or rather the origin of sin: This corresponded to the uncertainty about one's salvation, since it was this uncertainty that could lead one to commit the essential sin, to despair of one's salvation. Then there was the dread that was the consequence of sin: This corresponded to the uncertainty about one's works, since it was because of the conscious or unconscious presence of sin that there was uncertainty as to whether one's works proceeded from reliance upon God or from despair of God and reliance upon oneself. Both of these forms of dread were forms of uncertainty about oneself, about one's salvation or about one's works. Finally there was the dread that was a "saving experience by means of faith": This, according to a definition of faith he formulated later, corresponded to the "objective uncertainty due to the repulsion of the absurd held fast by the passion of inwardness."[41] This too was a form of uncertainty about oneself, the ultimate uncertainty about oneself. For the absurd in Christianity, the thing that makes it uncertain, according to Kierkegaard, is the individuality of Jesus Christ, which tends to hurl a man back upon himself as an individual. The upshot is that the dreadful thing is the self, and what a man fears most is to be hurled back upon himself as an individual.[42]

This final point about dread, that it is ultimately dread of oneself, is probably something that comes to light only when all mediation is taken away, temporal as well as spiritual, and man stands utterly alone before God. The ambiguity of this situation can be taken as an uncertainty pure and simple, the way Kierkegaard took it, or it can be taken as a probability, the way Newman took it. "I say that I believed in a God on a ground of probability," Newman wrote in his autobiography, "that I believed in Christianity on a probability, and that I believed in Catholicism on a probability."[43] Kierkegaard and Newman were not only contemporaries; they found themselves in rather similar circumstances, Kierkegaard dissatisfied with the established Christianity of Denmark, and Newman dissatisfied with the established Christianity of England. They reacted differently, though, Kierkegaard trying to come directly to grips with ambiguity, and Newman searching for mediation. Perhaps it was only to a man in search of mediation, as was Newman, that the ambiguity could seem anything better than uncertainty.

The probability Newman saw in the ambiguity was an uncertainty too, but an uncertainty with a direction. "My argument is in outline as follows," he wrote, describing the history of his own religious opinions, "that that absolute certitude which we were able to possess, whether as to the truths of natural theology, or as to the fact of a revelation, was the result of an assemblage of concurring and converging probabilities."[44] If Newman were to define faith in Kierkegaard's terms, he could go so far as to say that faith was an "objective uncertainty held fast by the passion of inwardness." He did not believe that his "concurring and converging probabilities" were enough to create what he called "logical certainty"[45] and Kierkegaard called "objective certainty." There was needed what he called "real assent" and Kierkegaard called "the passion of inwardness." Where he would differ from Kierkegaard would be in this, that he could not say that the objective uncertainty was "due to the repulsion of the absurd."

Where Kierkegaard saw the repulsion of the absurd, Newman saw the concurring and converging probabilities.

Whether one sees probability in it or mere uncertainty, there does seem to be a profound ambiguity in modern religious experience. It was interpreted variously in the sixteenth and seventeenth centuries as a duality in God or an uncertainty of man about himself, and various methods were found in the seventeenth and eighteenth centuries for resolving it. Its root, though, appears to be the lack of anyone or anything to mediate between the modern man and God, a situation that became more acute in the nineteenth and twentieth centuries when the breakdown of the system of temporal mediation completed the process that had begun with the breakdown of the system of spiritual mediation. The fear or dread or anxiety to which this ambiguity gives rise has been so prominent in modern religious experience that Freud could plausibly reduce religion to an "anxiety neurosis."[46] It might be more plausible, though, to extend to the experience of uncertainty the kind of pragmatic thinking Anton Boisen applied to the experience of despair. Just as there is a religious response to despair, according to Boisen, which is the successful counterpart of the psychosis, so there would be a religious response to anxiety, which would be the successful counterpart of the neurosis.

Two successful responses to despair and anxiety could be envisioned. One would be a search for mediation in which the search itself would have something of the effect of mediation. This was the response, it seems, of Erasmus, Pascal, Ligouri, and Newman. The uncertainty is incorporated into this response in the spirit of the search, the spirit of the quest that embodies the question expressing the uncertainty, and yet it is the spirit of the search not to be satisfied with uncertainty but to seek something better, something like an answer to the question. The other successful response would be rather a form of unmediated existence, an assurance in the face of the ambiguities of unmediated existence. This was the response, it seems, of Luther, Bunyan, Wesley, and Kierkegaard. The uncertainty is incorporated into this response as that which is faced. In both responses, to the extent that there is a movement that goes out of uncertainty or goes in the face of uncertainty, there is an experience of assurance.

The New Heaven: Assurance

The third phase of religious experience, according to Luther's formula, was just this: a heavenly assurance in the face of the hellish despair felt in the first phase and the purifying uncertainty felt in the second. It was, in fact, a confidence that was compatible with despair and uncertainty. A man could despair of his own ability and be uncertain about the value of his works and yet be supremely confident of being accepted by God. Or he could, if being accepted by God did not depend on his own ability and his own works. This is the kind of confidence Luther had in mind when he spoke of being justified by faith rather than by works. Such confidence or "security," according to Luther's formula, was an anticipation of heaven. It was a heaven, nevertheless, that was compatible with purgatory and hell. Dante's heaven had been the place where Christ and the saints reigned in glory. Luther's heaven was the assurance man could derive from the anguish, the abandonment, and the despair experienced by Christ on the cross and shared by the saints during this life.

The difference between the two heavens in Luther's terms was the difference between the "theology of glory" and the "theology of the cross." Glory was "invisible," but the cross was "visible": The glory in which Christ reigned with his saints was above and beyond the experience of this life, but the cross suffered by Christ and his saints in this life was a matter of experience. "The man who perceives the invisible things of God through the medium of created things," he asserted in the *Heidelberg Disputation*, "is not worthy to be called a theologian, but rather the man who perceives the visible things of God, God's 'hinder parts,' through the medium of sufferings and the cross." "The theologian of glory calls the bad good and the good bad," he went on to say, "but the theologian of the cross calls a thing what it is."[47] The theology of

glory, as Luther conceived it, was a wisdom based on the Law of
God. A man trying to learn about the invisible things of God
from created things would learn about the requirements man
must satisfy to reach heaven. The theology of the cross, on the
other hand, was a wisdom based on the Gospel. A man trying to
learn about the things of God made visible in the sufferings and
the cross of Christ would learn about the good tidings of forgiveness and salvation.

It was important to keep these two ways of thinking separate,
Luther believed, and not to combine them as Erasmus had done
in his diatribe, *On Free Will.* The teaching of Erasmus on free
will, Luther maintained, involved a confusion of the Law and the
Gospel, which led Erasmus "to mix up everything, heaven and
hell and life and death."[48] As for himself, Luther confessed that
it was a comfort to him to know that salvation did not depend on
so-called "free will," since if it did, he could never be "certain and
secure"[49] that he pleased God, but would always be doubting
whether he had done enough. Erasmus had tried to surmount
Luther's dichotomy between man's ability, or rather inability,
under the Law and God's grace under the Gospel by maintaining
that man's ability was the ability he had by God's grace. This
effectively took away the certainty and security of which Luther
spoke. If man's ability were his ability by God's grace, then God's
demand would be possible of fulfillment. If God's demand were
possible of fulfillment, then the comfort of not having to worry
about fulfilling it would be taken away, and along with that
comfort the assurance that one was saved.

It was no help toward certainty and security to resolve, as
Erasmus had done, the ambiguity of man's existence under the
Law and the Gospel. The certainty and security actually depended on the ambiguity. As long as man stood simultaneously
under boundless demand and boundless acceptance, he was simultaneously a sinner and a saint, a sinner under the Law because he could never hope to meet its boundless demand, a saint
under the Gospel because he was the object of its boundless
acceptance. He could be assured, therefore, of being righteous,

even though he was quite sure at the same time of being sinful. If the ambiguity were taken away, though, the "both-and" would be replaced by an "either-or," and the certainty of being both a saint and a sinner would be replaced by an uncertainty as to whether he was a saint or a sinner. This was the strength and the weakness of Luther's position. He was able to turn ambiguity to advantage and make it the basis of assurance, but he could not afford to let it be resolved.

If assurance in Lutheranism depended on leaving the ambiguity unresolved, assurance in Calvinism depended on resolving it. A Calvinist like John Bunyan could not be sure of his salvation without determining whether he stood under God's grace or God's wrath. Either God had accepted him or else he had rejected him. There was no question of standing like Luther under grace and wrath simultaneously. Yet the way Bunyan did manage to resolve the ambiguity resembles very much the way Luther arrived at assurance. The passages from the Bible that led Bunyan to believe God had rejected him were ones Luther would have called Law, while those that led him to believe he was accepted were ones Luther would have called Gospel. He tried to find signs that he was accepted in the quality of his life, in the fulfillment of the Law that is supposed to follow upon being justified and saved through the Gospel. But he did not succeed in this. He was dismayed instead by his sins and shortcomings. "Are these the fruits of Christianity?" he asked himself. "Are these the tokens of a blessed man?"[50]

After this had driven him to one last bout with despair, Bunyan thought of statements in the Bible to the effect that "not by works of righteousness that we have done, but according to his mercy he has saved us,"[51] and with this he reached his final assurance of salvation. This assurance was quite similar to Luther's. The title of Bunyan's autobiography indicates as much, *Grace Abounding to the Chief of Sinners*. Under the Law Bunyan was "the chief of sinners," but under the Gospel he was the object of "grace abounding." And yet there was a difference. Luther was assured that measured by the Gospel he was a righteous man, although measured by the Law he was a sinful man. Bunyan's assurance answered to a further question: "Does God, then, measure me by the Gospel or does he measure me by the Law?" There was no doubt in Bunyan's mind but that any man would be a sinner if he were measured by the Law, and any man would be a saint if he were measured by the Gospel. To be assured of one's salvation, however, was to be assured that God actually measured one by the Gospel.

Uncertainty as to one's salvation could not be resolved in this manner in Catholicism, since one could not be assured, according to the Council of Trent, of being and persevering in God's grace. A kind of assurance or confidence, nevertheless, could be attained. "Someone told me once," Pascal said, "that he felt a great joy and confidence on coming from confession. Another told me that he remained in fear. I thought thereupon that these two would together make one good man, and that each was lacking in that he had not the feeling of the other."[52] The reason for remaining in fear was what Pascal elsewhere called "the uncertainty of the judgement," the uncertainty of God's judgment upon a man, the uncertainty of the present judgment, the question whether the man stood at the moment in God's grace, and the uncertainty of the final judgment, the question whether he would persevere in grace. The reason for joy and confidence was what Pascal called "repose and sureness of conscience," the sureness a man could derive from the truth in matters of conscience, and the repose he could attain by the sincere search for such truth.

There was contention within Catholicism on this last point. The Jesuits had maintained that probability could yield certainty in matters of conscience. "But is it probable," Pascal retorted, "that probability assures?" "There is a difference," he said, "between repose and sureness of conscience: Nothing gives assurance but truth; nothing gives repose but the sincere search for truth."[53] Whether or not the certainty was thought to arise from probability, though, it was characteristic of Catholicism to combine certainty of conscience with uncertainty of salvation. This was more or less the inverse of the situation in Lutheranism, where certainty of salvation was combined with an uncertainty as to the goodness or sinfulness of one's works. The feeling of the combination in either case, still in all, was not very different. What Pascal said about the two men coming from confession could well have been said by a Lutheran. Only if a Lutheran had said it, he would have assumed that the one man was joyful and confident about being accepted by God and that the other remained in fear about the motive of his actions.

These combinations of certainty and uncertainty, of confidence with fear, were considered makeshift at best in the evangelical movements of the eighteenth century. They were not countenanced at all by the Moravians. Wesley too, though he himself experienced just such a combination of joy and confidence with fear and trembling, sought always what he called the "fullness of faith,"[54] the certainty that would cast out all doubt, the veritable heaven on earth. This certainty, as he conceived it, seems to have consisted of a combination of certainty of salvation with certainty of conscience. Wesley called the one certainty "justification" and the other "sanctification."[55] The one was the beginning of the Christian life; the other was its perfection. In Lutheranism he found a deep understanding of justification, but practically no understanding at all of sanctification, while in Catholicism he found an understanding of sanctification, but practically none of justification. In his own Methodism the Christian life began with a first conversion, in which one experienced justification and reached a certainty of one's own salvation, as Wesley himself had done in his experience at Aldersgate, and it came to its perfection in a second conversion, in which one experienced sanctification and attained a certainty of conscience.

Among Wesley's followers those who experienced the second conversion and witnessed to this before others were called the "greatest professors" of faith. It is significant that Wesley himself never became a "professor" but always remained short of absolute assurance in his own mind and in his claims for himself.[56] Still he was willing to believe that others attained such assurance, though he cautioned those of his followers who were "professors," warning them against pride, enthusiasm, antinomianism, sins of omission, desiring anything but God, and schism.[57] The combination of certainty of conscience with certainty of salvation was a heady mixture. It led some, according to Wesley, to believe that they would never die, others to go from house to house persuading people otherwise lacking inner certainty to believe that they were perfect, others to believe that God had given them the gift of discerning spirits, others to believe that they could not err, others to believe that they could not sin and fall, and others to denounce preachers who did not subscribe to these claims.

When certainty of conscience is added to certainty of salvation as it was in Methodism, it could well be taken, as Wesley took it, for "full sanctification," and there was danger of all sorts of over-confidence. When it is separated from certainty of salvation, on the other hand, as it was in Catholicism, there could be some question of its value for sanctification. Much depended then on the manner in which the certainty of conscience was attained, whether it was based on probability according to the method of the Jesuits or based instead on a more all-out search for truth such as Pascal advocated. Certainty of conscience when attained by the latter method could verge on certainty of salvation as in Saint Thomas More's statement on the scaffold that he died "the King's good servant, but God's first." More had rejected the recourse to probability, which was proposed to him, that "in whatsoever matter the doctors stand in great doubt, the King's commandment, given upon whither side he list, solveth all the doubt."[58] He entered instead upon a search for truth in the matter which led him to the conviction that he must resist the King's wishes even though it meant going to the scaffold.

According to the method of "probabilism" advocated by the Jesuits during the next century, ironically enough, there would have been libtery, "in whatsoever matter the doctors stand in great doubt," to do what he liked and thus to have saved his life. There was another way, however, of acting on the principles of probabilism which was practically equivalent to the more exacting search for truth. This amounted to resolving conscience by weighing the probabilities of the matters at issue themselves rather than by simply weighing the opinions of the doctors of morality. Ligouri was an example of how this could lead to a confidence in one's own conscience and to holiness. "In the choice of opinions it was always a matter of great concern to me," he said in the preface to his *Moral Theology*, "to put reason before authority,"[59] to put reason, he meant, before the authority of the moralists. "I follow my conscience," he wrote in 1764, "and when reason persuades me I make little account of moralists."[60] The power with which assurance of conscience like this could fill a life was great but, as Ligouri's temptation to despair at the end of his life demonstrated, not so great as assurance of conscience combined with assurance of salvation.

The cause of both uncertainty of conscience and uncertainty of salvation, as also the cause of despair of ability and despair of salvation, according to the diagnosis Kierkegaard worked out in the following century, was individuality. Living as he did in a time when dread and despair in both forms seemed to him particularly imposing, Kierkegaard wished to make a point of affirming individuality. He wanted the inscription on his tombstone to read "That Individual."[61] Faith for him consisted of facing this dreadful thing, his own individuality, and accepting it, like Saint Francis of Assisi kissing the leper. Each man had a leper to kiss, we might say, but the leper was not another person as it was for Francis; it was himself in his own individuality. The assurance of faith was the kind of assurance a man would attain who had completely conquered dread and despair within himself. As victory over dread Kierkegaard defined faith as "the inward certainty which anticipates infinity,"[62] an inner assurance in the face of the infinity of possibilities concerning himself that makes a man uncertain of himself.

As victory over despair he defined faith as the state in which, "By relating itself to its own self and by willing to be itself, the self is grounded transparently in the Power which constituted it."[63] This definition he proposed under the pseudonym Anti-Climacus, and it purports to be a definition from the inside by a man of faith. Earlier, under the pseudonym Climacus, he had proposed a definition that purported to be from the outside by a man who had not yet attained faith: "the objective uncertainty due to the repulsion of the absurd held fast by the passion of inwardness."[64] These definitions, too, described what it was to kiss the leper, to face the dreadful, the one beforehand, the other afterward. Beforehand and from without there was absurdity, repulsion, uncertainty; afterward and from within there was transparency. What the transparency was like in his own life Kierkegaard suggests when he says, "I every day ascertained and convinced myself anew that a God exists."[65] When one has an inward certainty that anticipates the infinity of possibilities that concern oneself, as Kierkegaard did, then every possibility that eventuates becomes a confirmation of one's faith.

An inward certainty that anticipates the infinity of possibilities, however, does not seem capable of resolving matters of conscience and the question of salvation. It is essentially an assurance that "no matter what . . ." It seems capable of resolving only among the alternative attitudes—despair, dread, and faith—that could be taken by an individual toward the issues that face him. One might compare and contrast on this score the kind of transparency that Kierkegaard found in faith with the peace of mind Newman found at the end of his search for mediation. Newman's conception of faith was not far removed from Kierkegaard's. "Real assent, then, as the experience which it presupposes," he said, "is an act of the individual, as such, and thwarts rather than promotes the intercourse of man with man."[66] Yet Newman does not appear to have simply faced and accepted the dilemmas of individuality without resolving them as did Kierkegaard. All the dilemmas Newman had personally experienced appear to have been resolved for him at the end of his search when he underwent his conversion.

On the one hand Newman acknowledged, "I was not conscious to myself, on my conversion, of any change, intellectual or moral, wrought in my mind. I was not conscious of firmer faith in the fundamental truths of Revelation, or of more self-command; I had not more fervour."[67] So it was not faith that he found, faith being understood in his meaning of the term as "real assent" and not merely "notional assent." On the other hand he could go on to say "I have no variations to record, and have had no anxiety of heart whatever. I have been in perfect peace and contentment; I never have had one doubt . . . it was like coming into port after a rough sea; and my happiness on that score remains to this day without interruption." What he had found, evidently, was mediation, the mediation for which he had been searching. This had the effect not of increasing his faith or his self-command or his fervor, but of resolving the ambiguity of unmediated existence, of dealing with the situation that had apparently been the cause of his anxiety of heart, his lack of perfect peace and contentment, his doubt, his unhappiness.

Running all through the history of religious experience in modern times we find a combination of certainty and uncertainty. After being tempted to despair of his salvation and actually despairing of his own ability, Luther found an assurance of salvation, an assurance that left him, however, in uncertainty of conscience and dread about the holiness or sinfulness of his deeds. Erasmus held for a freedom of will, which would have deprived Luther of this assurance that he had and left him with only an assurance of the possibility of salvation. Bunyan, after despairing not only of his ability but also of his salvation, came at length to an assurance of salvation. Pascal thought by sincere search for the truth in matters of conscience to attain a sureness and repose of conscience which, nevertheless, would leave him in uncertainty as to God's judgment on his life. Wesley sought throughout his life to attain a complete assurance which would eliminate all anxiety but succeeded only in attaining a measure of assurance which failed to cast out fear and doubt. Ligouri attained a high degree of confidence in his own conscience but was overwhelmed toward the end of his life with scruples of conscience and temptations to despair of his salvation. Kierkegaard underwent both dread and despair and attained at length to an assurance and transparency, by facing, though not abolishing, the ambiguity that was the cause of his dread and despair. Newman, after a long and anxious search, attained a peace of mind, but the peace he attained was only that which he had sought and not such as to increase his faith or his self-command or his fervor.

The problem in each instance seems to have been the "double God," or perhaps to speak more traditionally we could say the "double man" or, more accurately, the ambiguity in the relationship between God and man. The great psychologist C. G. Jung provoked considerable reaction in religious circles in the twentieth century by maintaining that God was not altogether good but was possessed of a "dark side" as well as a "bright side." The reaction was not altogether warranted, nor was Jung's view as unconventional as he thought, if one considers the history of the "double God" in religious experience from Luther to Kierkegaard. It appears from Jung's autobiography[68] that this view of his was not merely a theory based on a psychological study of religious experiences. It was his own experience of God. His own reaction to his experience and the one he would have others share was to confront the ambivalence of God, to face the fact that God has a dark side as well as a bright side. This was, as we have seen, the reaction of Luther and of Bunyan and perhaps we could say also of Kierkegaard, and it is the opposite of the reaction of Wesley. Such a confrontation bespeaks a great deal of assurance and was clearly in Jung's own life a successful response.

The ambivalent nature of Jung's God, however, like that of Luther's and Bunyan's and Kierkegaard's suggests that his religious experience was, in the terms we have been using, an experience of unmediated existence. It was an experience of a situation in which there is nothing human between man and God to put man in touch with God or to shield him from God. This could be taken the way Jung took it as a challenge to man to be courageous. "The spiritual adventure of our time," he said, "is the exposure of human consciousness to the undefined and the indefinable."[69] It could also be taken as an indication of another possible solution, that of a search for something human to mediate between man and God or a search for a situation in which the ambiguity is resolved and man is neither too far from God nor too close to God. This seems to have been the way of Erasmus, Pascal, Ligouri, and Newman. Erasmus, Pascal, and Ligouri searched for a situation in which the ambiguity is resolved and man is neither too far from God nor too close to him; Newman searched for something human to mediate between man and God.

Maybe the conclusion we should draw is that both the experience of unmediated existence and the search for mediation are essential components of the modern religious experience. The spiritual adventure of our time does seem to be, as Jung said, "the exposure of human consciousness to the undefined and indefinable." The exposure to the undefined and indefinable, though, leads to the search for mediation. Christ is often felt to be the archetype of the contemporary man exposed to the undefined and indefinable, for he is exhibited in the Christian message undergoing all the ins and outs of unmediated existence, the heaven of assurance, in which he calls the unknown and uncontrollable by the name "Abba," the agony of uncertainty, in which he asks "If it be possible, let this cup pass from me," and the hell of abandonment, in which he cries "My God, my God, why have you forsaken me?" In fact, the contemporary man seems to be faced, as we have suggested, with the alternatives either of trying to be the Christ himself by undergoing this alone or else of experiencing mediation by undergoing it in fellowship with Jesus. As for Jesus, he seems to have been compelled to undergo it alone against his own will: In the beginning the Spirit "drove him into the desert," and in the end he had to pray "not my will but yours be done." The question remains whether the contemporary man, too, is somehow compelled to undergo it alone.

NOTES

1. Cf. my article "Realpolitik in the Decline of the West" in the *Review of Politics* (1959) XXI, 131 ff.
2. Cf. my book *The City of the Gods*, pp. 172 f.
3. There is what amounts to a list of the points at issue in the Reformation in the "Rules for Thinking with the Church" given by Saint Ignatius of Loyola in his *Spiritual Exercises*, tr. by John Morris (Westminster, Md., Newman, 1943), pp. 121 ff.
4. The translations are my own. Cf. Luther's own commentary on his theses in Jaroslav Pelikan and Helmut T. Lehman, *Luther's Works*, (Philadelphia, Fortress, 1957), XXXI, 119 ff.
5. Cf. my discussion of Luther and Calvin on this point in *The City of the Gods*, pp. 186 ff.
6. Cf. the anonymous treatise, *The Cloud of Unknowing*, ed. by Phyllis Hodgson (London, Oxford University Press, 1944). The full title is "The Cloud of Unknowing in Which Cloud a Soul Is United to God."
7. Dante, *Inferno*, III, 9.
8. On the need for despair cf. also Luther's essay *The Freedom of a Christian* in Pelikan and Lehman, *Luther's Works*, p. 348.
9. Erasmus, *De Libero Arbitrio*, ed. by Johannes von Walter (Leipzig, A. Deichert, 1910), IV, 16.
10. Cf. the *Heidelberg Disputation*, theses 19-24.
11. Bunyan, *Grace Abounding*, ed. by Roger Sharrock (London, Oxford University Press, 1962), #130, p. 43.
12. *Ibid.*, title page, p. 2.
13. Pascal, *Pensées*, ed. Brunschvicg, pp. 435, 524, 526 ff.
14. Cf. *John Wesley*, ed. by Albert Outler (New York, Oxford University Press, 1964), p. 66. For Luther's preface to Romans cf. *Martin Luther*, ed. by John Dillenberger (New York, Doubleday, 1961), pp. 19 ff. For Wesley's later criticism of Luther cf. Outler, *op. cit.*, pp. 107 and 366.
15. Outler, *John Wesley*, p. 49. Cf. James 2:19.
16. *Ibid.*, p. 41.
17. Ligouri, *Theologia Moralis*, ed. by Leonard Gaude (Graz, Akademische Druck–U. Verlagsanstalt, 1954), I, p. 62.

18. *Ibid., iv.*
19. Kierkegaard, *The Journals,* tr. by Alexander Dru (London, Smith, Peter 1938), #1325.
20. Cf. *ibid.,* #1025. It is a central thesis of Kierkegaard's *Concluding Unscientific Postscript* that Christianity is not a doctrine but an "existence communication" (p. 536). It is especially under the pseudonym Anti-Climacus that Kierkegaard discusses the individuality of Jesus as "offense." Cf. *The Sickness unto Death,* pp. 214 ff., and *Training in Christianity,* tr. by Walter Lowrie (Princeton, N.J., Princeton University Press, 1941), pp. 79 ff.
21. Kierkegaard criticizes Hegel's "mediation" *passim* in the *Concluding Unscientific Postscript* (esp. pp. 330 ff.) and elsewhere. Cf. Hegel, *The Phenomenology of Mind,* pp. 82 f. where Hegel uses "mediation" and "reflection" as synonyms.
22. Cf. Newman, *The Development of Christian Doctrine* (London, Longmans, Green, 1888), pp. 33 ff. Cf. Hegel, *Concluding,* p. 758.
23. Cf. Newman, *Grammar of Assent* (New York, Longmans, Green, 1870), pp. 34 ff.
24. Hegel, *Phenomenology,* p. 135.
25. William James, *The Varieties of Religious Experience* (New York, 1902) (Modern Library ed.) pp. 125 ff. Cf. *ibid.,* pp. 19 ff. on judging religious experiences by their fruits rather than their origins.
26. Anton T. Boisen, *The Exploration of the Inner World* (New York, Harper 1962), p. viii. Cf. his autobiography, *Out of the Depths* (New York, Harper, 1960).
27. *Heidelberg Disputation,* Theses 7, 8, and 11.
28. *Ibid.,* Thesis 12.
29. Erasmus, *De Libero,* III, 13.
30. *De Servo Arbitrio* (Weimar edition of Luther's works), XVIII, 636.
31. Max Weber, *The Protestant Ethic and the Spirit of Capitalism,* tr. by Talcott Parsons (New York, Scribner's, 1958), p. 221.
32. The Council of Trent, Session VI, c. 9 (Denzinger 802)—on uncertainty as to state of grace, c. 13 (Denzinger 806 and 826)—on uncertainty as to predestination and perseverance.
33. *Pensées,* 518.
34. Cf. Wesley's personal concern about assurance in Outler, *John Wesley,* pp. 50, 65, and 68; his doctrinal summaries on the point, pp. 149, 159 f., and 165 ff.; and his discourse on this theme, pp. 210 ff.
35. Cf. his critique of Catholicism *ibid.,* p. 405; of Luther, pp. 107 and 366; and of Calvinism, pp. 425 ff.
36. *Ibid.,* p. 69.
37. Cf. *ibid.,* pp. 68 f., 356 f., and 359 ff.

38. Ligouri comments on Romans 14:23 and the principle of certainty of conscience in *Theologia Moralis,* pp. 4 ff.; then he treats the scrupulous conscience, pp. 6 ff.; the doubtful conscience, pp. 11 ff.; the probable conscience, pp. 21 ff.; and concludes with his "moral system for the choice of opinions which we can licitly follow," pp. 25 ff.
39. Kierkegaard, *The Journals,* #754.
40. Cf. *The Concept of Dread,* tr. by Walter Lowrie (Princeton, 1957), Chapters 1 and 2 (pp. 23 ff.) on the first form of dread, chapters 3 and 4 (pp. 73 ff.) on the second, and chapter 5 (pp. 139 ff.) on the third, according to my interpretation.
41. *Concluding Unscientific Postscript,* p. 540.
42. It is often said that the object of dread as Kierkegaard understands it is "nothingness." Kierkegaard does say that, but he goes on to specify the nothingness as that of the projected self. Cf. *The Concept of Dread,* p. 38.
43. Newman, *Apologia pro Vita Sua* (London, Oxford University Press, 1964), p. 207.
44. *Ibid.,* p. 21.
45. *Loc. cit.*
46. Cf. Freud, *The Future of an Illusion,* p. 76 where he calls religion "the universal obsessional neurosis of humanity."
47. *Heidelberg Disputation,* Theses 19, 20, and 21. Cf. Theses 22 to 24 on the theology of glory as a wisdom based on the Law.
48. *De Servo Arbitrio,* p. 680.
49. *Ibid.,* p. 783.
50. Bunyan, *Grace Abounding,* ##256 ff., pp. 80 ff.
51. *Loc. cit.* Cf. II Timothy 1:9 and Titus 3:5.
52. *Pensées,* p. 530.
53. *Ibid.,* p. 908.
54. Cf. Outler, *John Wesley,* pp. 251 ff.
55. Cf. *ibid.,* pp. 107 f.
56. *Ibid.,* p. 22.
57. *Ibid.,* pp. 298 ff. and 305 (extremes to which some went).
58. As quoted by R. W. Chambers, *Thomas More* (New York, Harcourt, Brace, 1935), p. 303. It was Cranmer who proposed this way out to More. Cf. *ibid.,* pp. 349 f. on More's last words.
59. Ligouri, *Theologia Moralis,* p. lvi.
60. As quoted by Harold Castle in *The Catholic Encyclopedia* (New York, Encyclopedia Press, 1913), I, 340.
61. Cf. "The Individual" in Kierkegaard, *The Point of View of My Work as an Author* and *Two Notes About the Individual,* tr. by Walter Lowrie (London, Oxford University Press, 1939), p. 101.
62. *The Concept of Dread,* pp. 140 f.
63. *The Sickness unto Death,* pp. 147 and 262.

64. *Concluding Unscientific Postscript*, p. 540. On these two definitions of faith by Climacus and Anti-Climacus cf. my article "The Metamorphoses of Faith" in *The Review of Politics* (1967), XXIX, 299 f.
65. *The Point of View of My Work as an Author*, p. 66n.
66. *Grammar of Assent*, p. 80.
67. *Apologia pro Vita Sua*, p. 247.
68. C. G. Jung, *Memories, Dreams, Reflections*, recorded and ed. by by Aniela Jaffé, tr. by Richard and Clara Winston (New York, Vintage, 1961). Cf. the introduction by Jaffé on the reaction caused by Jung's ideas on God.
69. *Psychology and Religion: West and East*, tr. by R.F.C. Hull (New York, Pantheon, 1958), p. 105.

The Autonomous Man

IMAGINE ALL MEN STANDING around the circumference of an immense circle. There are an infinity of points on the circle and each man stands at a different point. There is also a center. The task of each man, let us say, is to go from the circumference to the center. What situates a man on the circumference is the partiality of his self; what stands at the center would be the integral self. Say the problem is one of integrating thought, feeling and action, the basic dimensions of human life. As long as thought, feeling and action are separate from one another, a man stands on the circumference. As they are integrated with one another, he moves toward the center.

A man will tend, when his self is yet fragmented, to retreat into his most powerful component. One man will retreat from feeling and action into thought; another will retreat from feeling and thought into action; another will retreat from thought and action into feeling. The mastery of life that a man attains by retreating into his most powerful component simulates integration, but it amounts in actuality to falling prey to the power principle. Perhaps we could distinguish an initial stage in which one is prey to the conflicting forces in one's life, for instance prey to one's moods of exaltation and depression. Then in a subsequent stage one learns to retreat into one's powerful component and master all such situations in this way, for instance to retreat from moods into action or into thought. Then in a further stage, now that one has developed one's retreat and is confident of being able to master anything that might arise, one might venture once more to confront the things from which one had fled and integrate them into one's life.

Many possible lives could be envisioned: In some of them no such retreat would occur; in others there might be no return from the powerful component. As illustrations let us consider the classics of modern autobiography, the lives of Rousseau, Wordsworth, and Goethe; and as parallel examples from the more recent period let us consider the lives of Sartre, Yeats, and Jung.

The Loss of Temporal Mediation

It has been said that a kind of malaise appears in modern autobiography, in autobiographies written after the classical works of Rousseau, Wordsworth, and Goethe.[1] The earlier autobiographies written in the sixteenth and seventeenth centuries are often marked by a confidence in the importance of the self which is based on religious belief; those written in the eighteenth century show a comparable confidence, though the basis is less often religious; but those written afterward in the nineteenth and twentieth century seem usually to lack any such confidence. The difference can be verified in a striking way by comparing the *Confessions* of Rousseau with *The Words* of Sartre. Rousseau says at the beginning of his autobiography, "I am like no one in the whole world. I may be no better, but at least I am different."[2] Sartre says at the end of his that he is "a whole man, composed of all men and as good as all of them and no better than any."[3] Neither Rousseau nor Sartre wishes to claim that he is better than others, and neither wishes to admit that others are better than he. Rousseau, however, wishes to assert his uniqueness; Sartre has no wish to assert his, but asserts his commonness and universality instead.

The change in the attitude toward the self can be related to a change in the prevailing attitude toward death. In the sixteenth, seventeenth, and eighteenth centuries, when the order ascribed to the world was hierarchical and life was organized according to ranks and distinctions, death appeared to be the great equalizer, the abolisher of all ranks and distinctions. Uniqueness at that time appeared to be a solution to the problem of death, a salvation from the common plight of mankind. "Prince, Subject, Father, Sonne, are things forgot," John Donne wrote, "for every man alone thinkes he hath got to be a Phoenix, and that there can bee none of that kinde, of which he is, but hee."[4] Afterward the seeming disorder of an absence of rank and distinction came to be seen as order from another point of view, the order that consists of uniformity. So in the nineteenth and twentieth centuries it was this uniform order that appeared to be disrupted by death, and death appeared to make each man stand out in his distinctness. Heidegger, for instance, has it that man is utterly alone, hence utterly distinct, in facing the prospect of his own death, since ultimately no one can take his place at death.[5] For a man in this frame of mind uniqueness is no longer a solution but a problem.

The spiritual journey men traveled in early modern times appears to have involved (a) living in terms of the hierarchical order of the world with all its ranks and distinctions among men, (b) facing the prospect of death as the common lot of mankind, and (c) searching with varying success for a uniqueness which would set one apart from the rest of mankind. These elements contrast sharply with the corresponding ones that tend to appear in more recent lives: (a) living in terms of the uniform order of the world in which there are in principle no ranks and distinctions among men, (b) facing the prospect of death as something that has to be undergone alone and that singles one out from the rest of mankind, and (c) searching with varying success for a bond that will unite one to the rest of mankind. The difference between the later lives and the earlier lives seems to be due to the breakdown of the hierarchical order of society and thus of temporal mediation. What is common to the earlier and later lives, on the other hand, seems to be the fact that death is seen as over-turning the order of the world or of life, whether that order be hierarchical or uniform.

In the life and thought of Rousseau the first pattern appears, an initial experience of hierarchical order, the prospect of the disruption of that order, and the search for uniqueness. These elements are implied in Rousseau's teachings in the *Social Contract* on the inherent equality of men, the general will as the basis of government, and the corruption and degradation of human nature by civilization. What Rousseau meant by "civilization" was the hierarchical society. This was his initial experience of order. With the prospect of the disruption of that order went a sense of its artificiality. Hence Rousseau's belief in inherent equality and in the general will as the proper basis of government and his conviction that "civilization," i.e., hierarchical organization, was corrupting and degrading. The search for uniqueness was for him a search for naturalness, an attempt to shake off the artificiality of the hierarchical society and to be true to himself, to exchange the mask for the mirror, to live according to the ideals of sincerity and self-expression.

The second pattern appears in the life and thought of Sartre, an initial experience of uniform instead of hierarchical order, the prospect of loneliness in the failure of that order, and the search for a bond to unite the lone individual to the rest of mankind. The fundamental thesis of Sartre's existentialism, that there is no human nature, implies that the uniform order of liberty, equality, and fraternity established by the French Revolution has no positive basis in man. The basis is negative instead. It is simply the lack of any basis for a hierarchical order, the lack of any natural distinctions. When the masks have all been removed, as Rousseau desired, and man turns to the mirror, he finds that he is faceless. He has, according to Sartre, to choose his own essence, to invent himself. When he tries to be true to himself, as though he had a determinate self to be true to, when he tries to live according to the ideals of sincerity and self-realization, he finds himself implicated in "bad faith," and he learns that "man is impossible."

The thing that had undermined the hierarchical order was apparently the prospect of death as the common lot of mankind. Rousseau had experienced the prospect of death during an illness at the age of twenty-six.[6] This period of his life, he says in his *Confessions*, was the one time when he was truly happy. He was living with Madame de Warens, his mistress whom he called "Mamma," in a country retreat. The happiness began before the illness, but the prospect of death deepened it rather than taking it away. Madame de Warens did not believe in hell, and by convincing Rousseau that there was no hell, she was able to take the terror out of death for him. Reconciled with death, he was able to enjoy himself with her in the country, for his illness, outside of making him sleepless, was not painful. All this seems to have given Rousseau a vivid image of man happy in a state of nature. All the vanities and false distinctions of hierarchical civilization had vanished for him in the country, in the presence of Madame de Warens, and in the face of death. The thought of the hierarchical order vanishing before the prospect of death had long been current, ever since the Dance of Death, but the thought that man is happier without it became current with Rousseau.

That it is the prospect of death that also undermines the uniform order, plucks a man out of the crowd and makes him stand out in his uniqueness and aloneness, has been denied by Sartre.[7] Death, according to Sartre, is always accidental. A man cannot know whether he will die of old age, of sickness, of starvation, or of violence. If he attempts suicide, he cannot be sure that he will succeed. Death, therefore, cannot enter concretely into his plans and prospects except as a factor that eliminates all plans and prospects. What makes a man stand out in his uniqueness and aloneness, Sartre thinks, is his freedom of choice, for in choosing one alternative, he excludes others, in living one life, he excludes other possible lives. The finiteness of a human life is not so much the fact that it is terminated by death as the fact that one life excludes another. This kind of finiteness and uniqueness would hold even if man were immortal. Sartre admits, nevertheless, that the uniqueness of man is a problem to man. His way of saying this is to say that "man is condemned to be free." The necessity of living one life to the exclusion of all others is felt as a condemnation. One could say, though, that this is not so unrelated to death as Sartre imagines. The thought that "I have only one life to live" has a remarkable similarity to the thought that "I must die."

The sense of living one life to the exclusion of other possible lives goes with the nineteenth- and twentieth-century idea that "man makes himself." Rousseau had assumed, on the contrary, that the self is to be discovered rather than invented, that nature makes man. "Whether nature did well or ill in breaking the mould in which she formed me," he said in the preface to his *Confessions*, "is a question which can only be resolved after reading my book."[8] To say that nature broke the mold in which she formed him was a way of saying that he was unique. If it were said that nature did well in breaking that mold, it would mean that his bad qualities outweighed his good ones and that it was better for there to be no more men like him. Rousseau would have been quite content, it seems, if some of his readers were to draw this conclusion, for it would still leave him with the thing he valued most, his uniqueness. This unique self of his, he evidently believed, was able to cover a multitude of bad qualities. Perhaps this is how he found courage to confess some of the more embarrassing features of his life, for instance that the pleasure he desired most from women was a kind of masochism, or that he bore false witness against a girl in Turin, or that he abandoned in Lyons an old music master who was an epileptic, or that he abandoned his five children and had them raised in an orphanage.

If one believes that one is responsible for one's own bad qualities, as Sartre does, and that there is no mold, broken or unbroken, in which one has been formed, then one's unique self can no longer cover the multitude of one's bad qualities. There is no "given" in man. There is only what Sartre calls a "nothingness" out of which a life is created. The idea that man has no nature may be as important and as commonplace in our time as the opposite idea was in the time of Rousseau. Man's emptiness and

artificiality have become as much a problem for Sartre, at any
rate, as the emptiness and artificiality of "civilization" was for
Rousseau. As the problem of loneliness, being confronted with
emptiness when one is alone with oneself, it is widely felt in our
time and is met with a wide range of solutions, from membership
in the organization to the interpersonal relationship. Sartre in his
later years seems to agree with Marx that the solution to the
problem is *praxis*, revolutionary activity by which one creates
something out of the nothingness, but to judge from his autobiography, *The Words*, he seems to believe that he has solved the
problem rather poorly in his own life, that nothing has come out
of his emptiness but words.

Anguish, abandonment, despair,[9] the terms Heidegger used to
describe the experience of man facing the prospect of death and
that Sartre uses to describe the experience of man facing the
nothingness within himself, have a remarkable similarity to the
kind of terms Luther used to describe religious experience. Like
Luther's terms, *despair, uncertainty, assurance*, they seem to describe the experience of unmediated existence. It is noteworthy,
on the other hand, that Rousseau used no such terms. Maybe the
reason for this is that Sartre experiences unmediated existence in
the loss of temporal mediation much as Luther experienced it in
the loss of spiritual mediation. Rousseau, on the contrary, experienced the presence of temporal mediation as something artificial
and undesirable. Longing as he did for unmediated existence, he
could hardly use terms like *anguish, abandonment*, and *despair* to
describe it.

The difference between these terms and those Luther used
is that these are meant to describe an experience that is not religious. Sartre, in fact, wishes to describe an experience that is
positively irreligious. The experience of unmediated existence,
though, is an ambiguous one. A man undergoing it feels both
religious and irreligious, he feels at once close to God and far
away from God, for he feels that there is nothing either to separate him from God or to unite him to God. This suggests a hypothesis about the rise of irreligious experience in our time. As

long as mediation was temporal, as it was in the early modern period when the "lords spiritual" had been overthrown by the Reformation but the "lords temporal" still remained, unmediated
existence tended to be felt more as a religious than an irreligious
experience, for it stood in place of the experience of spiritual
mediation. Now that the "lords temporal" themselves have been
overthrown by the Revolution, it can just as well be felt as an
irreligious experience, or better, its full ambivalence can be felt.

The New Childhood: the Father of the Man

Each step in the abolition of the medieval system of spiritual
and temporal mediation seems to have had a considerable effect
on the ages of life, childhood, youth, manhood, age. This is particularly clear with regard to childhood. When the system of mediation was intact, childhood was conceived to be simply the years
before the "age of discretion." That age, about seven years, was a
fairly sharp dividing line: Prior to it the child was considered
incapable of personal sin, even "venial sin," but after it the person
was considered suddenly capable of ultimate moral decisions and
not only of venial sin but also of "grave" or "mortal" sin.[10] Of
course the mere belief that the child was incapable of important
personal acts did not make the child actually incapable of them.
It did, nevertheless, mean that children were treated as being
incapable of such acts, and this undoubtedly did make a difference in the actual experience of the child.

As long as it was believed that no important personal acts
could occur in a life before the "years of discretion," the only way
in which a child could conceivably be received into Christianity
was through the mediation of other persons. With the decline of
the system of spiritual mediation, however, it began to seem that
no one could enter into Christianity except by a personal act of
his own. Hence the tendency among some of the Reformers to
reject infant baptism. This had the effect of making the line between childhood and the rest of life much sharper, of placing the
child outside Christianity and reserving Christianity for adults.

Perhaps the mentality underlying this tendency had some affinity with the new consciousness of the distinctiveness of childhood, which appeared in the art of the time. In the earlier medieval art the child had been represented as having on a small scale the proportions and features of an adult, whereas in Renaissance art it came to be represented as having its own proper proportions and features.[11]

When temporal mediation began to go the way of spiritual mediation, and hierarchical civilization began to seem artificial through and through, the child began to emerge as the embodiment of unspoiled nature. Noble birth began to lose significance, and education of the child began to gain significance. Rousseau was the great spokesman for this conception of the child, the critic of the artificiality of hierarchical civilization, and the advocate of an education that would be simply the "course of nature." The difference he saw between this idea of the child and the one that had hitherto prevailed was very much like the difference between the image of the child in Renaissance art and that in medieval art. He complained in the preface to *Emile*, his educational romance, that educators were always looking for the man in the child, without considering the child in the child.[12] They were like the medieval painters who could not draw a child except as a tiny adult. As a result they could not grasp the importance of childhood in life, but were under the impression that nothing important occurred until adulthood.

Rousseau evidently believed that the events of his own childhood were of prime importance for determining the future course of his life. He did not see some of the connections that might appear obvious after Freud, for instance, between the fact that he lacked a mother during childhood (she had died in giving birth to him) and the fact that he called Madame de Warens, his later patroness and mistress, by the name *Mamma* and treated her as a mother. He did realize, however, that the pleasure he desired from women was a kind of masochism, and he saw the origin of this in the pleasure he experienced as a child in being punished by Madomoiselle Lambercier, who for a time exercised the authority of a mother in his life.[13] He was also able to weigh the effects of the tender loving care he received in early childhood and the ill treatment he received in late childhood and early youth.

By the time of Sartre the idea that the events of childhood are decisive for the future course of one's life had become widespread and well established. The hierarchical civilization Rousseau had considered a corrupting and degrading influence on human development had largely disappeared. Instead of following the "course of nature" as Rousseau expected, however, human development seemed capable of following any number of courses. When nature was allowed to take its course, it was discovered that nature had no course, at least for man. Thus human life came to be conceived as something artificial rather than natural, as a drama in which man is essentially an actor, and the ages of life became once more, as they had been for Shakespeare, roles a man plays. Sartre, for example, has it in *The Words* that as a child he was essentially an actor, that he was always playing a role. A new turn was given to the old idea of life as a drama, though, by the more recent idea that the events of childhood are decisive for the future course of one's life. According to this, the plot, the characters, the thought, the words, and all the essentials of the drama of life are determined in childhood.

One thing that seems to have been very important for determining the plot and the characters of Sartre's life was the fact that his father died soon after his birth. As Rousseau lacked a mother, Sartre lacked a father during childhood. Sartre's own estimate of this is that he was thereby delivered from the Freudian problem a father ordinarily creates. "I have no Superego," he said.[14] The Superego in Freudian terminology is the conscience, insofar as it is felt as being the will of one's father. Probably Sartre meant to include here also the fact that he had no belief in God, no "father in heaven." There is a connection, though, which he may not have seen between his having no father and his philosophical teaching on man. He has it that man is "the desire to be God,"[15] the futile endeavor to become a *causa sui*, to become his own foundation and the sufficient reason for his own being. The desire to become one's own cause, one's own begetter, sounds very much like the desire of a man who has no father. Acting in the drama of life means for Sartre inventing or creating a self and thus attempting in effect to beget oneself and to be one's own father.

The idea that childhood decides the course of life and that a man is his own father is implicit in Wordsworth's famous line, "The Child is father of the Man," but here as in Rousseau it is separated from the idea that life is a drama. Yeats has it that Wordsworth is often flat and heavy because his moral sense is a discipline of mere obedience and has no theatrical element.[16] The ethical meaning of the line "The Child is father of the Man" becomes clearer in the two lines that follow it: "And I could wish my days to be bound each to each by natural piety." These three lines are the opening verses or the inscription of his ode "Intimations of Immortality from Recollections of Early Childhood." The "natural piety" of which Wordsworth speaks embodies the "moral sense" Yeats mentioned. If the child is father of the man, then one should honor one's childhood in the spirit of the commandment "Honor thy father and thy mother." One's childhood is one's unspoiled nature, oneself at one's best. To honor it, to return to it in recollection, to live by it, is to honor, to remember, to live by what is best in oneself. This is an ethic of obedience, "mere obedience" Yeats called it, like obedience to one's parents; it is an ethic of sincerity requiring one to be true to oneself or to what is best in oneself and forbidding all theatrics. On the other hand, it is an ethic; it implies that one should make childhood decisive in one's life, not, as would be thought after Freud, that childhood is already decisive of itself.

The thing about childhood that Wordsworth admired and wished to make normative was not the human relations between child and father and mother and brother and sister, with which Freud was afterward concerned. It was rather the child's relations with nature. For the child "all things are full of gods," as Thales said, but for the adult the world is ordinarily empty of gods.

When Wordsworth tells the story of his childhood in his autobiography, *The Prelude,* there is nothing about his father and his mother, his brothers and his sister. It is all about the "Presences of Nature in the sky and on the earth,"[17] which he knew when he was a child. The subsequent ages of life, according to the view he takes of them in "Intimations of Immortality," are a decline from childhood.[18] It is like the traditional myth of the four (or five) ages of mankind: the first is the golden age and each subsequent age is darker until the present age, which is darkest of all. Freud, too, when he left aside the question of human relations, knew something about a decline from childhood. He spoke of the striking contrast between the "radiant intelligence of a healthy child," and the "feeble mentality of the average adult."[19] The emphasis here is different, on the questions the child asks rather than the presences that people his world, but the point is ultimately similar, the child's sense of wonder, which is lost by the adult.

A rather more far-reaching sense of loss and disappointment is implied in the melancholy sentence with which Yeats concludes his *Reveries over Childhood and Youth:* "all life weighed in the scales of my own life seems to me a preparation for something that never happens."[20] Instead of saying that the child is father of the man, he is saying that childhood (and youth) is a preparation for manhood. Somehow, though, the manhood never eventuates, not at any rate the manhood that the preparation would lead one to expect. It was not that he had accomplished too few of his plans, he explained, or that he experienced a frustration of ambitions. It was rather that the extent of the preparations would lead one to anticipate something more than what actually comes about. Yeats felt this way, he said, when he thought of all the books he had read, and of the wise words he had heard spoken, and of the anxiety he had given to parents and grandparents, and of the hopes he had had. So much trouble goes into the preparation for life in childhood and youth that the actual life that occurs in manhood seems a disappointment.

The specific nature of the disappointment Yeats felt with his life was apparently, despite his preparation, that he was "gentle

and passive," while he wished to be "creative and overmastering."
The archetype of the passionate man in his life was his grandfather—he begins the story of his childhood and youth with his
relation to his grandfather and ends it with his grandfather's
death—but he feared his grandfather and "confused him with
God."[21] At one point in his life he reversed the thinking of
Rousseau and came to believe that the doctrine of sincerity and
self-realization makes a gentle and passive person, and that the
way to become creative and overmastering is through imitation,
"by turning from the mirror to meditation upon a mask."[22] When
he tried himself to turn from the mirror to meditation upon a
mask, though, he failed and ultimately had to give up the idea.

His final judgment, "all life weighed in the scales of my own
life seems to me a preparation for something that never happens,"
contrasts sharply with the judgment one finds in Goethe's autobiography, "what one longs for in youth, that one has in age in
abundance."[23] Goethe was unlike Rousseau and Wordsworth, although he lived in the same era, for he did conceive life as a
drama, and his greatest work, *Faust*, was cast into dramatic form.
Life for him was drama, however, in the sense that it was material for drama. In itself it was nature for him or "truth," as he
called it, just as it was for Rousseau and Wordsworth. He entitled
his autobiography *Poetry and Truth* with the idea that his
method was to transform the truth of his life into poetry rather
than to try to make poetry come true in his life.[24] He would
probably have considered Yeats' turning from the mirror to the
mask an endeavor to transform poetry into truth. Because poetry
can never be successfully transformed into truth, life will always
seem to a man like Yeats "a preparation for something that never
happens." Because truth can successfully be transformed into
poetry, on the other hand, it will seem to a man like Goethe that
what one longs for in childhood and youth one possesses in
abundance in manhood and age.

The "truth" of Goethe's childhood already contained some of
the material he later transformed into poetry in *Faust*. The account of his boyhood in his autobiography ends with his ill-fated

love for a girl older than himself named Gretchen. The form of that girl, he admitted, followed him afterward on every path he took.[25] When their relationship came under suspicion, and she had told the authorities who questioned her that she had always regarded him as a child and herself as a kind of sister to him, he was cured of his passion for her and convinced that he must abandon any thought of her. Yet he was never able to rid himself of her image. In the drama Faust seduces Gretchen and abandons her and then goes on to marry Helen of Troy and ends finally in pursuit of the Eternal Feminine. The story of Faust and Gretchen does not reproduce the story of Goethe and Gretchen nearly so closely as do Goethe's own subsequent love affairs with Annette, Frederica, and Lilli. These subsequent affairs, however, pertain to the truth of Goethe's life, while the affairs of Faust with Gretchen, Helen, and the Eternal Feminine pertain to the transformation of truth into poetry.

This idea of the truth of a life being transformed into poetry is paralleled by Jung's idea of the unconscious elements of a life being made conscious. Jung, in fact, thought that there was an "inner relationship" between his own life and that of Goethe.[26] He rejected Freud's idea that the course of life is determined by the events of childhood. Instead of the characters and plot of the drama of life being determined by the persons and events of childhood, he believed that, vice versa, the elements of the drama of life were innate exigencies, and that they determined what should happen and who should matter in childhood. The process by which the elements of the drama of life entered into the life he called the process of "individuation." This process, he believed, goes on unconsciously during childhood, but should become conscious in youth and manhood. If one remains a child and does not become conscious of the plot and the characters (which Jung calls "archetypes") in the drama of one's life, one becomes a victim of the process of individuation and is dragged along by fate toward the inescapable goal one might have reached walking upright.[27]

The experiences Jung considered most important in his own

childhood were revelations of unconscious elements in his life which seemed to be innate rather than once-conscious items that had been repressed. One experience was a dream of a phallus in an underground temple, another was a mannequin which he carved and wrapped and hid away with a colored stone, and a third was an involuntary thought sequence about God sitting on his throne in heaven and befouling his church on earth.[28] The first two experiences foreshadowed the access he was to have in later life to the secret world of the unconscious. The third foreshadowed his rejection of organized religion in the name of raw religious experience, his conviction that God could not be kept in bounds by the church. These elements would have entered his life with or without his consent and knowledge, he believed. He would have had access to the secret world of the unconscious, but he could have been overwhelmed by it and could have lost his sanity. He would have rejected organized religion, but he could have done so without knowing why and could have lost rather than gained by it. As it was, his individuation was conscious, and his transforming of the unconscious materials of his life into consciousness became a deliberate undertaking.

With Jung we have come full circle and are back to something resembling the medieval idea of childhood, the idea of time before the "years of discretion"—with the difference that the unconsciousness of the child is now conceived to have a positive content. Rousseau's child was unspoiled nature ready to take its course if it were only permitted to do so by culture. Wordsworth's child was the natural being who was father to the artificial being of later life. Goethe's child was the man made of truth, out of which the man made of poetry was to emerge. Sartre's child was the nobody always trying to be somebody and setting the stage for a lifetime of theatrics. Yeats's child was the elaborate preparation in early life for something that never happens in later life. Jung's child was the unconscious being out of which the conscious being was to emerge.

To me it seems that the child is the immediate man out of

which the existential man is to emerge. By "immediate man" I mean one who is concerned primarily about the here and now; by "existential man," one who is concerned primarily about the time of his life. The differentiation between immediate and existential states may be a post-medieval way of thinking, like the differentiation between the proportions and features of children and adults in Renaissance painting. The way in which childhood will be evaluated in a life and a time will depend on how immediacy is evaluated and how it stands with mediation. When the system of mediation seems an incubus, as it did in the time of Rousseau, Wordsworth, and Goethe, the immediacy of the child is likely to seem more a virtue than a defect. The child has the development of immediacy but not yet that of existence, which by comparison can seem a corruption; he has the natural being of immediacy but not yet that of existence, which by comparison can seem artificial; he has the truth of immediacy but not yet that of existence, which by comparison can seem poetry. When the system of mediation is gone and its absence is felt, as in the time of Sartre, Yeats, and Jung, our own time, the immediacy of the child can seem rather less an advantage than a necessary beginning. The child is no-body existentially, though he is somebody immediately and is trying to become somebody existentially; he is a preparation on the immediate level for something that never happens on the immediate level but only on the existential level; he is relatively unconscious of past and future, though conscious of the present. As immediate awareness is enhanced with existential awareness, as concern about the child's background and future becomes his own and not merely his parents' concern, the child changes into a youth.

The New Youth: the Unfinished Man and His Pain

The young man in his thirties who experiences enlightenment and determines thereupon the course of his life is a kind of archetypal figure. According to his most ancient image, when he attains enlightenment he is sitting under a fig tree. This occurs in the story of Gotama, who after seven years of searching attained enlightenment while sitting under the bo tree and became thereby the Buddha; it occurs in the story of Nathaniel, who was seen by Jesus sitting under a fig tree and received the call "Come and see"; and it occurs in the story of Augustine, who was converted as he sat under a fig tree in the garden and heard the voice "Take and read." There is a corresponding figure (though a different image) in medieval times which is the archetype of the young man like Bernard of Clairvaux who withdraws from the world to enter the monastic life. Then during and after the time of the Reformation there is the archetype of the young man like George Fox or John Bunyan who without leaving the world is converted to full Christianity. And finally in recent times there is the general archetype of the young man who, after a period of searching, discovers himself and decides the way of life that he is to follow in the subsequent course of his existence.

The problem of discovering oneself and determining the course of one's life has become more acute with the vanishing of the hierarchical society. As long as the hierarchical society existed with its ranks and distinctions, a man's future was largely determined by birth. His only problem was to come of age and enter upon his responsibilities. The great exception to this was the monastic life—to which one could not be born, and which, at least in principle, had to be entered by a strictly personal act. As the system of spiritual mediation broke down, and the monastic life fell into disregard, this was replaced by the conversion. The conversion, however, did not entail an actual change of one's walk in life unless perhaps it was associated with a call to the ministry. It was only when the system of temporal mediation began to go down after the system of spiritual mediation and the ranks and distinctions of the hierarchical society were abolished or became meaningless that the entire mode of one's existence became generally a matter of decision. When this came about, it began to seem necessary for all young men who could to discover themselves and to make a decision concerning the course of their lives. This discovery and decision, when it existed, was to be the end point of youth and the turning point into manhood.

The existence of a turning point, though not of a discovery and decision of this sort, seems implied in Rousseau's division of his autobiography into two parts, the first dealing with the first thirty years of his life, the period of his childhood and youth, and the second dealing with the remainder of his life until the age of fifty-three, the period of his manhood. He begins the second part by saying that he now has an entirely different kind of story to tell. There is no suggestion, however, of making a decision about the course of his life or even of discovering himself in some manner but only of a change in course. Rousseau lived when the hierarchical society still existed, before the time when the young man was called upon to bring about the change himself through self-discovery and decision. He lived in a period, nevertheless, when the hierarchical society was felt to be artificial and was near dissolution, when it was no longer enough simply to come of age and enter upon one's responsibilities, when maturity began to be postponed and immaturity prolonged.

Rousseau's immaturity was certainly prolonged. None of his attempts to enter upon a way of life during his first thirty years came to anything. He was apprenticed to an engraver, then entered the service of two noble families in succession, then entered a seminary, then studied and tried teaching music, then worked a short time as an interpreter, then went to Paris to enter the service of a colonel, then became a land surveyor for a short time, then a music teacher again, then a tutor, and finally went to Paris hoping to establish a reputation with a new system of musical notation. The only thing that seems to have carried through during this part of his life was his relationship with Madame de Warens, his patroness and ultimately his mistress. It was when this relationship broke up and he was supplanted in her affections by another that he regarded this period of his life as brought to a close and his youth ended. Another man at this point might have attained an insight into the failure of everything that he had attempted to do so far and then·turned that insight to advantage in determining the subsequent course of his life. One can imagine Rousseau at this time arriving at the point of view he formulated later as "The Creed of the Savoyard Vicar."[29] Actually he had already met and been influenced by the two priests whom he afterward fused into the figure of his Savoyard Vicar. The turning point was more in the nature of a weaning: his dependency on Madame de Warens, his "Mamma" as he called her, was ended by her act, and he was thrown upon his own resources.

The feeling of being thrown upon one's own resources has become commoner and stronger with the disappearance of the hierarchical structure of society in which each person was given a determinate place. Now a man tends to feel like a stranger in a world in which he has no place; he tends to feel "thrown" into or "abandoned" in a world in which he must make a place for himself. The project of making such a place for himself, the project of self-realization, is what Heidegger and Sartre have called the "life project." Traced through the different stages of life this project is the principle that gives unity to the life story. Sartre has used the idea to construct biographies of Baudelaire and Genet and also to construct his own autobiography. The life project of Baudelaire, according to this conception, was to become Baudelaire, that of Genet to become Genet, and that of Sartre to become Sartre. As understood in these lives, self-realization appears to have been an undertaking that was prepared in childhood, resolved upon in youth, and carried through in manhood.

"Atheism is a cruel and long-range project," Sartre said in his late fifties. "I think I have carried it through."[30] This is a statement he could make in late manhood, at the time when the life project is supposedly carried through. He saw the preparation of his atheism in his childhood: "I was led to disbelief," he said, "not by the conflict of dogmas, but by my grandparents' indifference."[31] His resolution to undertake the "cruel and long-range project" of atheism, however, was made in his youth. "At the age of thirty," he said, "I executed the masterstroke of writing in *Nausea*—quite sincerely, believe me—about the bitter unjustified existence of my fellowmen and of exonerating my own."[32] He undertook the project of atheism at this point but did not yet realize how cruel and long-range it would be. It is cruel and long-range, he believes, in that it involves liberating oneself from illusions about oneself. This is why it is a life project, a project of self-realization. At the age of thirty he knew it meant that human existence is "bitter and unjustified," but he did not yet fully realize that his own existence was therefore bitter and unjustified. "Later, I gaily demonstrated that man is impossible," he explained. "I was impossible myself and differed from the others only by the mandate to give expression to that impossibility, which was thereby transfigured and became my most personal possibility."[33] It was only in later life, when he had "carried through" this project, that the illusion of his "personal possibility" was destroyed.

With Rousseau, Wordsworth, and Goethe, though the autobiography is in each instance the story of the "self" in the modern sense, the self involved in the ideal of being true to oneself, life was not yet, as it is for Sartre, a project of self-realization. For Rousseau it was an interaction between the self and culture; for Wordsworth it was more nearly self-realization, an interaction between the self and nature; and for Goethe it was still nearer, the creation of a poetic self out of the real self. For each of these three, though, and for their era there was already a self within man. Wordsworth's autobiography thus is not the story of a life project, how it was prepared in childhood, resolved upon in youth, and carried through in manhood, but is, according to its subtitle, the story of "The Growth of a Poet's Mind." This growth, as he conceived it, was a process resulting from the interaction of the self with nature, the self refining the raw experience provided by nature. If much was seen in experience, this, he believed, was because there was a self or a mind capable of seeing it. In this way the self or the mind had to "give," as he said, or else it could never "receive."[34]

The story of "The Growth of a Poet's Mind" is the story of Wordsworth's childhood and youth, not of his manhood and age. He finished writing it at the age of thirty-five, though he revised it in later life. Apparently, therefore, the process of growth of mind takes place, according to Wordsworth, in the first two ages of life, and manhood is characterized by the fully grown mind. He tells first of his childhood and of school time, then of his residence at Cambridge, his summer vacation, the books he read, his visit to the Alps, his residence in London, and his residence in France at the time of the French Revolution. There are also reflections on the love of nature leading to the love of man, and on imagination and taste, how they are impaired and how restored. What is basically being described is the interaction between the self and nature, but the reflections on the love of nature leading to the love of man are an attempt to integrate into the rest of his early life the enthusiasm he experienced for the French Revolution during his residence in France. The reflections on imagination and taste are then an effort to describe the fully grown mind of the poet as it emerged from youth.

The belief that there is already a self in man carried through to Yeats, but he felt dissatisfaction with it and desired to create another self, which he called the "antithetical self" or the "mask." Everyman, he thought, had an antithetical self, which he tried to realize, either on "paper and parchment" like a poet or in "flesh and blood" like a hero or a saint.[35] This view, it seems, is halfway between the view that man has a self to which he can return and be true and the view that he is faceless and must invent himself. The antithetical self, however, as Yeats understood it, was as determinate and fixed as the given self; it was, in fact, derivable from the given self by inversion. The man who is of a rational and law-loving character—temperate, restrained, and meditative in nature, measured, ordered and balanced in temperament—is likely to admire the opposite sort of character and to desire to be unbounded, lawless, and irrational in nature, sensuous, frenzied and orgiastic in temperament. And, vice versa, the creative and passionate type will desire to be rational and controlled. The Apollonian type of man, as Nietzsche termed the former, will desire to be Dionysian, and the Dionysian, as he termed the latter, will desire to be Apollonian.

Like Nietzsche, Yeats was an Apollonian type, "gentle and passive" in his own terms, who wished to be Dionysian, "overmastering, creative." The difference was that Nietzsche ended up glorifying the Dionysian type in the concept of the "overman," the *Ubermensch*. Yeats ended up thinking instead that each man desired to become his opposite and, therefore, that only an Apollonian would glorify the Dionysian, and only a Dionysian would glorify the Apollonian. Before he came to this generalization he found himself being the one sort and wishing to be the other. When he described youth in one of his poems with the phrase "The unfinished man and his pain, brought face to face with his own clumsiness,"[36] perhaps he meant the pain of this disparity between what he was and what he wished to be, the clumsiness of trying to be what he wished to be when he was competent to be only what he was. The Apollonian who wishes to be Dionysian is unfinished in a sense until he becomes Dionysian, or until he realizes, as Yeats did, that every man desires to be his opposite. He is already finished in a preliminary sense, though, when his antithetical self becomes definite for him and he sets his heart upon it.

The "transformation of truth into poetry," the essence of Goethe's life as he describes it in *Poetry and Truth*, is not yet the realization of an antithetical self on paper and parchment. For the poetic self, Faust, is not, or at least is not intended to be, the antithesis of the true self, Goethe. What the relationship is supposed to be is suggested in what Goethe has to say about his early work, *The Sorrows of Young Werther*. It was the story of the suicide of a young lover. The young Goethe, who had acquired the habit of sleeping with a dagger beside his bed and experimenting without success each night before sleeping to see if he had the courage to plunge the dagger into his heart, was relieved and freed of his suicidal feelings by expressing them in the figure of Werther. When the novel was published and translated into various languages, it caused a wave of morbid sentimentality and even of suicide across the world. "While I felt myself eased and illuminated, by having changed reality into poetry," Goethe

wrote in his autobiography, "my friends were perplexed by the
work, and thought one ought to change poetry into reality, and
that they must imitate such a romance, and in any case blow their
brains out."[37]

The poetic self, according to this, is the realization of tendencies of the real self which are not realized in flesh and blood.
Suicide, for example, is committed in poetry but not in reality.
The fullest poetic realization of Goethe's otherwise unrealized
tendencies would be *Faust*, and the most adequate expression of
the unfinished Goethe described in the autobiography (which
covers only the first twenty-six years of his life) would probably
be the *Urfaust*, the unfinished version of *Faust*, which he wrote
during his youth (from his twenty-fourth to his twenty-sixth
year).[38] The *Urfaust* contains the story of Faust being dissatisfied with the limits of human learning and seeking worldly experience with the help of the devil Mephistopheles; it describes
the drinking bout to which this leads and the love affair with
Gretchen and her betrayal by Faust. All this perhaps reflects the
young university student's dissatisfaction with the learning he has
encountered and his craving for experience, as well as his unfulfilled love affairs. What it lacks is the later Faust's concern about
aging and his desire to renew his youth, his craving for power
and along with this the bargain he drives with Mephistopheles,
that which Mephistopheles drives with God, and the exercise of
power, which was later described in the second half of *Faust*.

Jung speaks of Goethe's whole life being enacted within the
framework of *Faust* and being haunted by the great dream of an
archetypal world. "I myself am haunted by the same dream,"
Jung says in his autobiography, "and from my eleventh year I
have been launched upon a single enterprise which is my 'main
business.' My life has been permeated and held together by one
idea and one goal: namely, to penetrate into the secret of the
personality."[39] There is a noticeable difference between the
course of Jung's life, however, and that of Goethe's. It is that
youth and manhood for Jung are separated by a dramatic confrontation with himself. This crucial event is described in a chap-

ter of his autobiography entitled "Confrontation with the Unconscious." The events described in this chapter began when Jung
was about thirty-seven years of age, and they ran through the
period of the First World War. He had already become a psychiatrist, had been attached to Sigmund Freud, and had finally
broken his connection with Freud. Having rejected Freud's
views, he was left with nothing, and he began to feel the need to
come to grips with himself to find his own way in thought and
life. Given his background and his previous association with
Freud, coming to grips with himself meant to him coming to
grips with his own unconscious, with the unconscious elements of
his life. It meant discovering the plot and the characters implicit
in the drama of his life, discovering the "myth," as he called it, by
which he lived.

The effort to do this proved both absorbing and dangerous. He
had to abandon most of his activities, his teaching, and to some
extent his writing and his practice as a psychiatrist to devote
himself fully to self-scrutiny. He began recording his dreams and
fantasies and following his impulses. These fantasies and impulses, however, came near overwhelming him. "To the extent
that I managed to translate the emotions into images," he writes,
"that is to say, to find the images which were concealed in the
emotions, I was inwardly calmed and reassured. Had I left those
images hidden in the emotions, I might have been torn to pieces
by them."[40] It was not enough, though, to translate the emotions
into images; he still had to obtain insight into the images. This
was the work of the remainder of his life. "It has taken me virtu-
ally forty-five years," he wrote when he was about eighty-two,
"to distill within the vessel of my scientific work the things I experienced and wrote down at that time."[41] The fundamental
images, which were the subject of his later insights, were determined at this time of his life, and in this sense his lifework was
then decided. "The years when I was pursuing my inner images
were the most important in my life," he says. "In them everything
essential was decided."[42] All the images, as he later understood
them, were images of the self or of opposing or complimentary

aspects of the self. Thus to penetrate the meaning of them was "to penetrate into the secret of the personality," his "main business" in life.

This term, his "main business" in life, was one he borrowed from Goethe, who had said that *Faust* was his "main business" in life. Each one of the figures we have considered seems to have had a main business such as this in his life, and the determination of this main business seems to have been the task of each one's youth. This is especially true of the later figures, Sartre determining his "life project," Yeats determining his "mask," and Jung determining his "mythos." But it is also true of the earlier figures: Rousseau arrived in that time at the elements he put together later in his personal creed, the "Creed of the Savoyard Vicar"; Wordsworth achieved the "growth of a poet's mind"; and Goethe began the lifelong process of transforming the truth of his life into the poetry of *Faust*. The difference is that the earlier figures seem to have considered the main business of their lives the expression of their selves, as though their selves already existed or were given. The later figures, on the other hand, seem to have considered the main business of their lives the realization of their selves, as though their selves did not yet exist except in the form of a representation as a project or a mask or a mythos. For Rousseau, Wordsworth, and Goethe there was first a self and then self-expression; for Sartre, Yeats, and Jung there was first a representation of the self and then self-realization.

If for all of them youth terminated in a consistent expression or representation of the self, then we may say that for all of them the contribution of youth to the main business of life was the self-image. The self-image determines the main business of life, whether that business be conceived as self-expression or self-realization. Another way of putting it, I believe, would be to say that youth is the time when the immediate man becomes an existential man, when the person who in childhood had been concerned primarily about the immediate here and now begins to bring his whole lifetime to mind and become concerned about his past and future. For bringing the lifetime to mind amounts to forming the self-image, the initial expression of the self, or else the representation of the self to be realized. There is a self that already exists or is given, namely the self that has present reality and is concerned about past and future. The lifetime brought to mind is an expression of this self. There is a self, however, that does not yet exist and is to be realized, since the future does not yet exist, and the significance of the past to some extent depends upon the future. The lifetime brought to mind is a representation of this self as a self to be realized. The youth, the "unfinished man," becomes a "finished man" when he brings his lifetime to mind and establishes himself on the existential level. He is finished, though, only in that the main business of his lifetime is defined; it still remains to be accomplished.

The New Manhood: the Finished Man Among His Enemies

The archetypal young man who sits under the fig tree and attains enlightenment or receives his call does not spend the rest of his life sitting there and attaining further enlightenment or receiving further calls, but spends it communicating what he attained or received there to others. Gotama did not continue his search for wisdom, but spent the remaining forty-some-odd years of his life communicating to others the Four Truths he had discovered concerning suffering, the origin of suffering, the end of suffering, and the way of escape from suffering. Nathaniel did not continue to wait for the Messiah, but spent the remainder of his life bearing witness to others of what he had seen in response to the call he had received, "Come and see." Augustine did not continue to go from one ism to another but spent the remainder of his life teaching others what he learned in a lifetime of response to the call he received, "Take and read." Likewise in the modern epoch the young man, after confronting himself, confronts others, after coming to grips with himself, comes to grips with others.

There is, to be sure, a modern ideal of continuous quest and lifelong pursuit. Lessing, for example, said that if God held all truth in his right hand and in his left the lifelong pursuit of it, he would choose the left hand.⁴³ By comparison it would seem that the archetypal young man sitting under the fig tree chooses the right hand, chooses all truth, and spends the rest of his life communicating it to others. The choosing of the left hand, however, would be as decisive an act as attaining enlightenment or receiving a call, as decisive in fact as choosing the right hand, and the lifelong pursuit that followed would then be analogous to the life that followed upon the enlightenment or the call, rather than to the quest that preceded it. What is peculiarly modern about Lessing's point of view is not the idea of a pursuit of truth—this is what precedes the enlightenment or the call of the archetypal young man under the fig tree—nor even the idea of spending a whole life in pursuit of truth—this is implicit in the classical idea of *philosophia* as the love of wisdom rather than the possession of it, and in the Biblical idea of life as a pilgrimage—but in the preference of the lifelong pursuit of truth to the possession of all truth. This seems to reflect a rejection of a hierarchical world and society like the medieval, in which a man would have a fixed place, and a preference for a world and a society like the modern, in which he would have no fixed place but would be continually on the move.

There is something like Lessing's preference in the "Creed of the Savoyard Vicar," where Rousseau shows his preference for a religion of conscience over a religion of revelation. If God held all truth in his right hand, what he held there would in effect be revelation. If he held the lifelong pursuit of truth in his left hand, what he held there would in effect be conscience. By learning what God taught through revelation, a man could somehow enter upon the possession of all truth. By following his own conscience, instead, a man would have to enter upon a lifelong pursuit of truth. Rousseau certainly chose the religion of conscience. His *Confessions*, in fact, are as much an act of the religion of conscience as Augustine's *Confessions* were an act of the religion of revelation. The sincere acknowledgment of his guilt in the confession of his most embarrassing deeds, for instance the abandonment of his five children, put him at one with his own conscience, he believed, and thus had the effect of obtaining something like forgiveness or absolution. Instead of being reconciled with the God of revelation, he was reconciled with his own conscience or, as he could also say, with the God who spoke through his conscience.

His objection to the religion of revelation was that it was a religion of authority, not really of God's authority, as it claimed, but of the spiritual and temporal authority of the culture he knew. He considered the parallel objection to his own religion of conscience, namely that "conscience, they tell us, is the creature of prejudice," but he was sure that conscience, as he understood it, was not the product of the hierarchical culture, for it was frequently in opposition to the spiritual and temporal authority of the hierarchical society—"but I know from experience," he has his Savoyard Vicar say, "that conscience persists in following the order of nature in spite of all the laws of man."[44] It was his religion of conscience, especially the expression he gave to it in the "Creed of the Savoyard Vicar," that brought him into conflict with the hierarchical society in the second half of his life. Warrants for his arrest were issued in France and then in Switzerland after the publication of *Emile*, the book in which the notorious creed was contained. The second half of his *Confessions* is the story of these real conflicts and the rather more imaginary persecutions he believed himself to be enduring in the latter part of his life. It appears that he did not conceive this part of his life as a continuous pursuit of truth as much as a suffering for the sake of truth or for the sake of the pursuit of truth. He was as finished a man with his religion of conscience as Augustine, after his conversion, with his religion of revelation, and he had enough of a position in this part of his life to provoke opposition, real as well as imaginary, such as he had not encountered in the first half of his life, when his position was not yet taken.

When the hierarchical society with which Rousseau had come into conflict had disappeared, the position he had taken looked quite different. Sartre, for example, chose also the lifelong pursuit of truth over the possession of all truth, or, to rephrase Lessing's choice in Sartre's own terms, he chose the "pursuit of being" over "being." Man, according to the view Sartre adapted from Heidegger, is not so much a being as a quest of being. Humanity consists in the pursuit of being rather than in the attainment of it: if a man were ever to achieve being and cease to be in pursuit of it, he would cease to be human. Thus Sartre was led to maintain, as he says in his autobiography, that "man is impossible."[45] This is the position he formulated in *Being and Nothingness* in his late thirties. As he attempted to live out his position in the second half of his life, however, he came to realize that the pursuit of being does not take place simply within the horizon of the individual lifetime but is going on in the larger context of the time of man, that the pursuit of being in a life is not separable from the times in which that life is inserted. When he came to reformulate his position in the *Critique of Dialectical Reason*, in his fifties, he tried to insert his original existentialist view of life into the larger context of the Marxist view of history.[46]

Underlying this reformulation is the opposition Sartre encountered in the second half of his life. In the days of his simple existentialism he had been the friend of Albert Camus, for example, but the two were alienated from one another in their forties on the question of Marxism.[47] Like Rousseau, Sartre saw his position to be in conflict with class-structured society, but after the French Revolution had eliminated the hierarchical structure inherited from medieval society, opposition to class-structured society had to take the form of a continued revolution. A revolution that ceased would be like a pursuit of being that ended in being. The Marxist concept of continuous revolution, it seems, is the counterpart on the historical level of the existentialist concept of a lifelong pursuit of being. Camus in *The Rebel* rejected not only the permanent revolution but also the lifelong pursuit of being and returned to the idea that there is a limiting human nature, that man is a being rather than a limitless pursuit of being. Sartre in *The Words* describes his own movement in the opposite direction as an awakening, a bitter awakening to his own inclusion in the predicament of man. This amounted to realizing the inclusion of his life in his times, but instead of revising his interpretation of life, as Camus did, he was led by this to apply it more consistently to himself.

There may be some inherent problem in choosing God's left hand, some inevitable temptation to failure of nerve in the second half of life. The problem appears very markedly in the life of Wordsworth, both from his own point of view and from that of others. From the standpoint of others, the biographical standpoint, it appears in the fact that the period of Wordsworth's poetic greatness was from about his twenty-eighth to his thirty-seventh year, from the time he wrote "Tintern Abbey" to when he wrote "Intimations of Immortality." Why the gradual decline after his late thirties? From his own standpoint, the autobiographical standpoint, it appears in the context of the works written during the period of greatness. The idea of the "growth of the mind," which occurs in the subtitle of his autobiography, seems to correspond to the idea of the pursuit of truth or the pursuit of being. In "Tintern Abbey," written at the beginning of the great period, life is conceived of as a process of growth of the mind, but in "Intimations of Immortality," written at the end, it is conceived of as a process of decline from childhood. The irony is that from the moment Wordsworth conceived life to be a decline, his life became a decline.

This, it seems, is not something that happens inevitably at the end of youth and the beginning of manhood. Jung began his "confrontation with the unconscious," his pursuit of his inner images, at the age of thirty-seven, and in the years that followed laid the foundations for his most creative period. He has it that Hölderlin, Wordsworth's contemporary, was "shattered" by a corresponding experience[48]—this would have been the insanity that began its onset in Hölderlin's thirties. The comparison with Hölderlin, who was exactly the same age as Wordsworth and who was also a romantic poet, may be very revealing. The confrontation with the inner images that occurred in the life of Hölderlin apparently never occurred in the life of Wordsworth, and so neither did the disaster that overtook Hölderlin, but neither too did the new and higher phase of creativity, which, to judge from Jung's life, is an alternative outcome. Another possible outcome is indicated in the life of Coleridge, Wordsworth's fellow poet and best friend, who at this point in their lives became addicted to opium, and who afterward became Wordsworth's chief (though sympathetic) critic. The course Wordsworth's own life took is the very one he outlined in "Intimations of Immortality," a declining power of vision relieved to some extent by a continuing power of recollection.

One does not find a decline of this sort in the life of Yeats. Instead his later poetry shows, as he himself believed, an increase in "self-possession and power."[49] There is in his later life the thing one finds missing in the later life of Wordsworth, a confrontation with his unconscious self, a pursuit of his inner images. He had come to a very pessimistic conclusion about his life, it is true, in an autobiography he wrote at the age of forty-nine: "all life weighed in the scales of my own life seems to me a preparation for something that never happens." Three years later, though, there began in his life an "incredible experience," which he describes in a work called *A Vision*, and to which he attributed the growth in self-possession and power shown in his later poetry. "I know now," he said in a later autobiography, finished at the age of fifty-seven, "that revelation is from the self, but from that age-long memoried self, that shapes the elaborate shell of the mollusc and the child in the womb, that teaches the birds to make their nest; and that genius is a crisis that joins the buried self for certain moments to our trivial daily mind."[50] This buried self corresponds to the unconscious self Jung confronted, and the revelation it yields corresponds to the inner images he pursued.

On the eve of the new experience, the revelation from the buried self, Yeats had spoken of his futile effort to transform himself from a gentle and passive person into an overmastering, creative person by turning from the mirror to contemplation of a mask. Afterward he called this endeavor the "path of the chameleon,"[51] the way of imitation. Every man, he had believed, would find his path to greatness by contemplating his antithetical self—the timid man's way was through courage, the harsh and cruel man's way was through mercy and kindness. When he experienced the revelation that came to him, as he thought, from the buried self, he found that his own seemingly futile endeavor to become his opposite had a point after all. The buried self encompassed both the ordinary self and the antithetical self in an integral whole; it was the principle that drove a man toward his opposite; and its existence meant that a man was already the self he was striving to become. The great danger of later life, as Yeats saw it, was to reduce oneself to the ordinary self one saw in the mirror, especially in the mirror of other's eyes:

> *The finished man among his enemies?*
> *How in the name of Heaven can he escape*
> *That defiling and disfiguring shape*
> *The mirror of malicious eyes*
> *Casts upon his eyes until at last*
> *He thinks that shape must be his shape?*[52]

He himself had tried to escape by endeavoring to become his opposite, but when he discovered the "buried self" which encompasses the opposites, he discovered that he had already escaped, that at bottom he was already more than the self of the mirror.

The confrontation with the buried or unconscious self, though it prevents the second half of life from being an anticlimax, seems very much like a reversal of Lessing's choice, like choosing the right hand of God, which holds all truth, after becoming dissatisfied with the left, which holds the lifelong pursuit of truth. Goethe's method of transforming the reality of his life into poetry appears, by contrast, to have been a way of carrying out the lifelong pursuit of truth that did not end in any kind of failure of nerve. Goethe has it in his autobiography that his life was "planless,"[53] and ends the story with lines from his *Egmont* to the effect that living is like holding fast to the reins of a runaway chariot. This may seem surprising when we set it beside the idea expressed in the title of the autobiography, *Poetry and Truth,* that his life was a process of transforming truth into poetry. Yet when one considers what it would be to live a life such as this or one similar to it, for instance a life of transforming the reality of one's experience into doctrine or teaching, one can see that such a life would be planless in a very real sense. To be sure, there would be the plan of transforming the reality of one's experience into poetry or doctrine or whatever, but there would be no plan for the reality itself. The reality itself would be like Goethe's runaway chariot.

Two questions arise about this kind of life, questions that move in opposite directions. Doesn't the plan of transforming the reality of a life into poetry or doctrine or some other lifework leave a residue of unfulfilled reality, of desires and tendencies which are fulfilled only in poetry or doctrine and the like but not in reality? On the other hand, doesn't such a plan actually determine to some extent the reality itself, the course of experience, since the lifework is a considerable part of the reality? The second half of Goethe's life certainly made its way into the Second Part of *Faust*, just as the first half had into the original version of the First Part. His years as chief minister of the Duke of Weimar, his travels in Italy and the enthusiasm for the classical spirit that he acquired there, his further love affairs and eventual marriage, his contributions to science, were all transformed into the poetry of Faust's later life. The method of transforming reality into poetry, however, does not seem to account for what happened in the reality unless its effect was to allow Goethe to leave everything unfinished in reality. Thus, in answer to our two questions, it could at once have caused a residue of unfulfilled reality and by this same means have determined to some extent the course of the life. It would have led Goethe to begin one thing after another while finishing what he began only in poetry.

The residues of a life appear, according to Jung, in a man's human relations: He seeks in the beloved, as Goethe and Faust did in one woman after another, what he feels to be missing in himself; he hates in the enemy what he rejects in himself; he likes in the friend what he likes in himself. Or they appear in his fantasy life: there he dreams or daydreams of his integral self and of all its aspects, accepted, rejected, missing, and sought. To pursue one's inner images as Jung did in his late thirties and early forties is thus to confront the residues of one's life, to come to grips with the integral self. It is to reach for what Lessing's God holds in his right hand, all truth. When one has done this, however, to judge from Jung's life, there is still room in one's life for what Lessing's God holds in his left hand, the lifelong pursuit of truth. For at this point one will possess all the truth about oneself and one's life merely in the shape of images. It still remains to attain insight into the images. Jung has it that when he had done pursuing his inner images and confronting his unconscious self, he was in possession of the "prime matter" for a life's work, but only the prime matter. His lifework then was to transform this image material into doctrine. This parallels Goethe's transforming the reality of his life into poetry, but it differs in that Jung did not leave the reality of his life to chance. Where Goethe's life was "planless," Jung's had, if not a plan, at least a set of guiding images.

These images, like the ones Yeats described in *A Vision*, were rather esoteric. He related them in his later work to the symbols of religion, alchemy, and astrology. It is noteworthy that all three of these figure prominently in the truth of Goethe's life and in the poetry of Faust's life. Perhaps Goethe was wiser not to take such images as a guide and to consider his own life planless in this direction, but Jung seems to have been confident of his ability to understand such images and to make use of them as a principle of action. It is positively dangerous, Jung believed, to elicit the images without attempting to understand them or to stop short with some understanding of them. "Insight into them must be converted into an ethical obligation," he said, and "not to do so is to fall prey to the power principle."[54] A more explicitly religious man might say at this point that although one should not attempt to plan the reality of one's life, one should nevertheless follow God, seeking for illuminations and inspirations from God in one's life experiences. Jung's insights into the inner images are like the

illuminations, and his insights converted into ethical obligations
are like the inspirations from God that the religious man seeks.
To "fall prey to the power principle" would be to do what Faust
did, sell one's soul to the devil for knowledge and mastery, and
what Goethe was perhaps tempted to do, be less concerned about
the reality of one's life than about mastering the reality of one's
life by some such means as poetry.

Maybe to prefer the lifelong pursuit of truth to the possession
of all truth is always to fall prey to the power principle, to care
less about the truth than about the pursuit of it. Although the
finished man of the modern epoch does not always see the issue
of truth this way, he does usually see it as somehow a choice
between reliance on self and reliance on others for the truth.
Rousseau saw it as a choice between a religion of conscience and
a religion of revelation, and his preference for the religion of
conscience was something like preferring to find things out for
oneself rather than learn them from others. Sartre saw it as a
choice between a lifelong pursuit of being and an attempt to
achieve being during life, and his preference for the lifelong pursuit of being was like preferring to be the undefined being one is
to oneself rather than the well-defined being one is to others
(thus his refusal of various forms of recognition such as the
Nobel Prize). Wordsworth saw it as a choice between hope and
despondency[55] over the growth of the mind, and his preference
for hope was like preferring to use one's own mind directly on
nature or reality rather than imitate the work of others. Yeats at
first saw it as a choice between the mask and the mirror, and his
preference for the mask was like preferring to take another for
one's model rather than be a model to oneself, but afterward
he saw it as a choice between the buried self and the self that
appears in the mirror of other eyes, and his preference for the
buried self was like preferring to be what one is at bottom to
oneself rather than what one is to others. Goethe saw it as a
choice between transforming the reality of his life into poetry
and, vice versa, trying to make poetry come true in his life, and
his preference for the former was like preferring to let what one

is to oneself determine the mythos of what one is to others rather than let a mythos of this kind determine what one shall be to oneself. Jung saw it as a choice between confronting or fleeing the unconscious self, and his preference for confrontation was like preferring the esoteric knowledge that one must ordinarily keep to oneself to the exoteric knowledge that one can share easily with others.

In each case the self rather than the other is made normative: autonomy is preferred to alienation. The literal meaning of autonomy—self(*autos*), law(*nomos*)—is verified in each instance, and the literal meaning of alienation, "other-ation," is the purport of the rejected alternative. This setting of the self over against others makes a "finished man among his enemies" in a profounder sense than the term "enemies" would commonly suggest. The problem of falling prey to the power principle, however, the problem of caring less about his life than about the mastery of it through his lifework, can remain unsolved for such a man. The power principle is destructive not only of others in his life but also of himself, since he will be concerned to become to others what he is to himself without necessarily being so concerned about what he is to himself. The problem of the power principle, it seems, is the problem of the second half of life. It is the problem that arises as the existential man becomes a historic man, as consciousness and concern go beyond the confines of the lifetime to the horizons of the time of man, as the individual comes forward to play his part in history.

The New Age: the Child of the Man

A man, according to Nietzsche, passes through three metamorphoses: First he is a beast of burden, loaded down with the beliefs and values and prescriptions of other men, then he is a roaring lion who has thrown off all these burdens, and finally he is a child who is at one with all reality and says *Yes* to life.[56] Perhaps we could say that there are actually four metamorphoses if we count the child at the beginning as well as the child at the end. There is first the child at the beginning, who is the "father of the man"; then there is the "unfinished man and his pain," who is Nietzsche's beast of burden; then there is the "finished man among his enemies," who is Nietzsche's roaring lion; and finally there is the old man, who is Nietzsche's child at the end. This would mean that what is ordinarily called "second childhood" is a kind of parody of what the old man can be. Second childhood as it is ordinarily understood is the "senile psychosis," the loss of memory, judgment, and moral and aesthetic values that can occur in old age, and the confusion, irrationality, and disturbed emotionality that can result. It is, as Shakespeare described it, "second childishness and mere oblivion; sans teeth, sans eyes, sans taste, sans everything."[57]

The child at the end as Nietzsche described him, on the other hand, is an "overman" (*ubermensch*), who recollects his life as he lies on his deathbed and says "Is that life? Then once more."[58] He is the old man who is completely reconciled with his own life and with all the sufferings and disappointments of it, so much so that he is willing to live it all over again. Nietzsche's overman is in general the man who wills eternal recurrence, who affirms his life so radically that he is willing to live it over and over again eternally. The will to eternal recurrence or, more generally, the affirmation of life comes to a head, though, when life is largely behind a man, and he has nothing further to do except take an attitude toward it. The overman, as Nietzsche conceived him, was certainly a modern autonomous man. As the child at the end, however, he chooses autonomy in a somewhat different manner from the roaring lion who preceded him. The roaring lion, the "finished man among his enemies," chooses autonomy and strongly rejects alienation, the alienation of the beast of burden, the "unfinished man and his pain," who preceded him. The child at the end, on the contrary, is autonomous by appropriating his entire life, by accepting both the period of his alienation and that of his autonomy, both the period of his dependency and that of his independence. He says *Yes* to his life and is willing to live the entire thing once more. He does not lose his judgment and his values so much as transcend them; he does not lose his memory so much as transfigure it.

This consciousness was compared by Rousseau to that of the reverie, the daydream. He wrote his *Reveries of a Solitary Walker* in the last years of his life, from his sixty-fifth to his sixty-seventh year, the year of his death. Up to the time when he began them, he was suffering delusions of persecution. He had become the "finished man among his enemies" to the point of paranoia. When he was sixty-four, however, his obsession suddenly abated. It is not that he realized that the persons he had considered enemies were really not enemies, or that he forgave them. He simply ceased to struggle against them. He began to recollect his entire life once again with a very strong sense of self-approval. Certain things about his life still bothered him: He examined himself on his truthfulness and on his abandonment of his five children.[59] Although he had not always been truthful during his life, he was convinced that he had been truthful in his *Confessions*. As for his putting the children in a home for foundlings, he went on at great length, producing one proof after another that he loved children. He ended up saying that he would put his children in a foundling home again and with a better conscience if he had it to do over again, for they would have become monsters in their family surroundings.

All this sounds very much like Nietzsche's child at the end who says *Yes* and *Once more* to his life, though Nietzsche had little use for a man like Rousseau or for his ideas. There is some resemblance, it is true, between Rousseau's last state and ordinary second childhood. The resemblance lies in the mental state of reverie. Yet the daydream Rousseau's memory had become was not "second childishness and mere oblivion." His former sense of conflict with his enemies was transformed into a sense of being solitary, a "solitary walker." Instead of a loss of memory he experienced a transformation of his memory into a reverie of pure and simple awareness of his existence as a whole. Instead of a loss of judgment and of values, he experienced a transformation of his judgment and his values, which allowed him to accept this whole existence of his as it appeared to him in his reverie. Instead of the confusion, irrationality, and disturbed emotionality of second childhood, he experienced, at least for the most part, a kind of happiness and peace.

The problem of final acceptance for Rousseau was a problem of accepting his own uniqueness, of being solitary, but this was not ultimately difficult, since uniqueness was really a solution of life's problems, a solution of the problem of death conceived as it was in early modern times as the problem of common mortality. The final *Yes* for a more recent man, on the other hand, is likely to be a different matter. Sartre has not yet come to this last stage, but *The Words* shows that the problem of acceptance for him is a problem of accepting his universality, his involvement in the common predicament of man. His self-criticism in his autobiography seems very harsh at first. Then one notices that the things he criticizes in himself are things that, according to his theory of man, are true of all men. He has no tale like Rousseau's to tell about abandoning his children, nor does he make anything like Rousseau's admission that the pleasure he desired most from women was a kind of masochism, or that he bore false witness against a girl in Turin, or that he abandoned in Lyons an old music master who was an epileptic. Sartre calls himself a "traveler without a ticket,"[60] meaning that he can find no justification for his existence, but he would say the same thing about any other man. He speaks of his insincerity during childhood, but if one turns to *Being and Nothingness*, one learns that man is necessarily insincere, for sincerity would mean being true to oneself, and man never is himself but is always in the process of becoming himself and so is necessarily striving to be what he is not.[61]

Sartre's self-criticism is as benevolent in its way as Rousseau's: Rousseau gently reproaches himself for being unique; Sartre gently reproaches himself for being human. Sartre could well have given his autobiography the title Gertrude Stein gave to one of hers, *Everybody's Autobiography*. His conclusion in the last sentence of the book that he is "a whole man, composed of all men and as good as all of them and no better than any" shows that he is in possession of a solution in life's problems, a solution to the contemporary problem of loneliness in life and in the face of death. The final *Yes*, though he has not come to it, is well within his reach. It would be an acceptance of his participation in the human condition and would not be so difficult to make, since it would be a final overcoming of solitariness, just as Rousseau's acceptance of his solitariness was a final overcoming of insignificance and banality. This suggests that both for Rousseau and Sartre there could have been a much more destructive sort of self-criticism but also a much more far-reaching sort of self-acceptance. The hard thing for Rousseau would have been to acknowledge and accept an unrelieved commonness; the hard thing for Sartre would have been to acknowledge and accept an unrelieved idiosyncrasy.

The situation of Wordsworth is similar to that of Rousseau, that of the man who finds in his uniqueness a solution to the problem of commonness. His poetry involves a deliberate use of common ordinary language, but the best of it, from "Tintern Abbey" to "Intimations of Immortality," is autobiographical like *The Prelude* itself, his autobiography. It is as though the commonness of his language were the appropriate foil for the uniqueness of his subject. These, in fact, are the two usual criticisms of his work: that his language is banal, and that he talks too much about himself. They could be considered, however, his virtues as well as his vices. The solemn banality of his language shows his sense of the problem of human life and death as a problem of common mortality, the problem of being in the same predicament as all other men. The subject of his discourse, his own life and self, shows his sense of the solution as being the uniqueness that rescues him from the common predicament. The solution is also communicable, and his poetry communicates it to other men. Just as Wordsworth's uniqueness saves him, so the uniqueness of everyman will save everyman.

The final *Yes* as it appears in Wordsworth's life is apparently a *Yes* to both commonness and uniqueness, but to them in their compatibility, not to them as two separate components of his life.

He finished his autobiography originally at the age of thirty-five, but did not publish it. Then he finished at sixty-nine the revised version, which was finally published after his death. He wrote no comparable account of the second half of his life, but one can see the changes that occurred by comparing the original account of the first half of his life with the final account.[62] The original version of *The Prelude* was addressed to his best friend, Coleridge, and was read to him instead of being published; the final version was addressed to the general public and was published. The changes of his ideas on life and religion show a corresponding expansion of awareness and interest from the scope of his lifetime to that of history—the original shows the religion of nature, which is characteristic of his early life, while the final shows his later taste for traditional Christianity as an historical religion. With this goes an increased acceptance of the course of history: his disappointment with the French Revolution and with the British role in the affairs of France is much mitigated in the final version. There is also an increased acceptance of the course of his own life, specifically a much less critical attitude toward the education he received at Cambridge. All of these things add up, it seems, to a kind of *Yes* to his own life and times.

Commonness and uniqueness are also the two poles in the life and thought of Yeats, but they are in an opposite relation: uniqueness is problem, and commonness solution. In his "Dialogue of Self and Soul,"[63] a poem written in his sixties and containing the phrases we have been using to describe youth and manhood, "the unfinished man and his pain" and "the finished man among his enemies," Yeats comes to grips with the problem of the final *Yes* to life. Envisioning life from birth to death as day and pre-existence and afterlife as night, he has "soul" in the dialogue argue for night and "self" argue for day. The argument for night is that it delivers one from "the crime of death and birth"; it is a commonness that delivers one from uniqueness. Birth and death are unique acts a man performs or undergoes alone, but pre-existence and afterlife are a kind of common limbo. Night thus understood could attract a man for whom uniqueness is a problem, for whom it is painful to stand alone before the prospect of his death or to feel that his birth and existence is accidental. The only trouble with opting for night is that it would consign the problem to oblivion instead of actually solving it.

It is "self," accordingly, that has the last word in the dialogue, and the last word is a *Yes* to the life spanning birth and death. The manner in which Yeats accepts his life, though, transforms its uniqueness into a universality. It is something like Nietzsche's overman willing to recur eternally and thus transforming his life from something that is once and for all into something that can be repeated again and again. Yeats recounts the difficulties of all the various ages of life, the difficulty and pain of growing up in the first half of life and the difficulty and pain of facing the opposition of others in the second half. Then he declares that he is willing to live it all again, that he is willing to forgive himself and "cast out remorse," and he describes the sweetness and well-being he experiences when all regret is overcome. The willingness to live his life again apparently does not mean for Yeats that there is any serious likelihood of actually living it again. It is merely an attitude he takes toward the life he has actually lived. Yet the fact that he, like Nietzsche, casts his acceptance into this form is probably significant. It could mean that his life is acceptable to him in that it is something potentially universal, something that could be repeated.

The inverse problem of commonness and the solution of uniqueness appears in Goethe's autobiography in the discussion of the "demonic" with which he concludes the story of his life.[64] The autobiography, though it covers only the first twenty-six years of his life, was written in his sixties, and the concept of the demonic, as he understands it there, is really an over-all concept, it seems, of the uniqueness of a life. It represents the perspective of an old man considering the significance of his life as a whole. The demonic corresponds very closely to what would more ordinarily be called "genius." As Goethe describes it, the demonic is an element of power in a life which pertains not merely to a man's personality but to his circumstances, and again not merely to his circumstances but to his personality. If we take it to be the uniqueness of a life, we are perhaps making it clearer and more coherent than Goethe did himself. This interpretation, nevertheless, seems to make sense of everything that he has to say about it, both in terms of personality and in terms of circumstances. He speaks of having encountered the demonic in other persons in his life, some of them nearer to him and some of them further away. He is hesitant to claim it for his own life, though, beyond saying that some of the events of his life were at least clothed in a demonic appearance.

This part of his autobiography was written very late. It embodies the aspect of his life that made it most acceptable to him. The final acceptance, however, the *Yes* to life, appears most clearly in the Second Part of his *Faust*, which he completed just shortly before his death in his eighties. The original bargain Faust had made with the devil, Mephistopheles, was that his soul and his life were forfeit if ever he should say to a moment in his life "Tarry, thou art so fair."[65] When Goethe wrote this in the First Part of *Faust*, he was probably thinking of something along the lines of Lessing's choice, preferring the lifelong pursuit of truth, which God holds in his left hand, to the possession of all truth, which he holds in his right. To say "Tarry" to the moment would have been to claim the possession of all truth or being and to abandon the pursuit of it. In the Second Part, however, toward the end, Faust does say to the moment "Tarry, thou art so fair."[66] When he says it, he loses his life indeed, but he does not lose his soul. The reason he does not also lose his soul is apparently that it does not mean now the abandonment of the pursuit for the possession so much as the acceptance of the whole lifetime of pursuit. The original bargain is the poetic transformation of the younger Goethe's preference for the pursuit over the possession; the final settlement is the transformation of the older Goethe's acceptance of his life.

Jung, like Goethe, speaks of a "demonic" element in his life, but he does not mean, as Goethe apparently does, the uniqueness of his personality so much as the suprapersonal forces at work in his life. He reflects in this the more recent man's problem with uniqueness and his search for a solution in some sort of common bond with mankind. In the autobiography, which he wrote in his eighties, Jung distinguishes two personalities within himself, "personality number one," which is the ordinary unique self, and "personality number two," which is the unconscious collective self or universal self.[67] This universal self of his resembles the *atman* of Eastern religions, the universal self that comes to light as a man overcomes or makes little of his own egoism. The demonic element, the suprapersonal force in his life, which makes for creativity, Jung takes to be this universal self. His life task was the work of integrating his everyday unique self with this hidden self, which was universal. He felt, nevertheless, a kind of loneliness and isolation from other men in carrying through this task[68] just because the unique self is the ordinary everyday self, which is familiar in human relations, while the universal self, however universal it actually may be, is not ordinarily in evidence. To have dealings with the universal self, as a result, tends to isolate a man from his fellows.

In a profounder sense, though, because it is truly universal, the assimilation of the unconscious self by the conscious self, what Jung calls "conscious individuation," tends to unite a man profoundly with all his fellow men in all times as well as his own. This is the thought with which Jung ends his autobiography. He expresses at this point an inability to evaluate his own life, to choose between saying that it was meaningful or meaningless. At the same time he expresses a willingness to accept it both in its meaningfulness and its meaninglessness.[69] The combination of meaning and meaninglessness embodies his conception of the universal as the reconciliation of all opposites, truth and falsehood, good and evil. He is able to accept this, it seems, because the problem of life for him is not whether it is good or bad in some simple and straightforward way, but whether it is unique or universal. Actually he has settled for it being universal, and in this way he finds it completely acceptable. If his life had been something strictly unique with no universal significance, he would have found it very difficult to accept. It was probably because he saw his own uniqueness as consisting in a delving into the secrets of the universal self that he could accept it.

The problem of age in all the figures we have considered, the problem of the final *Yes* to life, seems always to have been one of reconciling a unique and a universal self. For Rousseau, Wordsworth, Goethe, universality was the problem and uniqueness the solution; for Sartre, Yeats, Jung, uniqueness was the problem and universality the solution. The first group lived in an epoch when the hierarchical order of things still existed to some extent, and the problem of death seems to have been one of general mortality; the second group lived in an epoch when the hierarchical order had largely vanished and had been replaced by a uniform order, and the problem of death had become one of personal mortality. The problem can also be put in terms of alienation and the experiences of despair, uncertainty, and assurance. The first group lived in an epoch when the problem was a general uncertainty and despair, and the solution a personal assurance, when uniqueness was needed to rescue a man from the common alienation of mankind. The second group, on the contrary, lived in an epoch when the problem was a solitary uncertainty and despair, and the solution an interpersonal assurance, when universality was needed to rescue a man from the loneliness of his alienation.

Consider again our image of all men standing around the circumference of an immense circle. There are an infinity of points on the circle, and each man stands at a different point, but there is only one center. The task of each man, we said, is to go from the circumference to the center. What locates a man on the circumference is the partiality of his actual self; what lies at the center is the integral self. This image may seem typically that of a more recent man for whom uniqueness is the problem and universality is the solution. The life of a man according to this image, nevertheless, is completely unique. The radial line he must follow to reach the center from his particular point on the circumference is a line no other man can take. His goal, on the other hand, is to reach the same center every other man must reach to be integral.

The idea of going from a partial to an integral self reflects the ideas of Yeats and Jung. The idea that a man starts with a unique self, already has a unique self, squares with the ideas of Rousseau, Wordsworth, and Goethe. The idea that a man must achieve an integral self reflects Yeats and Jung on self-integration, but it also squares to some extent with Sartre's notion that the self is not given but must be invented.

The image of the circle and the center and of moving from the circumference to the center is actually an ancient one, even an archetypal one.[70] The problem of reconciling uniqueness and universality is also quite archetypal. In ancient times, when the life story was told as a story of deeds, there were periods when the deeds were considered to be universal, deeds to be done ever and again, and there were periods when they were considered to be unique, deeds done once and for all. So also in later times, when it was told as a story of experience, there were periods when the experiences were considered to be universal, a common gamut of experience, and there were periods when they were considered to be unique, a personal course of experience. What differentiates modern times, it seems, is that the life story is lived and told as a story of appropriation. For Rousseau, Wordsworth, and Goethe it is the story of a unique self appropriating the common reality and thereby rendering it all unique with the self's own uniqueness; for Sartre, Yeats, and Jung it is the story of a unique self appropriating the common reality and thereby becoming itself universal with the universality of the reality it has appropriated.

As long as the life story is lived and told as a story of appropriation, each age in life will have a definite task. This seems to hold true whether the appropriation of reality is regarded as a process of making reality unique or a process of making the self universal. The task of childhood will be to set the pattern of the life experience; that of youth to determine the lifework; that of manhood to decide the relationship between the life experience and the lifework; and that of age to complete the appropriation by the final acceptance of the life. Our account of the ages and tasks of life has thus turned out to be somewhat more complex than the existentialist account of the "life project." The latter is simply a generalized description of the project of self-appropriation or self-realization. If one distinguishes as we have between the "life experience" (reflecting the old story of experience) and the "lifework" (reflecting the old story of deeds), then the autonomous self, the goal of the process of self-appropriation, becomes ambiguous. It could be a self that falls prey to the power principle, a self for which the life experience is simply material for the lifework, or it could be quite a different sort of self for which the lifework is the expression of insight into the life experience. It now remains to determine the nature of the insight that would make the difference.

NOTES

1. Cf. Roy Pascal, *Design and Truth in Autobiography*, pp. 160 f. and 50 f.
2. Rousseau, *Confessions*, tr. by J. M. Cohen (London, Penguin, 1954), p. 17. Compare Jerome Cardan (Giralomo Cardano), *The Book of My Life*, tr. by Jean Stoner (New York, Dutton 1930), chapter 38 (pp. 163 ff) where Cardano lists "five unique characteristics" he believes himself to have had.
3. Sartre, *The Words*, tr. by Bernard Frechtman (New York, Braziller, 1966), p. 160.
4. "An Anatomie of the World," lines 215 ff. in *The Complete Poetry of John Donne*, ed. by John T. Shawcross (New York, Doubleday, 1967), p. 278. Cf. Margaret Bottrall, *Every Man a Phoenix* (London, 1958), a study in seventeenth century autobiography.
5. Cf. Heidegger, *Being and Time*, pp. 281 ff.
6. *Confessions*, pp. 217 ff.
7. *Being and Nothingness*, pp. 531 ff.
8. *Confessions*, p. 17.
9. Cf. Sartre's essay "Existentialism Is a Humanism" in Walter Kaufmann (ed.), *Existentialism from Dostoevsky to Sartre* (New York, Meridian, 1956), pp. 292 ff.
10. Cf. St. Thomas Aquinas, *Summa Theologiae*, I-II, q.89, a.6.
11. For a general discussion of the charging concept of childhood cf. Philippe Aries, *Centuries of Childhood*, tr. by Robert Baldick (New York, Knopf, 1962).
12. *Emile*, tr. by Barbara Foxley (New York, Dutton, 1911), p. 1.
13. *Confessions*, pp. 25 ff.
14. *The Words*, p. 11.
15. *Being and Nothingness*, pp. 566 ff.
16. W. B. Yeates, *Autobiographies* (London, Macmillan, 1956), p. 470. He had repeated this remark in *Per Amica Silentia Lunae*, p. 28.
17. *The Prelude*, I, 464 f.
18. "Intimations of Immortality," Part V.
19. *The Future of an Illusion*, tr. by W. D. Robson-Scott (New York, Doubleday, 1964), p. 84.

20. *Autobiographies*, p. 106.
21. *Ibid.*, p. 20.
22. *Per Amica Silentia Lunae*, p. 26.
23. This is the inscription of Part II of *Goethe's Autobiography* (*Poetry and Truth from My Own Life*), tr. by R. O. Moon (Washington, Public Affairs Press, 1949), p. 185.
24. Cf. *ibid.*, pp. 519 and 639.
25. *Ibid.*, pp. 141 and 187.
26. Jung, *Memories, Dreams, Reflections*, 206.
27. Cf. Jung, *Answer to Job*, tr. by R. F. C. Hull (New York, Meridian, 1960), p. 185. Cf. also pp. 180 f. on unconscious child.
28. *Memories, Dreams, Reflections*, p. 12 (phallus); pp. 21 f. (mannequin); pp. 36 ff. (God); p. 41 (the three mentioned together).
29. In *Emile*, pp. 228 ff.
30. *The Words*, p. 158.
31. *Ibid.*, p. 63.
32. *Ibid.*, p. 158.
33. *Loc. cit.*
34. *The Prelude*, XII, 276 f.
35. *Per Amica Silentia Lunae*, p. 26.
36. "A Dialogue of Self and Soul" in *The Collected Poems of W. B. Yeats* (New York, 1951), pp. 231 f.
37. *Poetry and Truth*, p. 519.
38. Cf. Goethe, *The Urfaust*, tr. by Douglas M. Scott (Great Neck, New York, Barron's, 1957).
39. *Memories, Dreams, Reflections*, p. 206.
40. *Ibid.*, p. 177.
41. *Ibid.*, p. 199.
42. *Loc. cit.*
43. On Lessing's statement cf. Kierkegaard, *Concluding Unscientific Postscript*, p. 97.
44. *Emile*, p. 229.
45. *The Words*, p. 158. Cf. *Being and Nothingness*, p. 615.
46. *Critique de la raison dialectique* (Paris, Gallimard, 1960). The introduction is translated under the title *Search for a Method* by Hazel E. Barnes (New York, Knopf, 1963).
47. Cf. Sartre's "Reply to Albert Camus" in his *Situations*, tr. by Benita Eisler (New York, Fawcett, 1966), pp. 54 ff.
48. *Memories, Dreams, Reflections*, p. 177.
49. *A Vision* (New York, Macmillan, 1938), p. *i*.
50. *Autobiographies*, p. 272.
51. *Ibid.*, p. 270.
52. "A Dialogue of Self and Soul" cited *supra*, note 36.
53. *Poetry and Truth*, pp. 688 and 690. Cf. *ibid.*, p. 692.

54. *Memories, Dreams, Reflections,* p. 193.
55. Cf. Wordsworth, *The Excursion,* III "Despondency" and IV "Despondency Corrected."
56. Nietzsche, *Thus Spake Zarathustra,* I, 1.
57. *As You Like It,* Act II, scene 7, lines 165 f.
58. *Thus Spake Zarathustra,* III, 2.
59. The question of his truthfulness comes up in the Second Promenade, and that of his children in the Ninth Promenade of his *Reveries.*
60. *The Words,* pp. 69 and 159.
61. Cf. *Being and Nothingness,* pp. 47 ff. on "bad faith."
62. Cf. *Wordsworth's Prelude,* ed. by Ernest de Selincourt (Oxford, Clarendon Press, 1928). This edition contains both versions and has an introduction comparing the two.
63. Cf. *supra,* note 36.
64. *Poetry and Truth,* pp. 682 ff.
65. *Faust,* 1700.
66. *Faust,* 11582.
67. *Memories, Dreams, Reflections,* p. 45.
68. *Ibid.,* p. 356.
69. *Ibid.,* pp. 358 f.
70. Cf. Mircea Eliade, *Cosmos and History* (New York, Harper, 1959), pp. 12 ff. and 17 ff.

5

The Search Through Time and Memory

IN THE LAST BOOKS of his *Confessions* Augustine conducts a search for God in time and memory. Conceiving his life as a story of experience more than a story of deeds, he carries his search to the outermost limit of his past experience, to the nothingness that preceded his conception and birth. It is here that he finds God. The nothingness from which he comes is the same as the nothingness from which the world comes, and the beginning of his life is linked through it to the very beginning of time. Thus in his awareness of his own contingency he finds himself standing in consciousness before the creator God, who draws being out of nothingness.

If a modern man were to carry out a search like this through time and memory, he would have to unravel a life story which is more a story of appropriation than a story of experience. Recollection in terms of the story of experience is itself an experience of experience. In terms of the story of appropriation it is an appropriation of time. One reaches the limits of experience with the experience of nonexperience, the awareness of the nothingness from which one comes, the consciousness of one's contingency. One reaches the limits of appropriation when one has brought one's lifetime to mind, one's past through memory and one's future through anticipation. Beyond this in either direction, past or future, is a time that is really not one's own, though one can in some manner bring this time also to mind. The problem is that time in the larger sense, the centuries, is no one's lifetime. Maybe it would be fitting to call this time "God's time." It is as though time in the larger sense were God's lifetime, the greater past God's past and the greater future God's future. This would mean that in reaching the boundaries of one's lifetime or in going beyond them, one would somehow find God.

Talk about "God's time" can be no more than imagery if we conceive God to be entirely beyond time. Let us consider it imagery, at least to begin with, imagery, however, into which we seek insight. Indeed the stories about God that are told in our time tend characteristically to involve the imagery of a God in time. Perhaps we should take these stories to be something on the order of philosophical allegories like Plato's "myths." If we examine them, nevertheless, we may find the consciousness of God which comes with unraveling the life story in its modern form. Starting from them we can carry out a search through time and memory which may lead us to God, or at least to what God tends to be for us.

Life Stories and Stories of God

The striking thing about the *Stories of God* told by Rilke at the beginning of the twentieth century is that according to them God once was and God will be, but for the time being everything is as though there were no God. This is the direct point of the last story Rilke tells, "A Story Told to the Dark."[1] It is the story of a man who returned to the scene of his childhood, hoping to discover there some insight, some clue. He hears of the girl who was his playmate in childhood, that she left her husband, went off with another man, and was left by this other man with child. He seeks her out. They reminisce, recalling how he had once come to her house, and they had waited with her family in great expectation for an important guest. The guest never came. Surprised that she is not unhappy in her present abandonment, he asks if her serenity is not due to piety—he himself had ceased praying sometime before he was ten years old. She explains that really she was never pious. She had discovered, nevertheless, when she came to Florence with her lover, the traces of God, the evidence that God once existed. That was already very much. Now she sometimes thinks: God will be. When she says this, they both realize that her companion has come again to her house, as he did in childhood, to join her in waiting for an important guest. They decide then to wait together until God really comes.

This story combines the theme of the "death of God" with that of "waiting for God." The theme of the death of God was prominent in the nineteenth century, first in the teaching of Hegel, then with the additional note of the "funeral of God" in that of Heine, and finally with the further addition of the "murder of God" in that of Nietzsche.[2] The theme has been repeated in the twentieth century in many forms, even by theologians. Meanwhile the theme of waiting for God has become important in the stories of God told in the twentieth century, for example by Simone Weil and by Samuel Becket.[3] This story of Rilke's puts the two themes together, stands maybe at the historical point where the story of waiting for God begins to join or replace that of the death of God, and in any case reveals the connection between two stories which might otherwise seem incompatible. The two stories, according to this, would actually be two parts of a longer story. Probably the first part of the story, that God once was, had to come to light first, just as it did in Rilke's story, before the other part, that God will be, could be thought of, and the sense of waiting for God could arise.

The longer story for Rilke, however, is not only the story of our times but also the story of our lives. His *Stories of God* are told "to grownups for children."[4] There is a feeling running through them that many of the things said about God will be understood better by the children than by the grownups who relate the tales. Children are nearer to the darkness out of which man comes when he is born. If God lives in that darkness, then the child may be in a better position to understand him. Likewise the grown man who faces the darkness that lies at the other end of life, the darkness of death, if God lives also in that darkness, if that darkness is somehow akin to the other, may have a better sense of God than the man who is not facing death or waiting for it. The God who once was, who is not, but who will be, is present in the darkness that precedes and follows human life. He is absent in the light that intervenes.

This may be the life experience underlying the "death of God" in the nineteenth century and "waiting for God" in the twentieth. The dead God is a God of the past; the awaited God is a God of the future; but, as far as experience is concerned, that past and that future are really no other than the past that goes before and the future that comes after the lifetime. It could be said that in the nineteenth century the great mystery of life was birth, while in the twentieth it is death: God lay behind then; now he lies ahead.[5] Something parallel could be said about the deism of the seventeenth and eighteenth centuries. God, according to deism, does not intervene in the course of the world except at the beginning and the end of time, to create the world and to judge it. If for the "beginning and end of time" we read everywhere the "beginning and end of life," we begin to understand what deism must have been as an experience of life. Taken this way, it is not so far removed from the life experience that goes with the "hidden God" of the sixteenth and seventeenth centuries. The hidden God of Luther and Pascal, in fact, appears to be the prototype of the absent God, the dead God, and the awaited God.

The deeper connection between life stories and these stories of God comes to light when another figure is introduced alongside God, namely the "soul." What I mean by "soul" is something distinct from the "self" as in Yeats's "Dialogue of Self and Soul" or in Jung's theory of the *anima*.[6] The soul, according to Yeats's dialogue, is what in man loves the darkness which goes before and comes after the lifetime. It personifies, according to Jung's theory, the dark forces in a man as distinct from the bright forces embodied in the ego. An early example of this way of speaking about the soul is a mystical poem from the sixteenth century, "The Dark Night of the Soul" by John of the Cross, and the lengthy commentaries he wrote about it.[7] The poem has it that on a dark night when all was quiet the soul, filled with love and yearning, went forth secretly from her house to meet Christ her beloved; she met him, and he reclined upon her breast; as she parted his locks, he wounded her neck with his gentle hand, and all her senses were suspended, her cares were forgotten, and she slept. John explains in his commentaries and in the inscription of the poem itself that the dark night is the dark night of faith, that the soul passes through it by detachment and purification of itself, and that the consummation that takes place is union with God.

Here we have the hidden God and the darkness of faith, the soul of man which loves the darkness where God dwells, and the union of the soul with the hidden God. The detachment and purification of the soul is detachment and purification from the self. Detachment and purification, to be sure, could also work the other way, and it would be the self that is detached and purified of the soul. This may be what underlies deism and the Enlightenment of the eighteenth century. The religious darkness of the Renaissance, the Reformation and the Wars of Religion, was rejected then. The "soul" we are speaking of still existed, nevertheless, to the extent that in deistic life and thought there was a positive feeling of God's absence. An absence is felt only if there is something in us that calls for the presence. The "death of God" in the nineteenth century is still more evidently this. The positive sense of loss bespeaks of something in man which calls for a living God. "Waiting for God," on the other hand, implies something further. It implies turning once more to the darkness. The soul that waits for God in the twentieth century is like the soul that sought union with the hidden God in the sixteenth. It is a soul that loves the darkness that lies ahead of life; it passes into that darkness by detachment and purgation from the "self" which has become so central in modern life and thought; and it waits to meet the dark God concealed in death and the future.

A comparison with mythology is illuminating here. The stories of the soul, especially stories of the soul and Christ, like "The Dark Night of the Soul," have a certain similarity with stories of the great goddess and her consort in ancient mythology.[8] Innin, the great goddess in Sumerian mythology, longs to descend into the nether world, to go down into the land of the dead. This is like the soul of man, which loves the darkness that lies ahead in death and the future and the darkness which lies behind in the dead and the past. Innin goes down into the underworld, and there she is stripped of her garments and hung naked and dead upon a stake projecting from a wall. This makes one think of Christ and his crucifixion, but here the naked and dead figure is feminine rather than masculine. Innin, who has provided in advance for her death, is afterward revived by the food and water of life and released from the nether world on condition that she find someone to take her place there. This reminds one of Christ and his resurrection, but again the resurrected figure is feminine rather than masculine. Innin returns to the land of the living, surrounded by demons, seeking for someone to take her place; she finds her consort and lover, the god Dumuzi, and gives him over to the demons; and they drag him down to the nether world to undergo the fate she has left behind. Here the masculine figure appears at last, and one thinks of correlating the soul with the goddess and Christ with the god.

At first the correlation seems perfect. It would imply that Christ takes the soul's place, that he dies in order that the soul might live, that he undergoes the shameful death of the cross in the soul's stead. The resurrection, however, does not fit in very well.[9] In the Gospel story Christ does not remain in the land of the dead so that the soul can remain in the land of the living, nor does he periodically change places with the soul. Rather he dies and rises again, and the soul dies and rises with him. Some kind of transformation has taken place, some kind of alteration in the archetypal pattern. The modern story of God seems at first much nearer to the archetypal pattern than the ancient Christian story, for the death of God, especially as Hegel describes it, means the liberation of man's spirit.[10] God dies that man may live. Yet the spirit of man that is liberated by the death of God is the "self" rather than the "soul." In the modern story the soul dies with God, and in the longer version of the story it comes back with God in the future; or, to put it another way, the soul experiences loss at God's death, and it waits for God to return.

The goddess in the ancient myth reflects the darkest forces in man, the desire to die, the desire to die a grim and terrible death, the desire for another to die in one's stead, the desire for the other to die an equally grim and terrible death. On Jung's theory of the *anima* the best that a man can do is recognize these forces within himself, differentiate them from himself, and relate himself to them.[11] To personify them as a woman is a way of differentiating them from himself (and vice versa for a woman to personify them as a man). This prevents him from being hagridden, from being obsessed or possessed by them. The word "hag" means primarily a female demon; so to be hagridden is to be obsessed or possessed by a demoness. When the dark forces are differentiated, they are transformed, mythically from a demoness into a goddess like Innin, literally from an obsessive and possessive principle into a principle that is clearly distinct from the ordinary self of everyday life. The transformation shows up in the modern stories of God in the latter way, in the implicit distinction of the "soul" from the "self."

A deeper transformation of the dark forces seems possible, however, than the one envisioned in Jung's theory of the *anima*. The suicidal and murderous tendencies, the masochistic and sadistic desires, persist after they have been recognized and differentiated from the tendencies and desires of the ordinary self. What is gained is that they are no longer able to obsess or possess the person. It still remains to change them from destructive into creative inclinations, to change the soul from a destructive into a creative principle. This is the transformation that appears in "The Dark Night of the Soul." It seems connected somehow with the alteration that the story of Christ introduces into the archetypal pattern of the descent and ascent of the goddess. None of the grimness of the myth is taken away or even mitigated, but the basic experience is changed from a vicarious into a sympathetic experience. The soul in "The Dark Night of the Soul" does not seek to die and to have Christ die in its stead so that it may live. It seeks union with Christ; it seeks to share by sympathetic experience in his death and life.

There is something deeply transforming about sympathetic experience, something that can redeem the darkest urges in man. This seems to have been perceived in one way or another in all the great religions. In the religions of salvation there is the figure of the compassionate savior. In Buddhism, for example, the savior is called "the Compassionate Buddha." In the religions of prophecy there is the figure of the compassionate God. Every chapter of the Koran, for example, begins with the invocation "In the name of Allah, the Compassionate, the Merciful." In Christianity the two figures are linked, Jesus the compassionate savior and the compassionate God whom he called "Abba." In all the great religions the healing power of compassion is recognized. For compassion overcomes the closure of heart that is requisite for taking pleasure in one's own suffering or in the suffering of another, for desiring one's own death or the death of another. Compassion is a transformation of the dark pleasure taken in suffering, a transfiguration of the dark desire for death.

It is so close to these dark desires and pleasures that it can readily be confounded with them. Neitzsche did confound it with them when he tried to diagnose the sensitivity of Christ and Christianity in *The Antichrist*. There he has it that everything Christ said such as "Blessed are the poor . . . the hungry . . . those who weep . . . the hated and cast off and reviled . . ."[12] is an expression of a sensitivity dominated by the sentiment of pity. The rejection of Christianity in modern times, he believed, was a rejection of pity and of what pity does to man, both to the one who gives it and to the one who receives it. "God died of pity,"[13] he says, elaborating on the sentence "God is dead." What pity means to Neitzsche, however, is a vicarious experience of suffering and death inspired by a love of suffering and death. In reality there is such a thing as compassion, to use a term that has somewhat different connotations than "pity," which consists of sympathetic rather than vicarious experience. This too is an experience of another's suffering and death, but it is inspired not by love of suffering and death so much as love of the one who suffers and dies. All the grimness of suffering and death is present in compassion, just as it is in pity, in sadism and masochism, and in the death wish, but there is another love, a love that transfigures the dark love and transforms the significance of suffering and death for the person who gives and the person who receives this love.

The grimness of Christianity, the grimness of the crucifixion, of eating the flesh and blood of Christ under the appearances of bread and wine, has figured very profoundly in the modern stories of God. The image of the crucifixion and the idea of truly eating the flesh of Christ and drinking his blood became a problem, psychologically a very far-reaching problem, at the time of the Reformation. The crucifix exhibiting the suffering Christ was replaced by the bare cross, the bread and wine became mere symbols of the flesh and blood of Christ in some of the Protestant traditions. Perhaps the differentiation of the "self" from the "soul," which became so pronounced with the rise of the modern life story, the drama of the self, involved a strong differentiation of the bright forces from the dark forces in man. The soul is, as it were, the residue left by the movement from alienation to autonomy, and its story is the story left untold in the story of self-appropriation.

In the preface to one of his *Stories of God*, "A Tale of Death and a Strange Postscript Thereto," Rilke has it that God used to bury himself in the darkness and despair of men's hearts.[14] This was when they used to pray with their breast expanded and their arms spread out wide. But then men began to bury him in the brightness of their minds. This was when they began to pray with folded hands and build churches with slanting roofs and sharp steeples pointing toward the sky. It was like burying him in heaven instead of earth. The outstretched arms became an image of agony and death fastened to a cross. God, to escape these men and their prayers, fled from the sky into the outer darkness, which seemed to him much like the familiar darkness of the human heart. He went on and on, and the darkness grew denser and warmer like the darkness of the earth. The path of God's flight turned out to be like the path of a circle, leading him back once more to the place where he began. So someday, having fled from the bright sky and the lucidity of the human head, he will come to men again out of the dark earth and the warm darkness of their hearts.

The circle here, God burying himself in men's hearts, then being buried by them in their minds, escaping from their minds and ultimately entering once more into their hearts, could be compared to the circle described by the differentiation and trans- formation of self and soul. In the original situation the self is obsessed or even possessed by the dark forces of the soul: God buries himself in the darkness and despair of men's hearts. Then the self begins to be differentiated from the soul: God is buried in the brightness of men's minds, while the outstretched arms on the cross become a dark symbol of agony and death. When the self is fully differentiated from the soul, the light is fully separated from the darkness and the dark forces in man seem placed beyond redemption: God flees from the brightness into the darkness which needs salvation. When the soul itself, however, is ulti- mately transformed from a destructive into a creative principle, then there will be a harmony of self and soul: God will return to man once again through the darkness of man's heart.

Everything proceeds as if man's time, the time of man's "self," were a pause in God's time. If this were the whole truth, it would appear that our lives and times were much poorer than others in the experience of God. Further thought, however, reveals that there is actually a parallel with other lives and times. The time of man's "soul" is God's time. The structure of our life story and our story of God is quite similar to the one in the Gospel of John. In that gospel Jesus is said to have come from God into this world and to be returning once more to God. There is no question but that his life, according to that account, is full of God, and that his times, otherwise empty of God, are enriched by this. The difference is that God, according to John, dwells in light rather than darkness. Jesus has come from light into the darkness of this life and is going back to the light in which God dwells.[15] We think of ourselves, on the contrary, as having come from darkness into the light of our lives and times and to be going back to the darkness. Our days are full of God, as full as those of the Gospel, but ours is a dark God.

Stories of the Past: Once There Was a God

The story told in the Gospels has been retold in every age subsequent to the time of Christ. It has been told differently, though, according to the different preoccupations of each epoch. In our time it is told characteristically, it seems, as an "answer to Job," as a solution to the problem of human suffering. As it is told, for example, by Camus in *The Rebel* or by Jung in the *Answer to Job*, it begins with the problem posed in the Book of Job and goes from there to the solution found in the Gospels.[16] The problem is that man suffers, and his suffering cannot be explained away by saying that he has sinned and brought it all upon himself. The solution then is that God, instead of taking away the suffering, himself becomes man and shares the suffering.

The Gospels have existed and have been read for many centuries, the Book of Job for still longer, but this juxtaposition is a new one. Traditionally the Gospels have been read with the supposition that man has sinned and brought suffering upon himself. God becomes man, therefore, in order to save man from sin and all its consequences. The Book of Job, however, tells of a man who suffered without having sinned. Job lost everything he possessed, everyone he loved, and his own bodily health; his friends tried to explain it away by saying that God would not have allowed this if Job had not sinned; but Job maintained his innocence until the end, when God appeared and silenced him; then God took away his suffering, giving back everything he had lost and more. If we read the Gospels with Job in mind, we read the story that is told by Camus and Jung. Instead of silencing man with a show of power and then taking away the suffering, God becomes the man Jesus and shares the suffering even to the point of the anguish, abandonment, and despair of the cross.

It helps to understand the history of religious thought in modern times if we imagine it to be answering a Job. Luther and Calvin are answering a man who is maintaining his righteousness as Job was maintaining his innocence. They answer in the fashion of Job's friends by denying the righteousness he claims.[17] When Job's older friends fall silent, unable to convince him of sin, his younger friend Elihu comes forward, angry at Job for his self-righteousness and angry at the others for failing to refute Job, and proceeds to attempt a defense of God. In somewhat similar fashion religious thought turns in the seventeenth century from condemning man to defending God.[18] Milton, for example, tells the story of sin in *Paradise Lost* to "assert eternal providence and justify the ways of God to men."[19] Elihu is interrupted in the Book of Job by God speaking out of a whirlwind, and God answers Job by showing him all the wonders of creation. The defence of God in the eighteenth century takes a similar turn.[20] Leibniz, for instance, in his *Theodicy*, instead of justifying God's ways by man's sinfulness, tries to justify them by showing that the world God has created is the best of all possible worlds.[21]

In the nineteenth century a more radical turn occurs, religious thought begins to take the part hitherto reserved to antireligious thought, the part of Job. Kierkegaard feels like Job at the end, a man who has lost everything and hopes to receive everything back manifold, but it has occurred to him to pretend not to believe in God in order to take the blame for the suffering, to be unhappy ever after because God has required everything of him even though all should be returned, to feel guilty that he has been willing to give up his beloved for the will of God, not to trust God to return what has been given to him.[22] Melville, telling the story of the great white whale Moby Dick, feels like Job silenced by the splendors of God's nonhuman creation, Leviathan and Behemoth, but unanswered. Dostoevsky, speaking through the Brothers Karamazov, especially through Ivan Karamazov, is like Job speaking, replying to the arguments of his friends and questioning God's justice. Camus and Jung, writing within a year of one another in the middle of the twentieth century,[23] take Job's part more openly, speak for him directly in their own persons, Camus questioning the existence of a just God, and Jung affirming the dark side of God.

Why has the problem of suffering become so important in modern times? The problem is of course a perennial one, but it seems to revolve around the self, the central point of reference in modern thinking and living. If we draw upon sources completely outside the Western tradition on this matter, we can gain much further insight into it. The self, according to the Eastern religions, is the root of suffering.[24] Man is liberated from suffering, according to both Hinduism and Buddhism, by renouncing self and selfishness, for it is the self that suffers, and suffering consists in the frustration of selfish desire. Now in modern Western culture the life story has become essentially a drama of the self, a story of self-appropriation. No wonder, then, that suffering has become a central problem, that this age-old problem should suddenly have become so acute that it renders the very existence of God doubtful. No wonder that modern religious thought has reflected the Book of Job, and has gone from answering Job to taking Job's part in questioning God.

The problem of suffering as it is formulated in the Eastern religions, to be sure, is not the same as the question posed by the Book of Job. In Hinduism and Buddhism there is the axiom "existence is pain."[25] Life, according to this, is pervaded wth suffering. In the Book of Job, on the contrary, a man is described who was at first in a state of happiness, then afterward in a state of misery, and finally in a restored state of happiness. This implies that life on earth need not be unhappy. Job, before he lost his possessions and his loved ones and his health, enjoyed an exis-

tence that was not at all painful. It was only when he lost everything that his existence became pain. According to the axiom
"existence is pain," on the other hand, every form of human existence is pervaded by pain and frustration. The pain implied in the
axiom is that which comes from the desire for possessions and
loved ones and health, the hope for these things, the anxiety about
them, and the fear that one may lose them. It is a pain that
cannot be absent from existence, whereas the pain of actual loss is
one that can be absent. Hence the thing that Job asks of God is
not a happiness that is incompatible with human existence on
earth, but one that is quite feasible.

There is a close connection, nevertheless, between the Eastern
problem of suffering and the modern Western conception of the
self. One could compare the axiom "existence is pain" with the
existentialist principle "the essence of existence is care."[26] The
existentialist principle is one of the many modern definitions of
the self. The "care" of which it speaks is quite similar to the
"pain" of which the axiom speaks. Care about possessions, about
loved ones, about health, about life and death, this is the pain
pervading human existence according to Hinduism and Buddhism, and it is the heart of human existence according to existentialism. If care or concern is what defines the self, if the level
of care, immediate, existential, historic, is what defines the level
of self-consciousness, then the self of Western thought is quite
comparable with the self that is to be renounced according to
Eastern thought. And the self-awareness, which is such a central
value in Western philosophy, is very similar to the suffering that
is the problem of Eastern religion.

Care, therefore, while it is not the theme of the Western problem of suffering, probably does underlie the problem. It is because of care about health, loved ones, and possessions, that their
loss means suffering and unhappiness. The Western problem of
suffering, put into the form of a question, is this: "Why does God
allow man to suffer the loss or deprivation of the things man cares
about?" The question was posed in the Book of Job because of
the prominence in Hebrew thought of the all-powerful and be-

nevolent God who should have been capable and willing to prevent such loss or deprivation. It is posed in modern thought, it
seems, more because of the prominence of the self which cares
about these things. Man, no doubt, has always cared about these
things, and thus these things have always been important to him,
supremely important. He has not, however, always attributed so
much importance to the care itself and to the caring self. A great
weight of value has been shifted from the soul to the self, it
seems, and this has caused the old story of God and the soul to
undergo a revision.

Kierkegaard retells the story of God and the soul in the form of
a parable about a king and a humble maiden.[27] Once there was a
king, it goes, who loved a humble maiden. This king was so
powerful and well established that he could marry her without
being forced to abdicate. If he were to marry her, the king knew
that he would make her forever grateful. It occurred to him,
though, that something would be wanting to her happiness. She
would always admire him and thank him, but she would not be
able to love him, for the inequality between them would be too
great, and she would never be able to forget her humble origin
and her debt of gratitude. So he decided upon another way.
Instead of making her queen, he would renounce the kingship.
He would become a commoner and then offer her his love. In
doing this he realized that he was taking a great risk. He was
doing something that would be foolish in the eyes of most people
in his kingdom, perhaps even in her eyes. He would lose the
kingship, and he might also be rejected by her, especially if she
were disappointed at not becoming queen. Yet he decided to take
this risk. It was better, he believed, to risk everything in order to
make love possible.

Actually Kierkegaard did not carry the parable this far. When
he came to the king's dissatisfaction with a relationship of gratitude, he assumed that the king would merely disguise himself as
a commoner (as he would do in a fairy tale) to win the maiden's
love.[28] With that Kierkegaard shifted from the parable to a direct story of God, telling how God would not merely disguise

himself as man to win man's love but would genuinely become man to make real love possible. The story is that God loved man. God, moreover, was able to make man happy by removing all suffering from man's situation. Yet God saw something wanting in such a happiness. Man would be forever grateful to God, but he would not be able to love him because he would never be able to forget that God is God and man is man. So God chose another way. He decided to become man in order to make it possible for man's relationship to him to be one of love. In doing this, he risked giving offense to man. For, quite likely, man might prefer to be eternally grateful to God for ridding him of suffering rather than to have God share in the suffering and to be capable of being in love with God.

God's love for man thus became, according to Kierkegaard's story, an "unhappy love."[29] God's unhappiness was not merely the human misery he shared, but something deeper which only God himself could know. It was the sorrow of being an occasion of man's ruin. Before he became man, God's relationship to man was clear: he was the object of man's worship. His becoming man, though, was likely to meet with incomprehension. The purpose of becoming man was to make possible a mutual understanding, but its effect was likely to be the very opposite. For the mutual understanding to exist, man would have to understand why God wanted to share man's suffering instead of taking it away. Man would ultimately have to understand still more, he would have to see the possibility of the misunderstanding and the sorrow this caused God. Only thus could man understand God's heart; only thus could man ever fall in love with God.

There is no attempt in this story to avoid anthropomorphism. Some of the anthropomorphism is traditional; some of it is new. It is traditional to compare God with a king and to compare the soul with the maiden who is to be the king's bride. The Song of Solomon in the Bible has been traditionally interpreted as a love poem about God and the soul. It is echoed according to that understanding in "The Dark Night of the Soul" and "The Spiritual Canticle" by John of the Cross. The story told in the Song, however, takes a turn opposite that of Kierkegaard's parable, for the king makes the maiden his queen. When the story is told this way, the unhappy love of God does not appear, nor does the possibility of misunderstanding between God and man. If the king does not make the maiden his queen in Kierkegaard's story, it is because this would mean taking away man's suffering. Apparently it meant something else in the older story, some kind of union of God and the soul which would be compatible with suffering. The new anthropomorphism, the unhappy love of God, probably goes with a new sense of the other factor involved in the relationship between God and man besides man's soul, namely man's self.

The moral of the new story, however, that the relationship between God and man should be one of love and mutual understanding rather than gratitude, reflects the later stage of modern religious thought, the stage in which it has begun to take Job's part. When religious thought was taking the part of Job's friends answering Job, it wanted man to be grateful to God for the remission of his sins; when it was taking God's part answering Job, it wanted man to be grateful for the best of all possible worlds. Meanwhile irreligious thought, taking Job's part, wanted man to be in a position to be grateful for deliverance from suffering and was prepared to be bitterly disappointed that he is not. When religious thought itself began, in the nineteenth and twentieth centuries, to take Job's part, it envisioned God taking Job's part, sharing in the suffering, instead of making Job grateful by delivering him from suffering. Here, for the first time in the history of answering Job, a relationship to God was envisioned that was not basically one of gratitude.

Between man and man, according to Kierkegaard, there is ultimately no debt of gratitude.[30] Between Socrates and his disciple, for example, there is no indebtedness because Socrates only makes the disciple aware of his own self, of what he already has within himself. Socrates does not pretend to have conferred that self and what it contains on his disciple. Between man and God, on the contrary, there is an indebtedness, for the self of a man and all that is in it is a gift of God. The man owes everything to God. If God had not become man, therefore, this would have been man's relationship to God. Becoming man has meant that the relationship between man and God now partakes somewhat of that between man and man. Before, the relationship could only be one of submission of man to God; after, it could be one of mutual participation and fellowship. Before, there was only the immediacy of God to the self, which he creates; after, there is the distance of one self from another. Love between God and man before could mean only intimacy and submission; afterward it could mean also mutuality and consent to distance.

Does this answer Job? If we take it to be merely an answer to Job, it comes to the idea that God and man are "partners in misery." It would be reminiscent of the proverb "misery loves company." Actually, though, it is meant to be more than an answer to Job. This is the difference between religious thought that in effect takes Job's part and religious thought that takes that of Job's friends or that of God speaking out of the whirlwind. The point of God taking Job's part, according to religious thought like that of Kierkegaard, is really not to answer Job but to bring about something entirely different, a relationship with man based on love and mutual understanding instead of gratitude. Man can indeed be grateful to God for the love relationship. Thus Kierkegaard retains the notion of gratitude and of owing everything to God.[31] Yet this is not what man wanted to be grateful for. He wanted deliverance from suffering. If God had wished to make man grateful, he could have accomplished this much more effectively by taking away man's misery. If he becomes man, he has another end in view.

The compassionate savior in the Eastern religions teaches man to live by the soul rather than the self. The compassionate God in the religions of prophecy restores everything to the self and more, as he did to Job at the end. The God and the savior in Christianity, at least according to modern religious thought in its latter phases, takes Job's part, shares in man's suffering. The trouble with this last alternative is that if religious thought takes Job's part, it seems to be no longer religious, and if God takes Job's part, he seems to be no longer God. This was the implication of our modified and extended version of Kierkegaard's parable. If the king really becomes a commoner, if he does not merely disguise himself as a commoner, then he renounces the kingship. By doing this he makes something more than gratitude possible, he makes it possible for the humble maiden to be in love with him. But he also runs a grave risk of being rejected. Why should he be rejected? Because he was once a king and is so no longer.

Stories of the Present: Now There Is No God

Somehow when one approaches Jesus with the understanding of man implicit in the modern life story, the divinity of Jesus seems to fade and vanish and nothing is left but his humanity. This has been a general experience in the modern epoch. Camus pointed out in *The Rebel* that there has been a profanation of Jesus in modern times, and this has had the effect of stultifying the Christian answer to the problem of suffering.[32] The answer to Job contained in the Gospels depends on God sharing in man's suffering. But if the man described in the Gospels is not really God, then he is a Job, another innocent sufferer, another instance of the unanswered question Job asked. The cry "My God, my God, why have you forsaken me?" is a summary of all Job's complaints. If Jesus is not God, but only another man forsaken by God, then God becomes once again the God of Job. The problem of suffering is felt so acutely in modern times, though, that if God becomes again the God of Job, a man may well feel like saying with Stendhal "the only excuse for God is that he does not exist."[33]

If we search for the cause of the profanation of Jesus, we find it in the form of the modern life story. It is the fact that the life story has become a drama of the self. This has meant that Jesus has come to be conceived as a self. In earlier times, when the life story was rather a story of experience, it was possible to conceive Jesus as a divine person possessed of a human nature, this human nature being the basis of his participation in human experience. Nowadays, though, being human tends to mean being a self. This appears to conflict with being a divine person. Not that we need assume that "self" in the modern sense is equivalent to "person" in the ancient dogma, and that the difference is all in the adjectives "human" and "divine." The connotations of the two nouns are undoubtedly different by the very fact that the life story in ancient times was not contrued as a story of the self. The two nouns, nevertheless, both refer to what would be designated by the pronoun *I*. The *person* in the ancient dogma of the Incarnation and the *self* in the modern lives of Jesus both stand in place of the *I* which occurs in the sayings of Jesus.

Thus the self again appears to be the root of our difficulties with God. There is a positive connection between God and selfhood, however, which can further illuminate the profanation of Jesus and ultimately carry us beyond it. It is a connection that already appears in Biblical language about God in phrases like "the God of Abraham." With the prominence of the self in modern times it has become natural for us to speak of "the God of Paul" or "the God of Augustine" or "the God of Kierkegaard." The history of religious experience in this epoch is suggested by phrases like "the God of Luther," "the God of Calvin," "the God of Pascal." In fact, one can even speak of the Gods of deists and atheists, "the God of Voltaire," "the God of Stendhal," "the God of Nietzsche," meaning the absent God, the inexcusable God, the dead God. What is implied in every one of these phrases is an intimate link between the God and the self.

Such a link shows up very clearly in the modern epoch in the phenomenon of personal religion and personal creeds. To be sure, the personal creed usually has some direct relationship to a common creed. The prototype of the personal creed as a literary form is Montaigne's "Apology for Raymond de Sebonde."[34] Montaigne expressed there essentially his personal skepticism about the common creed of medieval Christendom. Sir Thomas Browne, writing in the next century, used much the same format in his *Religio Medici* to set forth his personal adherence to and reflections upon

the common creed of the English church of his time.[35] Lord
Herbert of Cherbury, on the other hand, writing at about the
same time, attempted in his *Religio Laici* to work out a reduced
creed which would rise above the religious differences of the time
by upholding only those articles that were common to the various
contending groups in Christianity and were shared even by the
non-Christian religions.[36] This became the pattern of personally
devised creeds in the eighteenth century, but Rousseau in his
"Creed of the Savoyard Vicar" managed to make such a generalized creed seem the intimate testimony of personal conscience in
its conflict with historically organized religion.[37] In the nineteenth century the critique of the common creed tended to be
made more in the name of the genuine "essence" of historical
Christianity than in that of personal conscience, though this
essence could be set out in explicitly personal creeds like Tolstoy's
My Religion.[38] In the twentieth century the attempt to recapture
the essence of historical Christianity has often been abandoned, as
it was for instance by Albert Schweitzer,[39] in order to put forward in the personal religion and the personal creed something
indeed for all mankind but something consciously new with respect to the historical religions.

A man who has a personal religion and who is capable of
composing a personal creed is "his own man" and has his own
God. This may be the source of his difficulties with historical
Christianity. His difficulties are not with common creeds as such
but with the common creed of Christianity, for this creed involves
the preeminence of another self, that of Jesus. It is much easier to
appropriate something universal than to appropriate something
individual. Appropriation means making the thing one's own, giving it the stamp of one's own individuality. This is very hard to do
when it already has an individuality stamped on it. Confronted
with this, the autonomous man may well be skeptical; he may
give it, almost in a patronizing way, his personal approval; he
may seek to eliminate the other individuality from it so that it can
receive the stamp of his own, reducing it to what it has in common with other religions, approving in it only what he finds al-

ready in his own conscience, trying to extract an essence from it which can be appropriated; or he may frankly set it aside for a religion and a creed of his own.

The difficulty with the individuality already stamped on Christianity existed before individuality itself became a problem. In the earlier centuries of the modern epoch, as we saw in Chapter 4, individuality was a solution to a problem; personal uniqueness was an answer to common mortality, a salvation from the common human predicament. The individuality of Jesus, however, which marks Christian religion, could already be felt as a difficulty, for it tended to prevent a man from marking Christianity with his own individuality. Hence the development of "natural religion" in the seventeenth and eighteenth centuries and the ability of men like Rousseau, Wordsworth, and Goethe to mark that kind of religion with their own individuality. In the later centuries, the nineteenth and twentieth, individuality became a problem, and the kind of universality that was needed to make religion capable of personal appropriation gave way to the kind needed to overcome the isolation of the individual man. Hence the recourse of men like Yeats and Jung to archetypal myths, the universal religious patterns of mankind, and the coupling in Sartre's mind of God's impossibility with man's impossibility, man's lack of a universal essence.

Personal religion and the personal creed are the religion and creed of the autonomous man, the man who has solved the problem of appropriation. If we move a step back, however, to the alienated man and the unsolved problem, we find a different kind of image of God and a different sort of connection with the self. Here it is less obviously true to say of an individual that he has his own God, for the God he has appears to him to be "wholly other," entirely different from himself. This goes with the fact that the man is actually "wholly other" to himself, that he is in a very real sense "not himself," not "his own man," since he has not yet appropriated his life and his world. Reality is yet to become his world; life is yet to become his life; and so it is no wonder that God is yet to become his God. The connection with the alienated self, therefore, appears in one way to be quite as close as it is with the autonomous self: God is alien to a man to the extent that the man is alien to himself.

It is only that the relationship is less simple than it is in the personal religion. The God can be a double God just as the self is double, being at once itself and other than itself. The double God of Luther, for example, the God of the Law and the God of the Gospel corresponds to the duality of Luther's self, the experience of being at once a sinner and a saint. The double God of Bunyan, the God of gratuitous rejection, and the God of gratuitous acceptance corresponds to an alternating sense of being rejected and being accepted. Sometimes the duality is only potential. Erasmus's God of free will and Pascal's hidden God correspond to the potential duality of a self that can opt or wager. Sometimes no duality appears, perhaps because the situation of the alienated man is experienced less as a state of alienation than as a quest of autonomy. Thus Wesley's God is that of a man single-mindedly seeking assurance of salvation; Ligouri's is that of a man seeking certainty of conscience; Newman's is that of a man seeking mediation.

Maybe, though, there is more to the sense of God as the "wholly other" than simply the experience of alienation. Kierkegaard, who uses this phrase to describe God,[40] uses it when writing under pseudonyms, when writing as an outsider to Christianity. He does not use it, as far as I know, when writing under his own name and as an insider. For him, therefore, it may be an outsider's sense of God, the sense a man has prior to the personal appropriation of Christianity that makes it his religion and makes its God his God. If we consider the fact, though, that the story of appropriation is not the perennial human story but only the form the life story characteristically takes in the modern period, we can guess that there is something else involved here besides appropriation. If the modern story of appropriation, the drama of the self, leaves something untold about man's life, let us say the story of the soul, then this may have something to do with God's resistance to being appropriated. Maybe there is a connection between the God and the soul, and what God is to the soul seems alien, "wholly other," to the self.

If we go back in history behind the modern epoch and the story of appropriation, we still find a close connection between the God and what would correspond to the modern self, but the connection, as with the modern alienated self, is not a simple one. The God of Paul the Christian was not the same as the God of Saul the Pharisee, though each was a God of righteousness, and the change of Gods seems to have involved a change of selves. So also the God of Augustine the Christian and that of Augustine the Manichee, the change of selves at his conversion was as radical as that at Paul's. Perhaps there can be not only a coming to oneself as in the story of appropriation but a change of selves. All this can be put, nevertheless, into the modern language of appropriation. It would amount to appropriating the God of another. Using our language to describe what they did, we could perhaps say that Paul and Augustine each appropriated the God of Jesus.

Thus we come finally to the God of Jesus. This is the God that Jesus called by the name "Abba," a name we ordinarily translate "Father" but which, as we saw in Chapter 1, is really the informal term like "Daddy" or "Papa." What this God is like we can see in the prayer of Jesus. Abba is intimately linked to the self of Jesus and also, as the prayer shows, to the soul of Jesus. The first half of the prayer, "Abba, who are in heaven; hallowed be your name; your kingdom come; your will be done on earth as it is in heaven," is a prayer of the soul, a prayer of that in man that loves the darkness that goes before and comes after the lifetime. The name itself, "Abba," suggests the originative power that lies in the darkness behind. This is the name that is to be hallowed. The kingdom of Abba, on the other hand, is to come, and so it lies in the darkness ahead. The soul longs for the dark forward, just as it hallows the dark backward. The will of Abba is done in heaven, where Abba is, where the kingdom is (which is also called "the kingdom of heaven"), in the time encompassing the lifetime, but the soul wishes for it to be done on earth, to be done during the lifetime. This would be the coming of the kingdom, the reign of Abba on earth.

The second half of the prayer, "Give us this day our daily bread; and forgive us our debts as we forgive those who are indebted to us; and lead us not into temptation, but deliver us from evil,"[41] is a prayer of the self. It would be the self, that in man that loves the daytime of life between birth and death, that would ask for daily bread. The prayer for forgiveness of debts shows that Jesus does not want to maintain a relationship of obligation with Abba or with other men but wants to have all obligations remitted. This would mean a relationship of love rather than of gratitude, for in the latter there would be the "debt of gratitude." The last petition, however, "lead us not into temptation, but deliver us from evil," implies that Abba, the God of Jesus, is capable of leading a man into temptation, just as the God of Job led Job into temptation.[42] This is what actually happened to Jesus himself, and this is what he complained of when he spoke of being forsaken upon the cross. The name "Abba," nevertheless, and the trust it implies, seems to stand valid for Jesus. On the cross after crying out his forsakenness he is still able to say "Abba, into your hands I commend my spirit."

All this carries us beyond the profanation of Jesus. Jesus is indeed a self, or has a self as well as a soul, like any other man. His self, moreover, like that of any other man, is intimately linked to his God. So far there is nothing we do not find in every man. Yet this God of his, Abba, when we consider him, is a God another man could well appropriate. To make the God of Jesus my God would mean a transformation of my self and my soul, but the transformation, to judge from the prayer of Jesus, could be a desirable one. Thus the God of Jesus, though intimately linked to the self of Jesus, could have a wider relevancy, even a universal relevancy. If, in fact, I were to make the God of Jesus my God, I would call his God "the true God," and I would call Jesus "my savior." The "truth" of his God would consist in Abba's being not only the God of Jesus but also my God. Jesus would be "my savior" in that the appropriation of his God would mean an assimilation of my self and soul to his. From my point of view, then, after I had made Abba my God, the intimate link of the self of Jesus with Abba would become something quite similar to the divine sonship traditionally ascribed to Jesus.

The transformation of the soul that this would involve amounts to a redemption of the dark urges of the soul. One could describe these urges as consisting of the will to die and, what is really the same thing, the will to return to nothingness from which one comes. The transformed soul would hallow its origin, calling it "Abba," and its goal, calling it "the kingdom." This would mean finding creative power rather than sheer nothingness at its origin and being rather than sheer nothingness at its goal. The will to nothingness would thus be transformed into a will to being. This might appear to be just a way of saying that the nothingness is desirable. There is a change of attitude toward the lifetime, how- ever, which shows that it is more than this. The untransformed soul could desire the abolition of the self and the lifetime, but the transformed soul desires the "will" of Abba to be "done on earth as it is in heaven." Instead of desiring to abolish the lifetime, it desires the encompassing time to pervade it.

The transformation of the self, accordingly, is not at all a kind of abolition of the self or its suffering. A self that still wants daily bread is still a self, still that in man that loves the lifetime, and it still can suffer, for it can be deprived of the daily bread it wants. A self that does not want to be led into temptation but to be de- livered from evil, moreover, is a self that does not want to suffer, not a self that would delight in suffering. A self, however, that remits all debts and wishes all its debts to God remitted is a self that prefers living on familiar terms with God to being in debt of gratitude to God for providing it with daily bread and delivering it from temptation and evil. It is transformed in its relationship to itself, to others, and to God. The remission of debts means that it can give freely to others, not placing them under obligation, and can receive freely from God, not coming under obligation. This utterly free giving on God's part and utterly free receiving on the self's part is, I believe, what is understood when the self says

"Give," "Forgive," "Lead not," "Deliver"; when it says "Abba."

The image that emerges here is not quite the one anticipated in the endeavor to answer Job. When Jesus is cast into the role of Job, an ambiguity arises. Jesus may be profaned, and God will become once more the God of Job. Or Job may be replaced by Jesus, and the God of Job replaced by Abba the God of Jesus. In the latter case Job is not actually answered; he is changed from a servant into a friend; and so his complaint is changed from that of a faithful servant into that of a faithful friend. The cry "My God, my God, why have you forsaken me?" still rings out, but the one who utters it is no longer a forsaken servant, but worse, a forsaken friend—worse at least from the standpoint of the problem of suffering. Something has happened, a transformation of man has occurred, but God still remains hidden in darkness, hidden in the darkness that goes before and comes after the time of man's life.

Stories of the Future: Someday God Will Be

When the story of Jesus is told as the story of a self, it has equal and opposite effects. One effect is to profane Jesus, to make him out to be only another man. This is the way Camus took the story in *The Rebel*. The other is to hallow man, to suggest that man is capable of being what Jesus was. This is the way Jung took the story in the *Answer to Job*. When it is taken this second way, it becomes a story of man's future. Although ideas of following Christ, imitating him, participating in his divine sonship are all quite traditional, the long centuries of worshiping him have never permitted the thought that man is capable of being what he was. The profaning of Jesus in the modern epoch made it thinkable. The thought was purchased too cheaply, however, by this means. It came by reducing Jesus to something man already is. Only when one gets beyond the profanation of Jesus, by realizing the relationship of his self to his God, does the thought become significant. Then it seems to reveal the deepest and greatest possibilities latent in man. It seems to be the clue to the future of man's spiritual evolution.

Man's spiritual history becomes in this light the story of an awakening, an awakening of man to God, and even, so Jung would have it, an awakening of God to himself through man. Max Scheler, propounding a similar notion, said, "this is an old idea which we find in Spinoza, Hegel and many other thinkers: the original Being becomes conscious of itself in man in the same act by which man sees himself grounded in this Being."[43] Out of this idea there has arisen in the nineteenth and twentieth centuries the image of an "unfinished God" or a "God in becoming."[44] This is in effect an interpretation of history as the process of God's self-realization. It clearly reflects the modern life story, the story of the self-realization of the individual man through a process of appropriation. No doubt it is natural for every epoch to understand history in terms of the life story, as a great story of deeds or of experience or of appropriation. The truth of the matter, though, is that this is what history is to one whose life story takes this form. The story of God's awakening to himself through man is really the story of man's awakening to God.

Jung saw man's spiritual history as going through three phases: first there is the phase exhibited in the Book of Job, where God's presence in man is unconscious; then there is that in the Gospels, where his presence is conscious in the One; and finally there is that which must follow, where his presence is conscious in the Many.[45] In the first phase man's relationship is that of Job; in the second there is a man, Jesus, who has another kind of relationship to God; in the third, other men have the relationship to God that Jesus had. The danger in the third phase, Jung admits,[46] is an inflation of the human ego; the danger already existed in the messianic consciousness of Jesus. It was forestalled for two millennia of Christianity by regarding Jesus as the one and only God-man. This, however, forestalled not only the danger of inflation but also the third phase, and it failed to explain how that danger was avoided in Jesus himself. Now in the beginning of the third phase, Jung believes, this danger must be met by differentiating the ego from its God. This is what we ourselves have just now done with the messianic consciousness of Jesus, differentiating the self of Jesus from the God Abba—though it has led us to something quite similar to the traditional conception of his divine sonship, according to which the Son is distinct from and correlative to the Father.

The real question here is about the nature of this consciousness, no matter whether we speak of God's presence being conscious in the One or in the Many. Is it really anything more than a consciousness of our own unconsciousness? It could well be that man's highest wisdom is a Socratic knowledge of his own ignorance. Being conscious of God, from this point of view, would amount to being aware of the unknown and uncontrollable in our lives as unknown and uncontrollable. The darkness encompassing human life can be penetrated, it may be, only in that man can become aware of it as darkness. Modern religious thought attempts to penetrate the darkness by answering Job. The failure of this attempt comes in profaning Jesus. The reversal of this failure, in turn, comes in hallowing man. Now it may be that in answering Job, we are simply answering the man whose life is encompassed by darkness; in profaning Jesus, we are realizing that Jesus is also such a man; and in hallowing man, we are realizing that it is one thing to be merely encompassed by darkness like Job and another thing to be conscious of this like Jesus. In the end, if this is so, the consciousness of the encompassing God is simply the consciousness of the encompassing darkness.

It is helpful to compare ourselves on this score with the pagans, when they were contemplating the possibility of accepting Christianity. In the story of England's conversion, as Bede gives it,[47] there was a solemn meeting of King Edwin and his councilors to decide whether or not Christianity should be accepted. One of the councilors, when his turn came to speak, compared human life to a sparrow's flight through a lighted hall in winter. The sparrow flies in by a doorway from the outer darkness and cold and wind; quickly it flies through the still air of the warm and lighted hall; then it flies out again by another doorway into the wind and cold and darkness outside. Human life, the councilor said, is like the brief interval of light and warmth and calm within the hall. What goes before life, though, and what follows upon it is unknown. It is like the darkness and cold and wind outside the hall. Thus if this "new doctrine," Christianity, could offer something more certain on these matters, he deemed it well worth receiving.

The parable of the sparrow's flight makes one think that the pagans had the same feeling for the uncertainty of life that we do, that they too thought of life as a lucid interval between the darkness before birth and that after death. When they turned to Christianity, it was to relieve the darkness. Are we back, therefore, to where they were in the beginning? Have we lost everything they believed they were gaining? Evidently we are, and we have, except that Christianity is no longer a new doctrine. To that extent we are not back where they were in the beginning. To them Christianity was something new; it promised to relieve the darkness they saw behind and ahead. To us it is no longer new; so we cannot bring ourselves to expect in quite the same way that it will relieve the darkness for us. This means that we have lost not only everything they believed they were gaining but still more. We seem to have lost also their hope of obtaining light.

The hopelessness goes with a certain sense of our knowledge of ignorance. We know, or think we know, not merely that we do not know, but that "man" does not know. So it is useless for us to seek further. This contrasts sharply with the attitude of King Edwin's councilor. He also said "we do not know," but he meant the "we" concretely, "we Northumbrians." So for him there was still hope that the "new doctrine" might bring light. Apparently, like ignorance itself, the knowledge of ignorance can be of two kinds, vincible and invincible. That which Socrates professed could be taken either way. Maybe Socrates believed he knew that "man" is ignorant. In that case his practice of cross-examining other persons would not have had the purpose of learning from them but simply of teaching them to know their ignorance. The Socratic "irony" in this supposition would have been quite heavy.

Maybe, on the contrary, Socrates thought only that he knew Socrates was ignorant. In that case he cross-examined others in order to discover if perhaps someone actually did have a knowledge or an awareness that he did not have himself.

There is an analogy between Socrates and Job, between Socrates' questioning of other men and Job's questioning of God. Job, too, could be understood in two ways. Maybe he was asking why it is that "man" is forsaken by God. This is the Job that much of modern religious thought has been answering. Maybe, on the contrary, he was asking why it was that he, Job, was forsaken by God. So also with Jesus on the cross. Maybe he was speaking for all men and was asking why God had forsaken "man." Maybe, though, he was speaking for himself and was asking why God had forsaken Jesus. When the question of Job or of Jesus is transformed into a question about man, it becomes a rhetorical question which expects no answer. It assumes that man has been abandoned by God. When it is man in general that is abandoned, then God is absent in principle; he is dead or simply nonexistent. If, on the contrary, it is a concrete man, Job or Jesus, who was abandoned, then the question "why" is a real one, and it expects an answer. The rhetorical question in the imagery of the twentieth-century stories of God expresses a hopeless "waiting for Godot"; the real question expresses a genuinely expectant "waiting for God."

When the question is real, there is an expectation that the situation described in the parable of the sparrow's flight can somehow be reversed. The reversal occurs when light and darkness change places. This is the sort of reversal that appears to have occurred between Socrates and Plato. In the Socratic knowledge of ignorance, life is a light encompassed by darkness; in the Platonic parable of the cave, where men sit contemplating shadows rather than realities, life is a darkness encompassed by light.[48] A contemporary example would be the reversal that occurred in the thinking of Martin Heidegger when he was about forty years of age.[49] In his earlier thinking Heidegger endeavored to throw light on "being" by examining human "existence." The dark thing for him during that phase was being; the bright thing was existence. In his later thinking he moves in the opposite direction, trying to clarify human existence by thinking about being itself. Now the dark thing is existence, and the bright thing is being. Before he did not speak of God. God did not appear in the light of human existence but was concealed, presumably, in the encompassing darkness of being. Now, while still speaking very little of God, he speaks of being with reverence. He calls being "holy"; he hails it, invokes it, thanks it.

The two kinds of thinking could be related to our distinction between "self" and "soul." We defined the "self" as that principle in man that loves the brightness of life itself, and we defined the soul as that which loves the darkness behind and ahead. To distribute the light and darkness this way, however, is to speak from the standpoint of the self. They would be reversed from the standpoint of the soul. The kind of thinking that is commonly associated with the name "existentialism" has the self as its point of reference. Existence is luminous for this viewpoint, while being is a surrounding darkness. The reverse of this sort of thinking makes existence a kind of shadow cast by the brightness of being. Such thinking probably has the soul as its implicit point of reference, for the soul, as we are conceiving it, loves being just as the self loves existence.

If this is what the reversal is, the great obstacle to its ever occurring is the importance of the self in the modern life story. As long as the standpoint of the self is assumed to be the true standpoint, there can be no going over to the standpoint of the soul. Only when the relativity of the self is perceived can the reversal occur. Only when I realize that the ignorance is mine, not man's, only when I realize that the forsakenness is mine, not man's, can anything happen to illuminate my ignorance or to relieve my forsakenness. As long as I assume that my ignorance is man's ignorance and my forsakenness is man's forsakenness, I am assuming that the standpoint of my self is the true standpoint. The self in the modern life story appropriates the common reality, thus giving all reality the stamp of its own uniqueness and becoming

THE SEARCH THROUGH TIME AND MEMORY   201

itself thereby universal. Nothing from this point of view seems left over. Only when it is realized that this is a point of view can anything else appear on the scene. One way of realizing this is to realize that there are other selves. I can still evade relativity here, though, by assuming that the others are simply counterparts of my self.

Ultimately the problem of the reversal is a problem not merely of thinking but of living. The life story is not only told as a story of the self, it is lived that way. A man not only thinks from a standpoint, he also lives from one. The problem thus is Archimedean. Archimedes said that he could move the world if he could be given a place outside the world to stand. A man can move the self only if he has a place to stand outside the self, namely the soul. If the terms of the problem are to move the world without standing outside of it, the problem is insoluble. When Job's question is appropriated by an absolutized self, it can be answered only by moving the world of the self, the world of suffering, without standing outside of it. The real Job stopped his mouth when the voice came from the whirlwind; the real Jesus, after complaining that he was forsaken, commended his spirit to Abba. An absolute self could never stop its mouth or commend its spirit; on the other hand, neither could it seriously complain about its forsakenness. Its moral indignation at a silent God is an empty posturing.

There is, to be sure, a kind of reversal upon the self which seems to have been taking place in the nineteenth and twentieth centuries with a rising sense of forces beyond the self's control. There is a sense of man being produced by his circumstances, a sense that underlies the rise of behavioral science, and there is also a sense of man being able to change his circumstances by violence, a sense that underlies the rise of revolutionary ideology. The force of circumstances is felt to be beyond the self's control; violence as exercised seems within but as undergone is outside the self's control. The actual experience of violence in the revolutions and wars of the two centuries, especially the twentieth, seems to have severely shaken the sense of the self's importance and power.[50] Against this background the individual self seems impotent to change the world; it seems able only to change its own relationship to the world. The life story in this light tends to become the story of the self's failure in the one respect and its success in the other, its insignificance in the one direction and its significance in the other.

This, however, is really the basic situation of the self from the beginning, the life encompassed by darkness. The dark backward was always felt to be beyond the individual self's control; the difference is that now it is conceived to be the circumstances of heredity and environment that produce the man and are susceptible of collective control. The dark forward was also felt to be beyond the self's control, though not so radically as the dark backward; the difference is that it is now felt, more than before, to be dominated by the power of violence. The genuine reversal, passing over from the self's standpoint to the soul's, would mean seeing the dark backward and forward not only as realms of force external to man, but also as realms of power within him. They appear to be realms of external force so long as man is equated with his self; they seem to be realms of inner power only when his soul is recognized. Violence ceases to seem purely external when a death wish is recognized within man; circumstances that produce a man, in like manner, could derive their force from an inner wish to return to his origin.

Indeed the real possibilities of the self, possibilities unrecognized in the myth of the self, appear only when the realm of the soul is recognized. There are Archimedean possibilities of moving the world of the soul by standing in that of the self, just as vice versa in the Eastern religions the world of the self and of suffering is moved by standing in that of the soul. The power of violence can be broken perhaps by renouncing the death wish, just as the power of suffering is broken in Buddhism and Hinduism by renouncing the life wish. The force of circumstances likewise can perhaps be broken by renouncing the desire to return to the origin, a desire that may be at bottom the same as the death wish. One could envision a kind of inverse Buddhism in which instead of the Four Truths about suffering, its origin and end, and the way to end it, there would be four parallel truths about death and reversion. The first would be that life is dominated by the force of circumstances and violence; the second that these forces get their power to some extent from man's will to die and to return to his origin; the third that these forces are broken or diminished when this will to die and revert is renounced; and the fourth that since the death or reversion wish is a flight from suffering, its renunciation would require the attainment of happiness in life or else the acceptance of suffering.

The trouble with renunciation of the death wish, as also with renunciation of the life wish, is that it could amount to a renunciation of one's humanity. The one is a renunciation of the soul, much as the other is a renunciation of the self. If one is going to accept his own humanity, he must accept his self and his soul, it seems, his life wish and his death wish. This leaves one powerless against suffering, against violence, and against the force of circumstances. To be powerless without having to be is a fairly significant thing. It merits some kind of name like "faith." It is reminiscent of Paul's statement "power is made perfect in weakness."[51] The proverb "act as though everything depended on you and pray as though everything depended on God" looks like simple unbelief up against this. For this would mean *not* acting as though everything depended on you. If it were up to man to conquer suffering, the thing to do would be to renounce the life wish that feeds suffering and gives it its power. If it were up to man to conquer violence and the force of circumstances, the thing to do would be to renounce the death or reversion wish that ministers to these forces. Not to make these conquests is to remain human. To leave oneself powerless, without having to, before suffering and violence and the force of circumstances is truly to wait for God. It turns out, in fact, that remaining human in the face of the suffering and the violence and the force of circumstances in the twentieth century and waiting for God are one and the same thing.

The dark God of the modern epoch, the hidden, absent, dead,

awaited God is related to the dark forces of man's soul. These forces are particularly dark for us because the soul is neglected in the modern life story. It is not part of the story, and so everything that belongs to it can appear foreign and exterior to the life. Once the soul and these forces are recognized, it is possible to do something about them. One possibility is the one we have just considered, a radical renunciation of them, comparable to the renunciation of the self in Hinduism and Buddhism. Another is the one we considered earlier, a transformation of them through compassion, comparable to the transformation of the soul, which occurs in those and other higher religions. If we wish to avoid any kind of renunciation of our own humanity, the latter possibility is the more promising. What we have to learn from the religions, according to this, is not renunciation but compassion. This then becomes a way of penetrating the darkness encompassing life, of penetrating the very darkness of the dark God.

If we refuse to renounce the soul, we have the dark forces to contend with. If we refuse to renounce the self, we are involved in answering Job or in taking his part. Here again we have learned something from the Eastern religions, namely that the self is the root of suffering and that suffering can be uprooted only by uprooting the self. Short of pulling up the root of suffering, nevertheless, it is possible to be happy as Job was before he lost everything. This means that Job has a point in questioning God about his suffering, and that he deserves an answer as was attempted in early modern religious thought, or else he deserves to have his part taken as has been done in subsequent thought. When we take his part, questioning God, it comes to light that in Christianity God takes his part. This implies a relationship with God that goes beyond that of gratitude for deliverance from suffering, a relationship in which there is love and mutual understanding instead of the debt of gratitude. Although it does not answer Job, this too is a penetration into the darkness of God.

These two ways of penetrating the darkness of God, compassion and the remission of the debt of gratitude, lead to similar results. Both reveal the dark God to be a compassionate God.

They agree in this with a third way, the appropriation of the God of Jesus. The transformation of the soul by compassion and the transformation of the self by the remission of the debt of gratitude is the very transformation that occurs when a man of the contemporary period relates to the dark God as if that God were Abba, the God of Jesus. A profanation of Jesus occurs when his God is reduced to the dark God, and he himself is reduced to something analogous to the untransformed self of a contemporary man. A transformation of contemporary man in self and soul occurs vice versa when the reduction is carried out the other way, when the dark God is trusted as completely as one would trust the God whom Jesus called Abba. As long as the contemporary man works as though everything depended on his self, he finds himself unable to pray with any kind of conviction "as though everything depended on God." Only when he actually takes a chance on God, so to speak, can he pray and does the dark God begin to resemble Abba.

What hinders him from taking that chance is the absoluteness of the self, its position as subject of the modern life story. Recognizing the relativity of the self is thus the fourth way we have found of penetrating the darkness of God. Life is richer, man can live out of deeper sources, when he is no longer reduced to his self, when his soul is recognized. The self too is more concrete, its ignorance and forsakenness is no longer that of man in general, and thus is no longer hopeless. The poverty of the absolute spirit is absolute and is not blessed. It is not surprising that we should have come to this, searching through the time and memory of the modern life, for our express purpose was to unravel the story of the self and to reach its boundaries. We have looked for a greater story, a story of God, of which the story of the self would be a part. We have found that there is a story of the soul which is left untold in the story of the self, that man does not live by self alone.

NOTES

1. Rainer Maria Rilke, *Stories of God*, tr. by M.D. Herter Norton (New York, Norton, 1963), pp. 115 ff.
2. Cf. the section on the "Death of God" in my book *The City of the Gods*, pp. 185 ff., and also my essay "The Myth of God's Death" in Bernard Murchland (ed.), *The Meaning of the Death of God* (New York, Random House, 1967), pp. 165 ff.
3. Cf. Simone Weil, *Waiting on God*, tr. by Emma Craufurd (London, Routledge and Paul, 1951); and Samuel Becket, *Waiting for Godot* (New York, Grove, 1954).
4. The original title was "Of God and Other Matters, Told to Grownups for Children." Many of the stories end with the narrator asking his listener to repeat his tale to children.
5. Cf. Charles W. Wahl in Herman Feifel (ed.), *The Meaning of Death* (New York, McGraw, 1959), pp. 26 f., on the obscenity of death in the twentieth century compared with the obscenity of sex in the late nineteenth. Also cf. Frederick J. Hoffman, *The Mortal No* (Princeton, Princeton University Press, 1964) on the changing role of death in the imagination of the nineteenth and twentieth centuries. The obscenity of death of which Wahl speaks could be connected with the rise of violence and the changed image of death of which Hoffman speaks.
6. Yeats's "Dialogue" is in *The Collected Poems of W. B. Yeats* (New York, Macmillan, 1951), pp. 231 f. Jung's theory of the *anima* is developed throughout his works, but the one most closely related to the discussion here of God and the soul is his late work *Mysterium Coniunctionis* (New York, Pantheon, 1963).
7. The commentaries are *The Ascent of Mount Carmel* and *The Dark Night of the Soul*, both tr. by E. Allison Peers (London, Sheed and Ward, 1953).
8. The myth I use here is "Innin's Descent into the Nether World," tr. by S. N. Kramer, *History Begins at Sumer* (New York, Doubleday, 1959), pp. 159 ff. Cf. my discussion of it (without comparison to Christ and the soul) in *The City of the Gods*, pp. 8 ff.
9. The retelling of the story of Adonis, Attis, Osiris, and similar figures by scholars in modern times is often influenced by the

story of Christ. It is important, therefore, to pay close attention to the differences in order to see the transformation of archetypal pattern that occurs in the Gospel.

10. Cf. Hegel, *The Phenomenology of Mind*, pp. 780 ff.
11. Cf. Jung's autobiography, *Memories, Dreams, Reflections*, p. 187.
12. Luke 6:20 ff.
13. *Thus Spake Zarathustra*, II, 3.
14. *Stories of God*, pp. 87 ff.
15. Cf. various statements on darkness in the gospel, John 1:5; 3:19; 8:12; 12:35, and in the epistle, I John 1:5 f; 2:8 ff.
16. Cf. Camus, *The Rebel*, pp. 32 ff.; Jung, *Answer to Job, passim*, especially pp. 74 ff.
17. Both Luther's central doctrine of Law and Gospel and Calvin's central doctrine of God's sovereignty in the bestowal of grace are directed against a man who would maintain his own righteousness. Naturally Luther and Calvin did not see themselves in the role of Job's friends, but in the role of Paul answering the Pharisees and Augustine answering the Pelagians. Just for the devil of it, though, I am casting them here into the role of Job's friends.
18. Cf. the rise of apologetics in the seventeenth century, great apologetics like Pascal's *Pensées*.
19. *Paradise Lost*, I, 25 f.
20. Cf. the rise of "natural religion" in the eighteenth century. Sample texts can be found in J.M. Creed and J.S. Boys Smith, *Religious Thought in the Eighteenth Century* (Cambridge, Cambridge University Press, 1934).
21. Leibniz's *Theodicy* appeared in 1710. The thesis that "all is for the best in the best of all possible worlds" was ridiculed in Voltaire's *Candide*, which appeared in 1759.
22. I am referring here to the four alternate versions of the Abraham story that Kierkegaard gives in *Fear and Trembling*, each of them corresponding to aspects of his own relationship to Regina Olsen. Cf. the end of his *Repetition* where the young man (who corresponds to Kierkegaard after losing Regina) compares himself to Job—the repetition or restoration is not a return of Regina but a return to himself, he is himself again. Cf. *supra*, chapter 2, Kierkegaard and the Story of Appropriation.
23. Camus' *Rebel* appeared in 1951; Jung's *Answer to Job* appeared in 1952. Note the feeling for Gnosticism in both (Camus, pp. 32 f.; Jung throughout but never by that name).
24. Cf. Mircea Eliade, *Yoga: Immortality and Freedom*, pp. 31 ff. on personality and suffering. Cf. my discussion of Buddhism and Hinduism in *The City of the Gods*, pp. 112 ff. and 123 ff.
25. Eliade, *Yoga*, pp. 11 ff.

26. Cf. Heidegger, *Being and Time,* pp. 235 ff. on care as the being of *Dasein.*
27. Kierkegaard, *Philosophical Fragments,* pp. 32 ff.
28. *Ibid.,* p. 39.
29. *Ibid.,* pp. 31 f., 34 f., 40 ff.
30. *Ibid.,* pp. 28 ff. (cf. *ibid.,* pp. 11 ff.).
31. *Ibid.,* pp. 17 ff.
32. *The Rebel,* p. 34.
33. *Ibid.,* p. 67.
34. Montaigne, *Essays,* II, 12.
35. Browne denies Montaigne's influence. Cf. *Religio Medici* and other works ed. by L.C. Martin (Oxford, Clarendon Press, 1964), p. 290, no. 6. Only after the old religion had become questionable, however, through the skepticism of men like Montaigne, was it possible to propose a new religion like Lord Herbert's or to make adherence to the old religion like Sir Thomas Browne's such a personal matter.
36. Herbert of Cherbury, *De Religione Laici,* ed. and tr. by H.R. Hutcheson (New Haven, Yale University Press, 1944).
37. In *Emile,* tr. by Barbara Foxley (New York, Dutton, 1911), pp. 228 ff.
38. Tolstoy, *My Confession; My Religion; the Gospel in Brief* (New York, Scribner's, 1922).
39. Cf. Schweitzer's essay "The Conception of the Kingdom of God in the Transformation of Eschatology" in Walter Kaufmann, *Religion from Tolstoy to Camus* (New York, Harper, 1961), pp. 407 ff.
40. *Philosophical Fragments,* pp. 55 ff.
41. It is "forgive us our debts as we forgive those who are indebted to us" in Matthew 6:12. In Luke 11:4 it is "forgive us our sins as we forgive everyone indebted to us."
42. Jung makes a point of this in *Answer to Job,* pp. 99 f.
43. Scheler, *Man's Place in Nature,* tr. by Hans Meyerhoff (New York, Farrar, Straus, 1961), pp. 92 f.
44. A prominent example would be the God of Whitehead—cf. his *Process and Reality* (New York, Harper, 1957), pp. 519 ff. Cf. also the God of Kazantzakis in his *Saviours of God,* tr. by Kimon Friar (New York, Simon and Schuster, 1960). Both Whitehead and Kazantzakis are greatly influenced by Bergson—cf. his *Creative Evolution,* tr. by Arthur Mitchell (New York, Holt, 1911).
45. Jung begins his *Answer to Job* with the Book of Job and the first phase; then he talks of God's intention of becoming man (pp. 74 ff.); and ultimately of continuing incarnation (pp. 136 ff.).
46. At the end of the book, *ibid.,* pp. 202 f.

47. Bede, *Ecclesiastical History*, II, 13.

48. *Republic*, VII, 514 ff.

49. Cf. William J. Richardson, *Heidegger: Through Phenomenology to Thought* (The Hague, M. Nijhoff, 1963). Cf. especially the preface by Heidegger, pp. *viii* ff.

50. Frederick J. Hoffman organizes his treatment of death and the modern imagination in *The Mortal No* (cited above in note 5) under three headings: "Grace," "Violence," and "The Self." The loss of grace and decorum in death brought about by the rise of violence, he believes, has shaken the sense and position of the self and has led to an effort to reestablish the self.

51. Corinthians 12:9.

6

Time Within Mind

"WHAT SEEST THOU ELSE," Prospero asked Miranda, "in the dark backward and abysm of time?" But Miranda could see no more. And what she did see was "rather like a dream than an assurance."[1]

The image of man you would expect to arrive at by bringing time to mind would be that of a man limited perhaps in space but greatly extended in time. This is the sort of image Marcel Proust creates in his *Remembrance of Things Past*.[2] It is the kind of image we were suggesting in the beginning of this book when we spoke of the immediate man, the existential man, and the historic man. The immediate man was restricted in his awareness and concern to the here and now; the existential man's consciousness was expanded to his past and future; the historic man's was extended beyond the confines of his lifetime to the past and future of mankind. When we examined the existential man's questions, however, questions like "Shall my future be like my past?" and "Is my past to be more necessary than my future?" we found that he was ignorant, though concerned, about his past and future; and so too the historic man; we found him concerned but ignorant about the encompassing time. Thus the image to which we actually came was that of a Socrates, a man who is aware of his ignorance. Our Socrates, nevertheless, is one who knows that Socrates is ignorant, not that man is ignorant.

The Socratic wisdom, the knowledge of ignorance, is one of the most central of all human insights. Any qualification of this wisdom would be of the utmost significance. We are proposing a qualification of it. If this qualification is valid, we are saying something that is of great importance. The qualification is a simple one. It is that the knowledge of ignorance is concrete rather than abstract, that it is a personal knowledge of personal ignorance. This is not meant to be an interpretation of the historical Socrates. It may well be that Socrates thought he knew that man is ignorant. If he thought that, then there was less hope and more irony in his wisdom than in this. What goes before Socratic wisdom, the ignorance of ignorance, would be an unawareness of the darkness encompassing human life; from within it would be like living in a room with no windows, brilliantly lighted by artificial light, a place in which there is no darkness. The knowledge of universal ignorance, if that is the Socratic wisdom, would be like experiencing a night that does not pass, a night like that of outer space. The knowledge of personal ignorance, however, would be like being outdoors in a night that can pass into day, a night like that of earth.

The passing of such a night into day would be a turning point in a life, the kind of juncture we found in the life of Jesus. The turning points in his life, according to our hypothesis, were the points where his life intersected with that of John the Baptist. At each of these junctures he went over from an ignorance to a knowledge. The first was in his baptism at the hands of John. That he presented himself for a baptism of repentance suggests that he was uncertain of his standing with God. His uncertainty, however, was changed into assurance as he underwent the baptism and experienced himself as beloved and well-pleasing to God. This left him still uncertain, nevertheless, as to whether the boundless acceptance he was receiving from God was for him alone or whether it was for others too. This uncertainty was removed at the second turning point, the imprisonment of John,

when he saw John silenced and felt himself called upon to step
into John's place and proclaim the kingdom of God. At this point
the uncertainty remained as to how the kingdom would come
about, whether it would come through ? conversion of Israel to
God by his preaching. The third turning point, the execution of
John the Baptist, seems to have been the beginning for Jesus of
the realization that the kingdom would not come in this way, that
instead his preaching would fail, and he himself would be put to
death.

The fourth turning point was the actual end point of his life.
There the darkness beforehand was that expressed in his cry "My
God, my God, why have you forsaken me?" The light that followed was that of his resurrection from the dead. No sooner is
this said, though, than it becomes clear that this turning point is
not as comprehensible as the others. The darkness that went before is accessible to a kind of sympathetic understanding, but not
the light that followed. The difficulty is that Jesus went over at
this point from the unfinished to the finished life. While your life
is still unfinished, the best you can do is relive in some measure
the experience of the turning points within the life of Jesus and
get some inkling from that of the turning point that lies at the
end. Bringing your own deathtime to mind makes you concerned
about that last juncture, but simultaneously makes you aware of
your ignorance of it. This ignorance corresponds in some manner
to that of Jesus himself at the end. Yet the consciousness of the
ignorance combined with the confidence that arises from the experience of the previous turning points can give some foretaste of
resurrection, some sense of human becoming heading toward
being rather than nothingness.

If there were no turning points of this kind during life, if there
were no truth for man beyond the knowledge of ignorance, then
Christianity would be like a Platonic mythos. The Gospel would
be like the stories Plato used to tell about the origin of the world,
the origin of man, the transmigration of souls. Plato told such
stories with an awareness that they were merely stories, with an
awareness, that is, of human ignorance in these matters. It would

be quite a sophisticated interpretation of Christianity to take it this way too, quite consonant also, at least in appearance, with Jesus's way of teaching by parables. The serious alternative to this, it seems to me, would be to acknowledge that the story form has varied from epoch to epoch in the Christian era, and that if Christianity is anything, it is the content that has carried over from story to story.

In each epoch, we surmised, there is a prevailing mythos, a fundamental story which appears in the many particular stories that are told, in drama, epic, biography, autobiography, and history. This story is the life story, the characteristic form life takes in a time. In the earliest part of the A.D. period the life story appears to have been essentially a story of deeds. This is the shape life takes in the New Testament itself, most evidently in Paul, with his concern about faith and works, but also in John, as he tells about the works of Jesus and the works of Satan, and also in such pagan literature of the time as Plutarch's *Lives* of men who were illustrious for their noble and immortal deeds. In a later period the life story seems to have become rather a story of experience, and it became necessary to retell all the old stories of deeds as stories of experience. This is the way it appears in the writings of Augustine, both in his account of his own life in the *Confessions* and in his account of history in the *City of God*. In the modern period the life story seems to have become a drama of the self, a story of appropriation. This is the form it takes for Kierkegaard, particularly when he contends that the truth of Christianity is a matter not of public knowledge but of personal appropriation and inwardness.

To get at the content of life in any one of these periods it was necessary to see through the mythos, to realize that the story was a story. Paul's conversion from Pharisaism to Christianity involved seeing, on the one hand, that it is impossible for man to justify his existence by deeds done in fulfillment of God's law and, on the other hand, that thanks to Jesus Christ his existence does not need to be justified. This amounted to seeing through the mythos of deeds. The conversion itself was like a participation in the first turning point of Jesus's life when Jesus experienced God's boundless acceptance, and it was followed by something like the second, Paul's discovery of his mission to the Gentiles, and the third, his facing persecution and death. Something similar came about in Augustine's conversion. Augustine went from Manichaeism, where good and evil were thought to be simply matters of experience, to Neoplatonism, where the story of experience was taken to be a changing image of eternity. This already amounted to realizing that the story was a story. His conversion to Christianity, however, led him to unravel the story of experience in memory until he came to the nothingness at his origin and stood before the God who draws being out of nothingness. This was like the original point, where Jesus stood before God and it led on to a vision of the city of God comparable to that of the kingdom of God and a sense that the city would stand despite the decline and fall of man's city.

The modern life story, the story of appropriation, especially as it is told by Descartes and Hegel, is like the course of a recovery from sickness. It is a process in which a sickness is induced to destroy itself, as in fever therapy, and thus bring about health. The sickness is alienation, estrangement from oneself, from one's life, from reality. Descartes diagnoses it as doubt; Hegel takes it to be also despair. The fever therapy lies in this, that doubt carried to the limit will end in the doubt of doubt, despair likewise will end in the despair of despair. It is as though disillusionment were to end at last in a disillusionment with disillusionment itself. So doubt ends in a certainty, and despair ends in a confidence. This, we could say, is the modern mythos in its most inward and conscious form. It is a drama in which there is no actor but the self. Seeing through the mythos, realizing that the story is a story, opens the way to a faith like that of Pascal in the face of doubt or a faith like that of Kierkegaard in the face of despair. Faith here consists of reliance upon God for a self, receiving the self from God. It replaces simple self-certainty like that of Descartes or pure self-confidence like that of Hegel. It puts man once again into the position of Jesus at the initial point, standing before God, going over from uncertainty to assurance.

Ordinarily, it is true, the story of appropriation would be lived outwardly rather than inwardly. A man would begin his life by going through a process of "socialization," acquiring the habits, beliefs, and accumulated knowledge of his society in the course of his preparation for adulthood. Then he might experience alienation as the feeling that he is merely the product of his circumstances, and he might set out to remedy this by changing his circumstances. The effort to acquire autonomy by changing circumstances might go on for some time, even for the whole of life. The nomadism would come to an abrupt end, though, if he were to realize that he carries his problems with him into each new set of circumstances. Then would come an inward collapse, a reorientation, a change of goals so that he would now seek like Descartes "to conquer himself rather than the world."[3] He would feel that he could not change the world but only his relationship to the world. He would begin to live the story of appropriation inwardly and would find himself trying to make his way somehow from despair and doubt to assurance.

The endeavor to find such a way out of despair and doubt began historically in the great religious revolution that occurred in early modern times. Luther compared despair, uncertainty, and assurance to hell, purgatory, and heaven. In the Middle Ages Dante had journeyed in imagination through the hell, purgatory, and heaven of the afterlife; in his *Divine Comedy* he had described hell according to traditional belief as a place where all hope is abandoned, purgatory as a place of unfulfilled hope, and heaven as a place of hope fulfilled. It is as though these dreams of the afterlife had become the waking realities of earthly life in modern times. The modern man, as Luther's comparison suggests, finds his hell and purgatory on earth in the form of despair and uncertainty, and he seeks accordingly to find his heaven upon earth too, outwardly perhaps in some ideal change of circumstances or inwardly in some kind of inner assurance. The search for the outward heaven runs through the great political revolutions of modern times; the search for the inward heaven runs through the great religious revolutions. A divine comedy is being acted out in life after life, but it seldom comes to its happy ending.

At bottom, we have suggested, the modern man's situation appears to be one of unmediated existence. There is no longer anything human between man and God. The mediators of the Middle Ages, the "lords temporal" who mediated between man and God as God of the living and the "lords spiritual" who mediated between man and God as God of the dead, have long since been deposed in political and religious revolutions. With nothing human between man and God, hell and purgatory seem to exist on earth, because there is nothing to unite man with God, but heaven too seems to exist on earth, because there is nothing to separate man from God. To be sure, there is still Jesus Christ the mediator according to religious belief, but, having no further mediator between himself and God, Jesus has readily become the prototype of man in the state of unmediated existence. Except Jesus seems to have lived the divine comedy in reverse in his earthly existence, going from the heaven of assurance to the hell of Godforsakenness on the cross. Perhaps there is a clue in this for the modern man: if, instead of seeking for the heaven of assurance, a man were to seek for something entirely different, maybe assurance and better than assurance would come to him.

If there is a lesson in the history of religious experience in modern times, it is that the quest for certainty is self-defeating. The more earnestly a man seeks for certainty, the more uncertain he becomes; the more strenuously he tries to remove all doubt, the more doubt he experiences. Among Protestant figures like Luther, Bunyan, Wesley, and Kierkegaard we observed a sustained endeavor to find certainty within the ambiguities of unmediated existence. Among Catholic figures like Erasmus, Pascal, Ligouri, and Newman we marked a persistent attempt to find a way back from these ambiguities to mediation. It may well be that certainty and unambiguous existence can be attained only if they are not sought. There is probably some paradox or irony here like that of the saying of Jesus "whoever shall seek to save his life shall lose it, and whoever shall lose his life shall preserve it."[4] Whoever shall seek to make certain about his existence, maybe we could say, shall become doubtful and perhaps desperate, and whoever shall abandon the quest of certainty shall be assured.

And yet assurance comes not simply from abandoning the quest of certainty. It comes, to judge by the history of autobiography, from undertaking an entirely different quest. The path of this other quest appears in the sequence of the ages of life. As a man goes from childhood to youth to manhood to age, he makes a journey in time which looks very much like a quest. Actually it might well be that he is being dragged through the stages of his journey instead of walking through them upright. Still the struggle in which he is engaged is likely to be along the same path that his quest would have followed. In either case the journey seems to take a characteristic form in each period of history, exhibiting the prevailing mythos or life story. The mythos, nevertheless, is not the first thing that emerges in the stages on life's way. The first thing, to judge from modern autobiography, is a feeling for life, a "sense of life" as one might speak of a "tragic sense of life" or a "comic sense of life" or an "ironic sense of life." This is a basic pattern of experience determined, it seems, in childhood.

Out of this feeling for life or this pattern of feelings there emerge images or a coherent set of images which could be called the "personal mythos." The primacy of feeling is suggested strongly in the autobiographies of Rousseau and Wordsworth; the emergence of the image from the feelings is prominent in the autobiography of Goethe. Eliciting the images from the feelings has the effect, we have seen, of liberating the man from the tyranny of his feelings. The personal mythos has all the elements of drama—plot, characters. This implies that man is to some extent an actor and an inventor of himself, as appears especially in the autobiography of Sartre. The eliciting of the personal mythos takes place primarily in youth, but, as the autobiographies of Jung and Yeats indicate, the process can run to the middle of life and past it. If childhood is the time for establishing the basic sense of life, then youth is the time for the mythmaking that goes into the personal mythos, and full manhood is delayed as long as the myth is in the making.

Manhood is the time for insight into the images. The danger in the images themselves, as Jung pointed out, is that a man might stop at them and so fall prey to the power principle. It is one thing to convert the "truth" of one's life into "poetry," to elicit the images from one's feelings, but to reverse the process and attempt to convert poetry into truth is liable, as Goethe pointed out, to destroy the life. Stopping at the image comes to this, for it means living by the personal mythos. Insight into the personal mythos would involve what we have termed "seeing through the mythos" and "realizing that the story is a story." It might consist simply of a knowledge of ignorance or, as insight into the personal mythos, a personal knowledge of personal ignorance. Or it might amount to such an actual turning point as we found in the life of Jesus, in which a man would go over from an ignorance to a knowledge. In both instances insight would effectively become the guide of life. In the first instance, however, the insight would be simply an experience of enlightenment; in the second it would be an experience of revelation. In the first instance we could say with Socrates "insight is virtue"; in the second we might even say "insight is grace."

The whole process, eliciting images from feelings, attaining insight into the images and converting insight into a guide of life, goes on throughout the lifetime. Childhood, nevertheless, seems the time when the basic pattern of feeling is determined; youth the time when the basic set of images becomes explicit as a personal mythos; manhood the time for attaining insight not merely into this or that image but into the personal mythos as such; and age the time for assessing the resulting life. The quest running through this entire process, to the extent that there is a successful quest in it, could well be called a "quest of understanding." The quest of understanding would verify the saying "seek and you shall find, knock and it shall be opened to you."[5] As long as a man is in quest of certainty, he seeks but does not find, he knocks but the door is not opened. Only when he abandons certainty and seeks for understanding is there finding and opening. But then as insights occur and he finds understanding, he becomes more and more confident that there is something to be understood and that he has understood something. This confidence seems to be, at last, the very assurance that always eluded the quest of certainty.

Confidence in the self, however, has been severely shaken in recent times. A disproportion has been felt between the prevailing mythos and prevailing sense of life, between the drama of the self and the contemporary experience of violence and the force of circumstances. The self seems to be at the mercy of powers much greater than it in scope; it seems to be produced by circumstances and destroyed by violence. This has led to a great loss of confidence in the self's importance. The lack of assurance is very noticeable in nineteenth- and twentieth-century autobiography. The uniqueness of the self was felt in the sixteenth and seventeenth and eighteenth centuries to be a solution to the problem of common mortality; it was what rescued the individual somehow from the common plight of mankind. In the nineteenth and twentieth centuries, on the contrary, the uniqueness of the self has come to be felt as a problem, that of personal mortality, of personal fragility and aloneness in the face of death and circumstance. The mythos of the self has begun to seem less and less adequate, and a search is underway for a more comprehensive image of man, which will take into account in some way the forces of violence and circumstance that are external to the self and beyond its control.

The images of "violence" and the "force of circumstances" themselves are probably the least adequate to describe what is untold in the story of the self. They imply that the forces external to the self are external to man, and thus assume that a man is nothing but a self. A second set of images associates these forces with God rather than the world. These are the modern stories of God, which tell of a God who was, who is not, but who will be. The dark backward of time, instead of concealing the circumstances that produce the man, conceals the God who once was; the dark forward, instead of concealing death and violence, conceals the God who will be; the luminous in-between, the lifetime, is the time of the self and is empty of God. Although these images seem far more mythological than those of violence and the force of circumstances, they are more adequate. For they represent the powers external to the self in terms of something that can be interior to man, namely God, and so lead beyond the reduction of man to his self.

A third set of images associates these forces directly with man. The chief image here is that of the "soul," as Yeats and Jung use the term, as distinguished from the "self" rather than from the "body." This is an image of that in man that loves the darkness that goes before life and comes after life. If there is such a love of darkness in man, it could well be the element that gives circumstances their force and violence and death their power. Also it would be this element in man, his love of the encompassing darkness, that would feel the absence of God, that God once was and is not, and would wait for God's coming, knowing that God will be. The inadequacy here is that this is not yet a unified image of man; it is the compound of the self and the residue that its story leaves untold, the soul. Insight into this complex image would be twofold. There would be first the kind of insight we find in Yeats and Jung, the insight that differentiates the soul from the self. This insight has the effect of breaking the obsession and possession of the self by the dark forces of the soul, the forces of violence and circumstance that are able to obsess and possess a man precisely because he sees them only as exterior and beyond his control.

A second kind of insight would be one which, converted into a guide of life, transforms the self and the soul. A transformation of the soul occurs when a man goes from secretly loving the circumstances that control the self out of the past and the death that destroys it out of the future to loving the God hidden in the darkness behind and ahead. The difference here is one of imagery, but it embodies a difference of relationship; it represents a change in a man's way of relating to the time encompassing his lifetime. A transformation of the self occurs along with this as a man goes from living on time borrowed from the encompassing time to living on time given him for his own. The change is from a relationship of indebtedness to God to one of companionship with God in time. The differentiating insight, which recognizes the dark forces in man and the relativity of his self, would be a Socratic insight, an awareness of the encompassing darkness. The transforming insight, which redeems the dark forces and saves the relative self, would be a passing over from darkness to light, as in the turning points in the life of Jesus. It would mean, in effect, appropriating the God of Jesus, sharing in his relationship to God.

The prime turning point in a life, we may conclude, is the point where a man goes over, if and when he does, from God as the unknown and uncontrollable to God as Abba. The prior state is simply an awareness of the unknown and uncontrollable, the knowledge of ignorance. The adage "act as though everything depended on you and pray as though everything depended on God" describes what prayer is like before going over. The man controls everything that he can control in his life, at least in the area of his chief concerns, but then he realizes that some things are beyond control such as death and circumstance. He fears the uncontrollable, and so he prays. If he were to cease believing in God in this manner, however, he would not change much. He would still act as though everything depended on him; he would merely cease to pray and would consider it impossible to do anything about the unknown and uncontrollable. Going over to a trust relationship with God from either of these states would involve a change that is quite radical. It would mean relinquishing control of his life in the central area, where he cares and where he also is able to exercise control. Looked at from the outside and before trusting, this means, so to speak, "taking a chance" on God, an awful chance. From inside and in the act of trusting, it means experiencing the trustworthiness of God.

The second turning point is the point where such a man begins to communicate to others what he is receiving from God. There is an old Greek maxim "Give away all that you have, then shall you receive."[6] The process we mentioned, eliciting images from feelings, attaining insight into the images and converting the insight into a guide of life, describes both the giving and the receiving, both a man's lifework and his life experience. Giving away all that he has means giving expression to all that is in him. If he does not elicit the images from his feelings, if he does not attain insight into the images, if he does not live by the insights, he fails to give expression to what is within him and fails to communicate to others. If, on the other hand, he does all this, he is receiving, for the process is one of discovery not merely invention. He is not making himself so much as discovering himself, and thus receiving himself and his life as a gift in the very moment of giving everything away to others. He is, in fact, becoming himself, for this process is that in which the basic dimensions of human life, thought, feeling, and action are integrated. The image mediates between thought and feeling while thought itself mediates between feeling and action.

The third turning point is the point where he faces the prospect of death. Here the temptation to panic and seize control of life becomes most acute. On the other hand, there is that within him that betrays him and hands him over to death, that in him that loves the darkness surrounding life. The awareness of his mortality is a tragic sense of life; it is a consciousness that deprives him of the illusion of immortality that can go with living merely in the here and now. The tragedy is transformed into comedy, however, in his personal mythos, the image of himself and his life that he elicits from his feeling for life. In the comedy he sees himself passing from doubt and despair at the prospect of death to assurance about his successful self-realization in life. The comedy is transformed into irony, though, when he sees through the mythos and understands that the attempt to achieve certainty defeats itself, that the harder he tries to make sure of himself, the more doubtful he becomes. The irony, nevertheless, is reversed when he goes over from the quest of certainty to the quest of understanding and discovers that certainty will come to him unsought, that the happy ending of the comedy will come to pass if he abandons the attempt to bring it about.

The last turning point is death itself. At this juncture the irony of life is harshest, and yet the possibility of its reversal is keenest. The irony is that there is a time for everything in the man's life, but the time for everything lapses. There is, to echo Koheleth,[7] a time to live and a time to die; a time for doing, for experiencing, for assimilating; a time to despair, to doubt, to be confident; a time for childhood, for youth, for manhood, for age; a time to remember God, to miss God, to wait for God. The obvious thing is that each time comes and goes. The thing that is not obvious is the point of the coming and going. The reversal of irony is that everything has a point, but the point is always concealed, for the point of becoming is not becoming itself but being, the lapsing time for everything is a becoming that ends in being rather than nothingness. Living means becoming a human being, dying means passing over to being; doing, experiencing, assimilating, are ways of going from nothingness to being; a hell is coming to be in despair, a purgatory in doubt, a heaven in confidence; the child is father of the man, the youth is the unfinished man, the man is the finished youth, the old man is child of the man; the time to remember God, miss God, wait for God is man's time of becoming, but God's own time is that of man's being.

The terrible irony of life is changed into humor, let us say, as in the song "Finnegan's Wake."[8] Finnegan is dead; he has drained the cup of life. The irony is that the cup, for all the drinking Finnegan did, is not really drained. Yet it turns to humor when you realize that this is because the cup is so full, because it is inexhaustible. When whiskey is spilled on Finnegan's body during the riot at his wake, he rises from the dead. . . . The face of God underlying all is neither the tragic mask nor the comic mask; it is not the wry face of irony; it is the compassionate face of humor.

NOTES

1. Shakespeare, *The Tempest*, Act I, scene 2, lines 45 and 49 f.
2. The last sentence of Proust's many-volume work, tr. by F.A. Blossom (New York, Randon House, 1932) is this:

   If at least, there were granted me time enough to complete my work, I would not fail to stamp it with the seal of that Time the understanding of which was this day so forcibly impressing itself upon me, and I would therein describe men—even should that give them the semblance of monstrous creatures—as occupying in Time a place far more considerable than the so restricted one allotted them in space, a place, on the contrary, extending boundlessly since, giant-like, reaching far back into the years, they touch simultaneously epochs of their lives—with countless intervening days between—so widely separated from one another in Time.
3. Cf. Descartes, *Discourse on Method*, p. 3, third maxim.
4. Luke 17:33.
5. Matthew 7:7.
6. Quoted by Jung in his *Memories, Dreams, Reflections*, p. 186.
7. Ecclesiastes 3:1 ff.
8. This is the song from which James Joyce took the title of his *Finnegans Wake* (New York, Viking Press, 1939). For the complete text of the song cf. Colm O'Lochlainn, *Irish Street Ballads* (Dublin, The Sign of the Three Candles, 1939), pp. 180 f. The last stanza goes like this:

   > *Then Micky Maloney raised his head,*
   > *When a noggin of whiskey flew at him,*
   > *It missed and falling on the bed,*
   > *The liquor scattered over Tim;*
   > *Bedad he revives, see how he rises,*
   > *And Timothy rising from the bed,*
   > *Says, "Whirl your liquor round like blazes,*
   > *Thanam o'n dhoul, do ye think I'm dead?"*

Index

Abba, *x*, 11, 12, 24, 113, 176, 192-94, 195, 197, 201, 222
Abraham, 15, 188
Agape, 42
Alienation, of self, 33, 34, 154, 155, 163, 177, 190-91, 192
Allah, 176
Anima, 172, 175
Answer to Job, 179, 195
Antichrist, The, 176
Antinomianism, 108
Apollonian type, 50, 51, 139
"Apology for Raymond de Sebonde," 188
Appropriation, of experience, 60, 61; life as story of, 164-65, 191-92, 196, 214, 215, 216; of self, 33, 62-63, 189-90, 196, 214, 216
Archimedes, 201, 202
Aristophanes, 8
Aristotle, 51
Atheism, Sartre on, 137-38
Atman, 162
Augustine, St., *ix,* 34, 67, 135, 144, 188, 192, 214, 215; and communication with God, 48-49, 54-55; dialectic approach of to understanding of experience, 49-50, 53; importance of *Confessions,* 45-46; inquiry and dialogue over state of own soul, 51, 52; on preexistence of the soul, 56-57; and question of man before God, 47-48; recollection of existential states by, 46-47, 53-54, 55-56
Aurelius Antoninus, Marcus, 47, 55
Autonomy, of self, 33, 34, 154, 155, 165, 177, 191, 216

Baptism, infant, 126; of Jesus, 9-10, 212
Baudelaire, Charles, 5, 137
Beatrice Portinari, 77, 78
Becket, Samuel, 19-20, 171
Becoming, as appropriation, 61, 62; and being, 1-2, 26, 27, 67-68, 213, 224; and death, 17-19, 21, 26-27; as exaltation, 21-22, 24, 25; as kenosis, 21, 24, 25; and life process, 17-19, 21, 26; and nothingness, 1-2, 26,

27, 67-68, 213, 224; as repetition, 61
Bede, 197
Being, and becoming, 1-2, 26, 27, 67-68, 213, 224; oblivion of, 56; pursuit of, 146-48, 153; relationship to existence, 199-200
Being and Nothingness, 147, 157
Beyond the Pleasure Principle, 57
Bergson, Henri, 16
Boisen, Anton, 92, 102
Book of My Life, The, 54
Browne, Sir Thomas, 188-89
Buddha, 135, 144, 176
Buddhism, 35, 176, 181, 182; suffering according to, 202-3, 204
Bunyan, John, 92, 96, 102, 111, 112, 135, 191, 217; doctrine of despair of, 85-86, 87; on salvation, 105

Calvin, John, 77, 180, 188; theology of the sovereignty of God of, 85, 86
Calvinism, 95, 96, 97-98, 105
Cardano, Geronimo, 54
Camus, Albert, 39, 40, 41, 81, 147, 179, 180, 181, 187, 195
Catholicism, 86, 88, 89; duality of God in, 96-97; and certainty of conscience, 98-99; and spiritual mediation, 96-97; and uncertainty of salvation, 106-7, 108
Cherbury, Lord Herbert of, 189
Childhood, decline from, 148; direction of course of life decided by, 129-34; effect of loss of temporal mediation on, 126-27, 134; as embodiment of unspoiled nature, 127, 128, 129-30, 133; and existential awareness, 133-34, 143-44; Goethe on, 131-32, 133; and immediate awareness, 133-34, 143-44; Jung on, 132-33; as preparation for manhood, 130, 137, 218, 219; Rousseau on, 127-28, 133; Sartre on, 128-29, 133; second, 155, 156, 157; Wordsworth on, 129-30, 133; Yeats on, 129, 130-31, 133
Christ, *see* Jesus
Christianity, 34, 36, 37, 40, 47, 53, 54, 56, 60, 85, 90, 91, 100, 101, 105, 135,

229

Christianity (*continued*)
159, 176, 177, 191, 196, 204, 215; at-
titude toward childhood, 126-27;
compared to Platonic mythos, 213-
14; England's conversion to, 197-
98; and problem of individuality
of Jesus, 189-90, 191
Church of England, 81
Cicero, 51
City of God, The, 46, 49, 214
City of the Gods, The, xi
Clairvaux, Bernard of, 135
Coleridge, Samuel Taylor, 149, 159
Communion, psychological problems of, 177
Compassion, healing power of, 176-
77, 204-5
Concept of Dread, The, 99
Concluding Unscientific Postscript,
xi, 60
Confessions (Augustine), *ix,* 45-46,
47, 48, 49, 53, 54, 55, 56, 67, 145,
146, 169, 214
Confessions (Rousseau), 47, 55, 120,
124, 145, 146, 156
Conscience, certainty of, 98-103,
106-7, 108, 109, 111, 191; and law
and liberty, 88-89; purgatory of,
99; and pursuit of truth, 145-46;
religion of, 145-46, 153; and salva-
tion, 110
Creation, from nothingness, 45, 55-
57, 67-68, 124, 125, 169, 215
"Creed of the Savoyard Vicar,
The," 137, 143, 145, 189
Creeds, personal, 188-90, 191
Critique of Dialectical Reason, 147
Cross, theology of the, 103, 104

Dante, 77-78, 79, 83, 93, 103, 216
"Dark Night of the Soul, The,"
173, 184
Death, despair in face of, 64, 65, 223-
24; as end to hierarchical order,
121-22, 123, 157, 163, 190, 220; as
end to uniform order, 121-22, 123-
24, 163, 220; faith in face of, 68;
ignorance before, 213; man's
changing attitude toward, 76-77,
78, 79, 120-22; as point of com-

pletion, 14-15; and process of be-
coming, 17-19, 26-27; and sin, 34-
35, 36, 37-41, 44; soul's union with
God in, 172, 173-74
Death, Dance of, 76-77, 123
Deeds, *see* Works
Deism, 172, 173
Demonic, concept of, 54, 160-62
Descartes, René, 63, 64-65, 66-67, 68,
215, 216
Despair, 95, 100, 102, 105, 125, 163;
Bunyan's doctrine of, 85-86;
Hegel's doctrine of, 90-91, 215; as
hell, 83-93 *passim,* 96, 103, 216,
224; highway of, 63, 64, 68, 91;
Jesuit-Jansenist controversy con-
cerning, 86-87; Kierkegaard's
views on, 90, 91-92; and doctrine
of Law and Gospel, 87-88; Lu-
ther's doctrine of, 83-86, 87, 90;
relationship to faith, 64-65, 66, 67,
109-10, 215; and relativism, 65-66;
of salvation, 109, 111; of self, 65,
86, 90
"Dialogue of Self and Soul," 159
Diogenes, 7
Dionysian type, 50, 51, 139
Divine Comedy, The, 77-78, 216
Donne, John, 121
Dostoevsky, Fyodor, 181
Doubt, as means to assert self, 63, 64,
66-67; path of, 63, 64-65, 66, 67,
68; relationship to faith, 64-65, 98,
215, 216
Dread, according to Kierkegaard,
100, 109, 110
Dumuzi (god), 174

Edwin (of Northumbria), 197, 198
Either/Or, 60
Egmont, 150
Emile, 127, 146
Enlightenment, attainment of, 134-35,
144, 145, 219
Enneads, 55
Erasmus, Desiderius, 87, 92, 102, 113,
191, 217; on Luther's doctrine of
despair, 83-84; on Luther's doc-
trine of Law and Gospel, 104; on
spiritual mediation, 85; on valid-

Erasmus (*continued*)
ity of works, 94
Eternity, relationship to time, 48, 50
Everybody's Autobiography, 157
Existence, as pain, 181, 182; relationship to being, 199-200; unmediated, 80-81, 82-83, 84-85, 87, 92-93, 94, 95, 96, 99, 102, 111, 112-13, 125-26, 217
Existentialism, 4, 5, 17, 33, 99, 122, 147, 165, 181, 200; see also Sartre, Jean-Paul
Experience, assimilation of, 59, dialectic approach to understanding of, 49-50, 52-53; existential level of, 2, 26, 46, 48, 49, 50, 52, 53-54, 55, 57-59, 60-61, 133-34, 143-44; historic level of, 2, 26, 49, 50, 54, 55, 60, 61; immediate level of, 2, 26, 46, 48-49, 50, 51, 52-53, 55, 57, 58, 59-60, 133-34, 143-44; life as story of, 34, 42-57, 169-70, 187, 196, 214, 215; religious, 92, 95, 97, 102, 111, 113, 125-26, 188, 217

Faith, assurance of, 88, 97-98, 99, 107-8, 109; darkness of, 173; degrees of, 98, 99; and doctrine of Law and Gospel, 87-88; and judgment, 68; justification by, 103; according to Kierkegaard, 63, 101, 109-10; mediation as mean to arrive at, 111; Newman's attainment of, 110-11, 112; relationship to despair, 64-65, 66, 67, 68-69, 109-10; relationship to doubt, 63-65, 68-69, 98, 215, 216; relativism as mean to arrive at, 65-67, 68-69; and self-acceptance, 62-63, 66; as way to righteousness, 42
Fall, The, 39, 41
Faust, 131, 132, 141, 143, 151, 161
Fiducia, 79
"Finnegan's Wake," 224
Fox, George, 135
Francis of Assisi, St., 109
Free will, 191; and salvation, 104
Freud, Sigmund, 4, 17, 18, 102, 127, 128, 129, 130, 132, 142; on repetition, 57, 58, 59-60

Future, greater, 16, 17, 61, 170, 174; orientation toward, 20-21; relationship to past, *vii*, 2, 4, 9, 10, 15-17, 172, 211; relationship to present, 2-4, 9, 10, 26, 53, 55; see also Simultaneity

Generations, contemporaneity of, 15-16
Genet, Jean, 5, 137
Glory, theology of, 103-4
God, absence of, 172, 173, 178-79, 199, 221; absolute sovereignty of, 85, 86, 87, 96, 97; acceptability of man before, 42-45, 84, 85, 86, 94, 95, 96, 97, 98, 103, 104, 191; according to deism, 172; awakening of man to, 196-97; communication with through recollection of experience, 48-49, 52, 54-55; consciousness of in darkness encompassing lifetime, 16, 17, 171-72, 173-74, 197-98, 204, 205, 220-22; dark side of, 181, 203-4, 205; of the dead, 76, 79; death of, 171, 172, 173-75, 176, 188, 199, 203; demand upon man of, 84-87, 89, 94, 95, 96, 97; despair of, 86, 100; duality of, 95-98, 102, 112, 191, 192; grace of, 86-87, 94-95, 96, 97, 98, 104, 105, 106; justification of to man in 17th century, 180, 185; kingdom of, 11, 215; of the living, 76; as man, 184, 186; man's desire to be, 128-29; mercy of, 86, 87, 105; passion of, 21-24, 27; question of existence of, 35, 36, 38, 40; relationship of Jesus to, *x*, 178-79, 192-94, 195-97, 205, 212-13, 215, 222; relationship of self to, 52, 53, 112, 187-95; search for, 169-70; sharing of man's suffering by, 179, 180, 184, 185, 186-87; seeming unrighteousness of, 38, 39-40; and the soul, 183-84, 185, 191-94; union with, 97, 173, waiting for, 171, 172, 173, 174, 199, 203-4, 221; Word of as found in history, 49, 54; wrath of, 86, 92, 95, 105; see also Jesus
Goethe, Johann Wolfgang von, 47,

Goethe (continued)
54, 55, 120, 134, 138, 143, 163, 164, 190, 218, 219; on childhood, 131-32, 133; on concept of the demonic, 160-61; final acceptance of life by, 161; on the poetic self, 140-41; and transformation of truth into poetry, 150-51, 152, 153-54
Golgotha, of absolute spirit, 22-23
Gospels, stories of, 179-80
Grace, doctrine of sufficient, 87
Grace Abounding to the Chief of Sinners, 85, 105
"Growth of a Poet's Mind," 138-39

Heaven, as assurance, 79, 80, 81, 82, 83, 96, 98, 103-13 passim, 216, 217
Hegel, Georg Wilhelm Friedrick, 2, 34, 49, 50, 53, 54, 66, 68, 90, 171, 175, 190; on absolute knowledge, 6-7, 22; doctrine of despair of, 63, 90-91, 215; on self-knowledge, 5
Heidegger, Martin, 56, 121, 125, 137, 147; on being and existence, 199-200
Heidelberg Disputation, 83, 93, 103
Heine, Heinrich, 171
Hell, as despair, 79, 80, 81, 82, 83-93 passim, 96, 98, 216, 224
Hinduism, 35, 181, 182, 202, 204
Hölderlin, Johann Christian, 148-49
Hus, John, 77

Individuality, see Self
Individuation, 132, 133, 162
Ignorance, knowledge of, 52, 66, 198-99, 211-12, 213, 219, 222
Innin, story of, 174, 175
Insight (Lonergan), xi
"Intimations of Immortality from Recollections of Early Childhood," 129, 130, 148, 149, 158
Isaac, 15
Isaiah, 11

James, William, 82, 92
Jansenists, 86-87
Jesus, viii, ix, x, xi, 22, 45, 49, 62, 68, 78, 88, 135, 201, 214, 218, 219; as

archetypal hero, 20, 113; baptism of, 9-10, 212; death and crucifixion of, 12, 13, 103, 174, 177, 199, 213; and death of John the Baptist, 11-12, 213; grace of, 83, 84, 87; humanity of, 9, 12-14, 21, 23-24, 41-42, 187-88; and imprisonment of John the Baptist, 10-11, 212-13; on judgment of man, 44, 68; kenosis and exaltation of, 21-22, 24, 25, 27; and kingdom of God, 11; life before and after, 19-20; as the Lord, 24-26; as mediator between God and man, 75, 80, 81, 113, 217; meeting with John the Baptist, 9-10, 212; participation in man's sinfulness, 41; passion of, 23-24, 25-26, 27; profanation of, 187-88, 193, 195, 197, 205; quest of the historical, 8, 9, 26; and quest of righteousness, 34, 37; and question of unmediated existence, 80-81, 82; relationship to God, x, 9-10, 11, 12, 14, 24, 178-79, 192-94, 195-97, 205, 212-13, 215, 222; relationship to the self, 90, 91, 92, 100-1, 113, 187-88, 189-90, 193, 195; relationship to the soul, 174, 176; relativism of subjective viewpoint of, 8-14, 24; resurrection of, 19, 36, 37, 174; and self-knowledge, 7-8; sharing of man's suffering by, 180; works as basis of faith in, 42; see also God
Jesuits, 106; controversy with Jansenists, 86-87; and method of probabilism, 108-9
Job, question of suffering of, 179-87 passim, 195, 196, 197, 199, 204
Job, Book of, 179, 180, 181, 182-83, 196
John the Baptist, death of, 11-12, 213; imprisonment of, 10-11, 212-13; meeting with Jesus, 9-10, 212
John of the Cross, 173, 184
John the Evangelist, ix, 7-8, 9, 12, 24, 25, 42, 44-45, 69, 178-79, 214
Judgment, of judgment, 44, 45, 68; of man, 43-45, 68; uncertainty of, 106, 111

Jung, Carl Gustav, *xi*, 120, 134, 163, 164, 179, 180, 181, 190, 195, 218, 219, 221; on childhood, 132-33; and concept of the demonic, 161-62; confrontation with the unconscious, 141-43, 148, 149, 151-53, 154, 162-63; on conscious and unconscious, 132, 133; on duality of God, 112-13; final acceptance of life by, 162-63; on man's spiritual history, 196-97; on the soul, 172-73; and theory of the *anima*, 172, 175

Justice, poetic, 38, 40

Kant, Emmanuel, 35, 36
Kierkegaard, Sören, *x*, *xi*, 15, 34, 68, 69, 76, 102, 109, 180, 188, 191, 214, 217; attitude toward mediation, 90; concept of dread of, 99-100; on despair, 90, 91-92; on God and the soul, 183-84, 185, 186, 187; on the life process, 2, 17-18; on Luther, 89; relationship of faith and despair according to, 64-65, 66, 67, 215; on repetition, 57-59, 60; on repulsion of the absurd, 101-2; on self-acceptance, 62-63, 109-11; significance of pseudonyms of, 61-62; on truth, 4

Koheleth, 224
Koran, 176

Law, fulfillment of, 34, 36, 37, 38-39, 44, 94, 214; and liberty, 88-89, 93
Law and Gospel, doctrine of: 84, 85, 87-88, 89, 90, 91, 93-94, 95-96, 97, 104-6, 191
Leibniz, Gottfried Wilhelm von, 180
Lessing, Gotthold Ephraim, 147, 150, 152; on pursuit of truth, 144-45, 161
Life, darkness encompassing lifetime, 172, 193-94, 195, 197, 200, 202, 204, 212, 219-20, 223-24; form of forms of, 33-34; interpretation of reality of, 151-53; and process of becoming, 1, 2, 17-19, 26; reconciliation with, 155-63, 164; as

repetition, 57; stages of, 14, 15, 61-62, 218; as story of appropriation, 34, 43, 61, 164-65, 169-70, 177, 191-92, 196, 214, 215, 216; as story of experience, 45-57, 61, 164, 169, 169-70, 187, 196, 214, 215; as story of works, 34, 41-42, 43, 45, 46, 61, 164, 165, 169, 196, 214; as succession of immediate states, 55

Ligouri, Alfonso Maria de, 92, 99, 102, 109, 111, 113, 191, 217; on law and liberty, 88-89

Lives (Plutarch), 43, 214
Lord, Jesus as the, 24-26
Lonergan, *xi*
Luke, St., *ix*, 8, 9, 10, 11, 24
Luther, Martin, *x*, 65, 76, 77, 92, 97, 102, 107, 111, 112, 172, 180, 188, 217; doctrine of despair of, 83-86, 87, 90; doctrine of Law and Gospel of, 84, 85, 87-88, 89, 90, 93-94, 95-96, 104-6, 191; and question of spiritual mediation, 78-81, 85, 89; theology of the cross of, 103, 104; theology of glory of, 103-4; three phases of religious experience of, 79-113 *passim*, 125, 216; on validity of works, 94, 95, 96, 98, 99

Man, abandonment by God of, 199; acceptability before God of, 42-45, 68, 191; ages of, 1, 2-3, 26, 59, 61, 126, 128, 130, 154-55, 218; archetypal, 75, 113; awakening to God of, 196-97; before God, 43-44, 47, 55, 63, 67, 93, 97, 101, 169, 215-16; before men, 43-44, 47; changing attitude toward death of, 120-22; guilt of, 39, 40-41, 42; impossibility of according to Sartre, 138, 147, 190; innocence of, 39, 40-41; and passion of Jesus, 25-27; and quest of certainty, 217-18, 219-20, 223-24; and quest of understanding, 219-20, 223-24; and question of unmediated existence, 80, 81, 82-83, 84-85, 87, 92-93, 94, 95, 96, 99, 102, 111, 112-13, 125-26, 217; relationship to the dead, 14-15, 16, 17; relationship to God,

Man (*continued*)
viii, 97, 112, 184-87; spiritual history of according to Jung, 196-97; subordinate identities of modern, 61-62; validity of works of, 94-95, 96, 100, 105, 107, 111; *see also* Self; Manhood

Manhood, childhood as preparation for, 130, 137; turning point into, 136, 139, 141-42, 144, 148, 219

Manichaeism, 34, 45, 53, 55, 56, 215

Mark, St., *ix*, 8, 9, 10, 24

Marx, Karl, 33, 125, 147

Matthew, St., *ix*, 8, 9, 10, 24

Mediation, *see* Spiritual mediation; Temporal mediation

Mediations (Marcus Aurelius), 47, 55

Melville, Herman, 180-81

Memories, Dreams, Reflections, *xi*

Mental illness, and religious experience, 92

Methodism, 87, 97, 107, 108

Milton, John, 180

Mind, and time, *vii*, *viii*, 1-3, 20, 27, 46, 48, 49, 50, 53, 55, 61, 143-44, 169-70, 211

Modernism, 81

Monasticism, 78, 135

Montaigne, Michel Eyquem de, 63, 188

Moral Theology, 88, 109

More, Saint Thomas, 108

Moravians, 88, 98, 107

Moses, 42

My Religion, 189

Mystery, and self-knowledge, 7-8, 23, 24, 52

Nathaniel, 135, 144

Nature, 123, 124, 127-28, 138, 139

Nausea, 137

Neoplatonism, 45, 53, 55, 56, 215

New Life, The, 77

Newman, John Henry, 91, 92, 101, 110, 113, 191, 217; on faith, 110-11; on spiritual mediation, 81; theory of concurring and converging probabilities of, 101-2

New Testament, *ix*, 2, 7, 34, 42, 44, 45

Nietzsche, Friedrich Wilhelm, 37, 50, 139, 140, 171, 188; on metamorphoses of man, 154-55; on the "overman," 155-56, 160; on pity, 176-77

Ninety-five Theses, 78

Nothingness, and becoming, 1-2, 26, 27, 213, 224; creation from, 45, 55-57, 67-68, 169, 215; recollection of, 45

Olsen, Regina, 59, 60

On Enslaved Will, 84

On Free Will, 83, 104

Paradise Lost, 180

Pascal, Blaise, 55, 66, 67, 68, 69, 86, 87, 92, 96, 102, 108, 113, 172, 191, 217; on faith, 63-64, 65, 215; on uncertainty of judgment, 106, 107, 111

Past, cumulative, 14-16; greater, 16, 17, 61, 170, 174; relationship to future, *vii*, 2-4, 9, 10, 15-17, 172, 211; relationship to present, 2-4, 9, 10, 26, 53, 55; *see also* Simultaneity

Paul, St., 19, 34, 46, 84, 99, 188, 192, 203; conversion of, 25-26, 36, 214-15; on death of Jesus, 37-38, 39-41; on doctrine of resurrection, 35-36; on judgement of man, 45; on righteousness, 34-35, 36-37, 38-39, 40-41, 42, 44; on sin, 44

Pensées, 87

Peter, St., 25, 26

Pharisaism, 34, 35-36, 38, 40, 42, 44, 45, 214

Phenomenology of Mind, 2, 22

Philosophia, 145

Philosophical Fragments, *xi*, 60

Pietism, 87, 97

Plato, 6, 8, 23, 48, 49, 50, 52, 53, 54, 56, 170, 199, 213-14

Plotinus, 55

Pluralism, 82

Plutarch, 43, 214

Poetry and Truth (Goethe), 47, 55, 131, 140, 150-51

Point of View of My Work as an Author, The, 60, 62
Predestination, 98
Prelude, The, 47, 55, 130, 158, 159
Present, pathway into, 21-22; relationship to past and future, 2-3, 9, 10, 26, 53, 55; *see also* Simultaneity
Probabilism, method of, 108-9
Protestantism, 85, 86, 87, 89, 177
Proust, Marcel, 211
Provincial Letters, 86
Psychoanalysis, 17, 33, 57; and self-knowledge, 4-5
Purity of Heart is to Will One Thing, 62
Purgatory, as uncertainty, 79, 80, 81, 82, 83, 93-103 *passim*, 216

Reality, appropriation by self of, 154, 164, 190, 200-1, 205; transformation of poetry into, 141, 150-51, 152, 153-54; unfulfilled, 151-52
Rebel, The, 39, 40, 147, 179, 187, 195
Recollection, as means to understand experience, 46-47, 50-52, 53, 55-57
Reformation, Protestant, 35, 76, 77, 78, 126, 135, 173, 177
Relativism, and faith, 65-67, 68-69; and judgment of man, 68; and subjective viewpoint of Jesus, 8-14, 24; and question of time, 16-17
Religio Laici, 189
Religio Medici, 188-89
Remembrance of Things Past, 211
Repetition, and appropriation, 60, 61; and assimilation, 59-60; Kierkegaard on, 57-59, 60; on immediate level of experience, 57, 58, 59-60; role of in modern philosophy, 57
Repetition, 57
Resurrection, Paul's views on, 35-36; *see also* Jesus
Retractations, 52
Revelation, religion of, 145-46, 153
Reveries of a Solitary Walker, 156
Reveries over Childhood and Youth, 130
Revolution, concept of continuous, 147

Righteousness, and death, 37-39, 40-41; and divine acceptance, 37-38; as experience, 45; and Job's suffering, 180; Paul's views on, 34, 35, 36-37, 38-39, 40-41, 42, 44, 192
Rigorism, 89
Rilke, Rainer Maria, 170-72, 177-78
Rousseau, Jean-Jacques, x, 47, 55, 76, 125, 129, 131, 134, 138, 143, 147, 163, 164, 189, 190, 218; on childhood, 127-28; final acceptance of life by, 156-57, 158; on hierarchical order, 122, 123; on religion of conscience, 145-46, 153; on the self, 120, 124; on temporal mediation, 125; youth of, 136-37

Salvation, assurance of, 98, 99, 100, 106, 107, 108, 109, 111, 191; despair of, 109, 111; and free will, 104; through God's mercy, 104, 105-6, 178
Sanctification, 107, 108
Sartre, Jean-Paul, x, 5, 20, 21, 27, 76, 134, 143, 163, 164, 190, 218; on atheism, 137-38; on childhood, 128-29, 133; on pursuit of being, 146-48, 153; on self-acceptance, 157-58; on uniform order, 122, 123; on uniqueness of self, 120, 123-25
Scheler, Max, 196
Schweitzer, Albert, 8, 189
Science of Logic, 22
Self, acceptance of, 62-63, 66, 67, 90, 109-10, 157-63, 181, 223; alienated, 33, 34, 154, 163, 177, 190-91, 192; antithetical, 139-40, 149-50, 153; appropriation of, 33, 62-63, 189-90, 196, 214, 216; appropriation of reality by, 154, 164, 190, 200-1; autonomous, 33, 34, 154, 155-56, 165, 177, 189, 191, 216; confidence in importance of, 120-21; despair of, 65, 86, 90; detachment from, 173-74; discovery of, 50-52, 135-44 *passim*, 149-50, 165, 218-19; effect of violence on, 201-2, 203, 220; of faith, 66, 67; and freedom of choice, 123-24; as gift of God, 185-86; and God's time, 178-79;

Self (continued)
and hierarchical order, 121, 122, 123, 135, 136, 137, 138, 145, 146, 147, 163; impotence of in modern period, 201-2, 220; integration of, 119-20, 150, 162, 163-64, 223; and man's changing attitude toward death, 120-22; nothingness within, 124-25; poetic, 138, 140-41; relationship to being and existence, 200; relationship to God, 52, 53, 187-95; relationship to itself, 52, 53, 62-63, 66-67, 100-1, 109-10, 122; relationship to others, 52, 53, 144, 149-50, 154, 222-23; relationship to the soul, 172, 175-76, 177-78, 183, 185, 186, 191-94, 200, 201, 202-5, 221-22; relativity of, 205, 221-22; and renunciation of the death wish, 202-3; and renunciation of the life wish, 181, 182, 202, 203, 204; and suffering, 181-83, 185-86, 194-95, 204; and uniform order, 121, 122, 123, 135-36, 137, 163; uniqueness of, 120, 121, 122, 123-25, 157, 158, 159-63, 164, 220; universal, 162-63, 164, 200-1; see also Man; Self-knowledge; Self-realization

Self-knowledge, ignorance as means to arrive at, 51-52; and mystery, 52; objective vs. subjective approach, 4-5; relativity of standpoints in arriving at, 4-8, 67

Self-realization, project of, 137-38, 143-44, 165

Shakespeare, William, 1, 61, 128, 155

Sickness unto Death, 63, 90

Simultaneity, 2-3, 26

Sin, 68, 97; and death, 34-35, 36, 37-41, 44; as experience, 45; grave, 126; mortal, 126; original, 100; participation of Jesus in man's, 41; as rejection of Jesus, 44; venial, 126

Sincerity and self-realization, doctrine of, 33, 39, 43, 62, 122, 131

Social Contract, 122

Socrates, 6, 8, 19, 23, 25, 26, 50, 51-52, 54, 197, 198-99, 211-12, 219

Soliloquies, 41, 48-49, 52, 55, 56, 67

Song of Solomon, 184-85

Sorrows of Young Werther, The, 140-41

Soul, change of from destructive to creative principle, 175-76, 178, 194; dark forces within, 175-78, 194, 203, 204, 221; and eternal truth, 52; preexistence of, 56; relationship to being and existence, 200; relationship to God, 175, 183-84, 185, 191-94; relationship of Jesus to, 174, 176; relationship to the self, 172, 175-76, 177-78, 183, 185, 186, 191-94, 200, 201, 202-5, 221-22; and renunciation of the death wish, 203; union with God in death, 172-74

Spinoza, Baruch, 196

"Spiritual Canticle, The," 184

Spiritual mediation, 92, 93, 94, 96, 99, 110, 125, 191, 217; breakdown of, 75-76, 77, 78, 81, 89, 100, 102, 135; as dialectic tool, 53; and duality of God, 112-13; effect upon medieval man, 77-78, 80-83; Hegel's idea of, 90-91; incorporation of death into life through, 76, 77-78, 79; as means to arrive at faith, 111; and the modern period, 81-83; points at issue concerning in the Reformation, 78; and question of distrust of God, 79-80

Stages on Life's Way, 60

Stein, Gertrude, 157

Stendhal, 187, 188

Stories of God, 179-72, 177-78

"Story Told to the Dark, A," 170-71

Suffering, God's sharing of human, 179, 180, 184, 185, 186-87; and renunciation of the life wish, 202, 203; and the self, 181-83, 185-86, 194-95, 204; see also Job

"Tale of Death and a Strange Postscript Thereto, A," 177-78

Temporal mediation, 81, 82, 100, 101, 217; breakdown of, 75-76, 79-80, 81, 102, 121, 135; effect of loss of on childhood, 126-27, 134; effect

Temporal mediation (*continued*)
of loss of on religious experience,
125-26
Thales, 129
Theodicy, 180
Thoughts, 55
Time, appropriation of, 169-70; encompassing the human lifetime,
16-17; and mind, *vii, viii,* 1-3, 20,
27, 46, 48, 49, 50, 53, 55, 61, 143-44,
169-70, 211; recollection of, 48, 50;
relationship to eternity, 48, 50
"Tintern Abbey," 148, 158
Tolstoy, Leo Nikolayevich, 189
Tractarian movement, 81
Trent, Council of, 96, 98, 100
Truth, eternal, 48-49, 52; as poetry,
131, 132, 133, 138, 140, 150-51, 152,
153-54, 219; search for, 33-34, 106,
108-9, 111, 144-46, 148, 150-51, 152,
153, 161

Uncertainty, doctrine of, 96-97
Unconscious, confrontation of, 141-
43, 148, 149-50, 151-53, 154, 162-63
Urfaust, 141

*Varieties of Religious Experience,
The,* 82
Vergil, 78
Vico, Giovanni Battista, 81
Violence, effect upon the self, 201-2,
203, 220
Vision, A, 149, 152
Voltaire, 188

Waiting for Godot, 19-20

Warens, Madame de, 123, 127, 136,
137
Wars of Religion, 173
Weber, Max, 95
Weil, Simone, 171
Weimar, Duke of, 151
Wesley, John, 84, 85, 89, 92, 102,
111, 112, 191, 217; on assurance of
faith, 97-98, 99, 107-8; on doctrine
of Law and Gospel, 87-88
Whitehead, Alfred North, 16, 33, 34
Words, The, 120, 125, 128, 147-48,
157
Wordsworth, William, 47, 55, 120,
131, 134, 143, 153, 163, 164, 190,
218; on childhood, 129-30 133; decline in life of, 148-49; final acceptance of life by, 158-59; youth
of, 138-39
Works, justification by, 103, 105,
107, 111; life as story of, 34, 41-42,
43, 45, 46, 164, 165, 169, 196, 214;
as way to righteousness, 41-42
Wycliffe, John, 77

Xenophon, 8, 54

Yahweh, 25
Yeats, William Butler, 33, 47, 62,
120, 134, 152, 163, 164, 172, 190,
218, 221; on the antithetical self,
139-40, 143, 149-50; on childhood,
129, 130-31, 133; final acceptance
of life by, 159-60
Youth, discovery of self in, 134-44,
218-19